THE SMART GUIDE TO

Getting Things Done

JEFF DAVIDSON

The Smart Guide To Getting Things Done

Published by

Smart Guide Publications, Inc.
2517 Deer Chase Drive
Norman, OK 73071
www.smartguidepublications.com

For information, address: Smart Guide Publications, Inc. 2517 Deer Creek Drive, Norman, OK 73071

SMART GUIDE and Design are registered trademarks licensed to Smart Guide Publications, Inc.

International Standard Book Number: 978-1-937636-70-8

Library of Congress Catalog Card Number:
11 12 13 14 15 10 9 8 7 6 5 4 3 2 1

Printed in the United States of America

Cover design: Lorna Llewellyn
Copy Editor: Ruth Strother
Back cover design: Joel Friedlander, Eric Gelb, Deon Seifert
Illustrations: James Balkovek
Production: Scribe
Exective Director: Cathy Barker

TABLE OF CONTENTS

PREFACE

You picked up this book because you're busy, ultra-busy, perhaps busier than you ever cared to be. In fact, you have so much to do you're not sure when you'll ever have the time, the energy, the resources, or the resolve. Each and every day is filled with lingering to-do items from the day before, the week before, the month before, maybe even the last year or two. What's more, you have a lofty long term goal or two, or three.

Add that to the new challenges that arise each day, plus those on the horizon, and you have the prescription for unrelenting time pressure, stress, piles mounting up, and that frustrating gnawing feeling that you're not going to get it all done. Technology was supposed to make our careers easier . . . and if we chose, simpler.

Decades and decades of management theory was supposed to result in more streamlined corporations, more effective workgroups, more enjoyable work settings, and shorter workdays. Your career trajectory, which once seemed rather clear, promising, and progressive, is perhaps now suspect. Should you turn this way or that, will you be here tomorrow, let alone next year, or in several years?

Real or Surreal

If you're feeling as if somehow reality has taken a major turn towards the surreal, you're not alone. An entire generation of career professionals, under the gun from dawn to dusk, feels as if the days are slipping by. They wake up and they're 30 and they don't know where their 20s went. They wake up at 40 and don't know where their 30s went, and then wake up at 50 and don't know where their 40s went.

No matter how many courses or seminars they take, or books and articles they read, on how to be more productive or accomplished, or how to have more or be more, too often for too many, it all seems like one big cultural hoax: a fabricated structure firmly anchored upon quicksand.

Over the course of twenty-six chapters, I'm going to lay out exactly what it takes to be both more efficient and effective, to start regularly accomplishing tasks which you set out to do on a daily and weekly basis, and feel good about the process.

I'm going to offer you insider tips, proven techniques, and general good sense that will read easy, sound right, and feel good in execution. While nothing I or any author can say in a book will turn back the clock or make society less rushed, fanatic, or hectic, you at least will have strategic tips and techniques to get the best of yourself, accomplish more in your career, and still have a life at the end of the day.

Yours truly,
Jeff Davidson

INTRODUCTION

Less than two decades ago, people came to work, put in their eight to ten hours, finished work, and still managed to have a life. Before tablets and smart phones, the workplace, as well as society as a whole, resonated at a slower pace.

People worked hard and it took a sterling effort to rise to the top. Along the way, the populous seemed to be better off mentally and emotionally than now. The need to pop anxiety-relieving or stress-relieving pills was not so prevalent. The number of distractions in a given day was much less than today.

Men and women remained in the same positions longer, worked with others familiar to them, reported to the same boss, perhaps even had the same parking space. The sameness in tasks and sequences of events that could seem kind of hum-drum today, nevertheless enabled the workers of yesteryear to achieve some sense of balance, centeredness, and certainly identity.

Fast Forward to Today

We are tormented by the sheer number of tasks we face from the minute we begin our work day. Our careers are daunting, boring, challenging, repetitive, irritating, intriguing, or, sometimes, overly-exciting. There is a LOT of everything.

Our work and personal environments today inundate us and over-stimulate us. A study at Cornell University found that low-level noise both lowered job motivation and increased stress levels. It appears as well that an open-office type environment can contribute to musculoskeletal problems, such as a stiff back or tense neck and even heart disease, due to increased levels of epinephrine, a stress hormone. In short, we often feel overwhelmed and powerless.

You already know about the pressures you face at work, but what you might not realize is that nearly everyone is feeling the same way; we all seem to be in a hurry. Is frantic any way to exist? Is it any way to run your career or your life?

The conditions we face have radically changed, even since the mid-1990s. Much of our day is consumed by activities that represent no more than "treading water," neither propelling us toward desired goals nor yielding any sense of balance.

We strive to pack more into each crevice of our already overstuffed workday, aware that we will still be confronted with a new onslaught of new tasks and distractions the next morning. There is always more to know and more to do. No end in sight. As such, this book addresses the all-embracing notion that you can complete most of what you want to get done at work and still stay sane. Indeed, as the result of reading this book, it's my fond and entirely feasible hope and that you'll be able to get more work done in a day.

Once you understand the plethora of benefits that come with getting things done, versus the stress and anxiety that accrues with having things remain undone, you will more easily gravitate towards completions and avoid incompletions like the plague.

May your days be cheery and bright and all your work days end before night.

Extras

Look for the little asides and comments I've added throughout the chapters to offer inside knowledge you need to succeed in getting more things done each day.

Dyna Moe

A hip career professional, who's been there, done that and has some pithy insights worth considering.

Word Power

Brief explanations of terminology employed.

Factoid

Useful, or at least interesting stuff, that embellishes your knowledge.

Coming Undone

Pitfalls and sand traps to avoid while accomplishing more.

ACKNOWLEDGMENTS

A non-fiction book such as this is a collaboration, first between author and acquisition editor, then between author and development editor, and finally between author and production editor. All the while, subject matter experts, interviewees, and authorities of all stripes play an important part of molding the perspectives and solutions an author has to offer.

As such, I would like to give a hearty thanks to the fine folks at Smart Guide Publications, including all the other department heads and managers who make things hum. All are dedicated and highly competent employees. Thanks to Heather Cozzie for her keen proof reading.

Thank also to subject matter experts and authorities, past and present, including Earl Nightingale, Steve Allen, Mark McCormack, Aldous Huxley, Allen Lakein, Edwin Bliss, John Kenneth Galbraith, Stephen Covey, and Alfredo Pareto, and on a more contemporary footing Robert Cialdini, Bert Decker, John Maxwell, Wayne McKinnon, David Lieberman, Paul Radde, Robert Fritz, Larry Rosen, Michelle Weil, Alvin Toffler, Rebecca Merrill, Bernie Seigal, Robert Fritz, Richard Chang, Deborah Benton, Soetsu Yanagi, David Meinz, and Robert Levasseur.

TRADEMARKS

The Challenge and Promise of Getting Things Done Each Day

Part 1
The Challenge and Promise of Getting Things Done Each Day

I believe that any book in this era of "getting things done," that does not first address the pervasive negative cultural developments and roadblocks to getting things done, impediments to information and communication overload, is not doing its job.

We'll attack this in Chapter 1. Chapter 2 delves into issues related to getting organized, managing your time, and improving your efficiency . . . while becoming more effective.

Impediments to Getting Things Done at Work

In This Chapter:

➤ Work distractions in all directions
➤ Information and communication overload
➤ More choices, more confusion
➤ Interruptions and productivity

This chapter explains that without distractions, our jobs would be much easier – still challenging, but easier. What gets in our way, and how do we keep that at bay?

Following World War II, and at least through the 1970's, time management specialists observed that the typical office worker earned a full day's pay for a 60 percent effort. In other words, over the course of an eight hour workday, the typical worker actually performed job-related work for 60 percent of the time, or 4.8 hours.

The rest of the time, totaling 40 percent of the day, was frittered away on daydreams (most often thinking about sex), personal phone calls, bathroom breaks, coffee breaks, extraneous reading, and even crossword puzzles!

Some studies indicate that, despite all the demands and responsibilities they face, workers today still waste away a sizable chunk of most days while facing more to do at work than their counterparts of, say, a generation ago. In this chapter, we will address the causes of information overload and the propagation of the human rat race.

Both Work Distractions and Productivity Are on the Rise

Without offering an involved and wearisome discussion about rising productivity levels, today's career professional, frittering and all, vastly exceeds the output of yesteryear's career professional at getting things done.

Today, workers in all types of organizations, including government, non-profit sector groups, health care, and education, as well as private industry,   devote a slightly higher percentage of their time to the tasks and responsibilities for which they actually were hired, and they have advanced tools that aid them in ways that the workforce ancestry could hardly imagine.

To be sure, intermittently many people goof off at the click of a mouse or voice command. Surveys show that non-job related web-surfing, emailing, and text messaging is rampant.

Who doesn't attend to personal business and personal frivolity during the workday? Even with the latest diversions, most workers are making diligent efforts a decent percentage of the time. This might be because they're dedicated, goal oriented, ethical, fearful of losing their jobs, or a combination of all the above. Or, it might be a result of improved workplace monitoring techniques. An employer's ability to gauge actual performance levels of employees has never been greater than it is today. Local area networks rule. So do surveillance cameras. No fun.

Factoid
Surveys show that more than 60 percent of employers monitor employees' activities and at least 15 percent of employers observe employees via hidden camera.

The Unrelenting Information Generation

Enhanced communication technology spawns information overload. In 1915, the typical person generated only a tiny amount of information in his or her entire life. Whereas notable people wrote dozens and dozens of letters, the typical person wrote only a handful. One hundred years later, by some estimates, today's career professionals have written so much (including email and text messages) that their collective output accounts for 80 percent to 85 percent of all original documents EVER written.

The Library of Congress catalogues 7,000 additional items each day. More than 2,000 new web sites go online each day. A minimum of two thousand books are published world wide each day.

Factoid

Researchers at the University of California at Berkeley in the Department of Information Sciences once concluded that if the total amount of unique information annually generated in the world were to be parceled out to every man, woman, and child on earth, each person have a personal library equivalent to 250 books.

In 1947, the first year *Books in Print* started collecting data, there were 85,000 titles in existence and 45 publishers listed. Sixty years later, there were more than 50,000 publishing houses in the United States alone.

A few quotes and statistics shed revealing light on a pervasive challenge to getting things done these days: so much information is available that it often becomes a hindrance to productivity.

➤ One-third of managers are victims of "Information Fatigue Syndrome." 49 percent said they are unable to handle the vast amounts of information received. 33 percent of managers were suffering ill health as a direct result of information overload. 62 percent admitted their business and social relationships suffer. 66 percent reported tension with colleagues and diminished job satisfaction. 43 percent think that important decisions are delayed and their abilities to make decisions are affected as a result of having too much information. (Reuters "Dying for Business" report)

➤ A single super bookstore offers 150,000+ titles; stocks 2,500 domestic and foreign newspapers, periodicals, and magazines; and can order 200,000 more book titles from national distributors. The children's section includes 15,000 titles; the music section has 25,000 CDs and cassettes. (Barnes and Noble Booksellers)

➤ More information has been produced in the last 40 years than the previous 5,000. The total quantity of all printed material is doubling every few years, and accelerating. A weekday edition of any major newspaper contains more information than the seventeenth-century man or woman would have encountered in a lifetime. (Reuters Business Information)

➤ Organizations are collecting so much data they're overwhelmed. Families are no different: we have more stored on disk, more photos, more songs, and more items than we'll ever have to allocate time for.

No matter how competent, adept, organized, or clever one might otherwise be, virtually all career professionals today find themselves in a daily tidal wave of information, a level which is unprecedented in the history of the human race. And the unvoiced expectation is that you're supposed to be able to handle it all.

Factoid

British author and psychologist David Lewis, Ph.D. says that "having too much information can be as dangerous as having too little. It can lead to a paralysis of analysis, making it harder to find the right solutions or make decisions."

More Choices, More Complexity

Your everyday supermarket now carries roughly 38,000 items —twice as many as a decade ago. So many products, brands, and sub-species of those brands, are available, that no consumer is safe from the bombardment of choice overload.

A huge variety of product offering doesn't aid consumers. It is insanity. From the vast array of athletic shoes to bagels to bottled water, a point quickly arrives when mega-choices, like mega-information, do not serve the consumer; they abuse him.

It seems everywhere you turn, people seek to complicate things. Many of the devices that we buy could serve us simply, but do they?

At the center of this information, communication, and technology glut, unquestionably, is the almighty microchip that plugs into the all-pervasive personal computer. Since 1971, when Intel invented the microprocessor, computer's labor-saving benefits have been widely touted. Computers provide us with the ability to accomplish a great deal of work in a relatively short amount of time, be it research, number crunching, document preparation, or communication.

We fiddle with our gadgets and try to take control of our little corner of the world. We communicate with staff, impress our bosses, and do our best to stay on top of things, but at the same time, we visit favorite blogs, comparison shop online, and pass jokes back and forth—not the essence of getting things done.

Management, with alarming irregularity, wants to know what we're typing, what we're watching, with whom we're communicating, and what we're passing back and forth. The temptation that an online connection provides can lure even the most diligent, loyal, and hard working among us. Who has not strayed during the course of the day, sometimes for prolonged periods?

Who has not taken chunks of time here and there away from their employer, proceeding all the while as if no one will know the difference? Though the word is rarely used, such forays are actually a form of theft. You can rationalize your escapades as long as you get the job done, i.e. who cares if you take a couple of minutes here and there for your own interests? Besides, you're not on the clock, you're a salaried or commission-based employee.

Still, if the tables were turned, you'd probably feel that you had a right to know when your staff was truly working versus not.

Dyna Moe

Hopefully, you're not among those who stray for large blocks of time throughout the day. You have the ability to self-regulate. You recognize that we live in an information overloaded society with too many web sites, publications, and electronic media bidding for your attention.

Traversing an Information and Communication Jungle

You buck up and decide to hack your way through the tangle of information and communication overload. You strip away anything that smells of excess or encroaches upon your ability to stay on the straight and narrow path to high productivity.

You speed up your routine so that you can sift through the day's deluge of emails, open the mail and address it, handle the memos, return the phone calls, and still come up smiling.

Word Power

Joie de vive is from the French which literally means "joy of life."

In deftly speeding through all that comes your way, a new kind of problem arises. In your quest to complete one thing done after another, your creativity, spontaneity, and joie de vive diminish.

When your brain is always engaged, when your neurons are always firing, when you find yourself in a continual mode of reacting and responding, instead of steering and directing, the best and brightest solutions that you are capable of producing rarely see the light of day.

A No-win Dilemma: To Accomplish More or to Have a Life?

You're firmly caught in a trap without realizing that you are. Like everyone else, you're adopting the same survival mechanisms, galloping along on the same treadmill, and defaulting into the same operational cycles.

If new insights or fresh perspectives spring forth, will you, can you, actually act upon them? Do you have any chance of thinking new thoughts, or are you simply generating permeations of all your previous thoughts?

In recent decades, Attention Deficit Hyperactivity Disorder has been on the rise, not only among children, but now among the adult population as well. The sudden rise of adult ADHD, while it might have genetic components, certainly receives a major boost from our kinetic, hyper-speed, information-bombarded society.

Adults with ADHD are likely to initiate more tasks and projects than they'll ever finish, become bored easily, seek thrills readily, have a propensity to be late, loath having to wait, and possibly be predisposed to taking foolish risks.

In 1965, the typical news sound bite lasted 45 seconds. By the year 2,000 it had dropped to eight seconds, and, by 2015, lower still. Ad clutter has increased annually since 1985 and has now exceeded the over-whelming level for many viewers.

While the typical TV advertisement was 53 seconds in 1965, by 2000 it had dropped to 25 seconds, and by 2014 15 second ads as well as three-second ads wewe peppering viewers at every turn. By 2002, every hour of daytime network TV offered nearly 21 minutes of commercials, up from ten to 12 minutes decades before. Some cable networks feature 60 seconds of ads for every 140 seconds of programming, in other words. 30 percent of the total broadcast.

Competition exists for every single moment you have to spare and those, you don't have to spare.

Danger: Never an Extra Moment

"Brave new world" is here. When you don't have, or feel you don't have, an extra moment to read philosophy, history, or science, when great literature, plays, and novels are as foreign to you as hieroglyphics, do you have any chance of seeing your work, career, or life in a new light?

You might be doing well in the race, but it's the same race essentially down the same track with the same opponents that might prove to be less than sufficient in enabling you to get those kinds of things done that you want to have completed.

Coming Undone

"People never are alone now . . . We make them hate solitude, and we arrange their lives so that it's almost impossible for them ever to have it." —Aldous Huxley, *Brave New World* (Doubleday, 1932)

Even if you're among the rare few who recognize how crucial safeguarding your day and work time has become, the chances are highly likely that you are not immune to the call of the modern day siren—the smart phone.

The All-Time Intruder

The results are in: the mobile phone has become the most disruptive aspect of work and everyday life. With now more than four-fifths of the population sporting them, it's nearly a given that any part of your day is subject to disruption.

On a plane, in a meeting, during a presentation, at a business lunch, or yes, in the restroom, some well-meaning but otherwise boorish soul will whip out a cell phone and engage in public space cell yell. And the conversations, oh my, are some inane!

It's not that you can't accomplish things with the use of a cell phone, indeed you can accomplish a great deal with them. However, the nature of what you handle is skewed. As the man with only a hammer sees everything as nails, the incessant cell phone user accomplishes a variety of tasks, understandably enough, that accrue directly to having a cell phone.

Factoid

An annual Lemelson-MIT invention index survey found that when asked to name the invention they hate the most but can't live without, 30 percent of respondents said the cell phone. Second to the cell phone were alarm clocks at 25 percent, followed by television at 23 percent and razors at 14 percent.

Sometimes this get-things-done kind of individual overdoes this stay-in-touch aspect of what he's trying to accomplish. How many times can you call a client? How often do you need to stay in touch with your office? Would every 60 minutes do it, or would 45 minutes be better, or 30 better still?

Many career professionals are uncomfortable with solitude. Increasingly, this discomfort tolerates only shorter and shorter attention spans. To retreat into one's own mind, to pause, to reflect, is now treated as if it were enemy territory.

Coming Undone

What kinds of new tasks and new responsibilities at work are you creating for yourself and others as a result of the constant communication and over-communication?

As the world wide web and interactive media begin to purvey our lives at even higher levels than they do now through the myriad of hand held and miniature devices as well as publicly pervasive audio/video displays, any career professional who wants a quiet, reflective moment is going to have to fight for it.

Work Distractions Feed Upon Themselves

Sadly, the higher the level of distraction, as with information overload, the greater we tend to seek information. You can get things done with electronic gadgetry, but beware: the types of things you complete will be of a certain ilk. Whole other realms of accomplishments might be unknown or out of reach for you.

It is vital to regain, or perhaps develop for the first time the ability to take quiet reflection. In doing so, at first, you will feel as if you've been left out of the party, but was it a party you wanted to attend in the first place? And even if you wanted to attend, did you want to attend all the time at that decibel level with no breaks?

Long-term types of accomplishment, grand achievements in your career—the big stuff— might require going where you haven't gone before, to that place and frame of mind where the best of your thoughts can emerge. In *The Unknown Craftsman*, Soetsu Yanagi says, "Man is most free when his tools are proportionate to his needs." For example, for optimal productivity, a carpenter needs woodworking tools and an environment conducive to his/ her work, not a steam shovel or an army tank.

When you learn to value quiet reflection over frenetic activity, the breadth and scope of what you can achieve notably improves. Silence can be golden if you respect it, harness it effectively, and recognize the gift that it has always provided.

Let's turn now to Chapter 2 and the four components of getting things done.

CHAPTER 2

The Four Components of Getting Things Done

In This Chapter:

➤ Oh, to be organized
➤ An inside time management secret
➤ Efficiency matters
➤ Effectiveness is critical

This chapter examines each of four vital components of getting things done, so that you'll have a firm understanding of them.

Long before the era of information and communication overload, and long after it, people looked for and people will continue to seek ways to get things done. Getting things done, however, can mean different things to different people. The terminology is hazy. As used throughout this book, getting things done will refer to one's ability to draw upon four components for success at work, including: becoming organized, managing your time better, improving efficiency, and increasing effectiveness.

Becoming Organized

The phrase "to get organized" as in "I've got to get organized!" serves as a rallying cry for some and invokes dread in others. The legions of career professionals who, I've met at more than 825 speeches I've given and more than 250 companies I've consulted for, seem to fall into one of two camps. They either:

➤ embrace getting and remaining organized and have reasonable skills in doing so, or
➤ are not good at getting and remaining organized and even if they have the skills, don't seem to employ them well.

No moral judgment is attached to "getting organized." If you're perpetually disorganized, you're still a good person. Some of the greatest geniuses throughout history have had poor organizational skills, and most were not considered ogres. Being organized in and of itself doesn't necessarily add up to a hill of beans in terms of getting specific things done.

Often, those who are proficient at getting things done also have organizational skills. Think of a political campaign with little coordination, construction of a new building where work schedules are unpredictable, or a hospital where the admitting procedure is unstructured. That candidate will lose, the bridge will be over budget (if ever finished), and the hospital admittance office, . . . well, don't go there, literally.

On a personal level, disorganization can cost one time, money, and even respect of one's peers (who might have otherwise been willing to be of assistance). If personal organization has been a continuing problem, perhaps what I offer here will make a huge difference in your career.

Organizing is Fundamental

You wouldn't drive your car and expect to cruise for 300 miles with a gallon or two of gasoline in your tank. Likewise, your range of professional capabilities will be limited if you're low on one of the key components that keeps your getting-things-done vehicle operating smoothly: organizing as a fundamental component to consistently getting a lot of things done.

Generally, people aren't born with organizing skills; they are acquired along the way. When you seek to become organized, do you quit after a short time, believing it's hopeless? As I discuss in, *Breathing Space: Living & Working at a Comfortable Pace in a Sped-Up Society*, the key to getting and staying organized is making the effort. For many, it is a minor relief to learn how long it will take. It depends on how long your work space has been disorganized, but for most career professionals, allocating the equivalent of three full weekends should suffice.

Being neat and being organized are not the same thing. Not everything needs to be in its place as long as you know where items are and can access them freely. Why do some people shun getting organized? For whatever reason, they approach it with fear and trepidation. Like natives who believe that a photograph of them captures their soul, some people proceed as if getting organized will strip them of their inner essence. They become anxious about doing nothing but getting organized.

Dyna Moe

Getting organized requires effort and thought, while saving time and offering peace of mind. The minor paradox is that you spend time to save time. If it's helpful, think of getting organized as preparation "to respond to challenges."

Many traps to getting started could occur even when you know it makes sense to "clean house." Here are some major excuses for failing to start:

➤ "I have been meaning to." If this proves to be a familiar self-lament, then make getting personally and completely organized a high-ranking item in your life.

➤ "I've never been good at organizing." Okay, all is forgiven! The difference between people "good at organizing" and "not good" is that organized individuals understand the level of effort needed to maintain the organization. Those who are not so good at organizing, think that items somehow "get out of order."

➤ "I don't know how to start." Keep reading.

➤ "I have so many other things to do." Of course you do; you will for the rest of your career. Becoming organized will support what you want to accomplish.

➤ "Organizing will take too much time." Initially, it requires about three weekends. Also, consider how much time disorganization has cost you.

➤ "I don't see any value in organizing." Many aspects of your career are already organized. Now you're going to extend the procedures to enhance your ability to get things done.

➤ "It makes me anxious; I don't feel that I am accomplishing that much." Tossing unnecessary files and papers to create more space in itself can accomplish a great deal.

Sometimes, people use getting organized as a stalling technique, but in general, being organized greatly enhances your ability to manage your time thereafter.

Don't Equate Organizing Time with Wasted Time

Sometimes it seems as if the energy and effort you expend in getting organized will be a waste. After all, if you're already feeling behind and have much to accomplish, wouldn't good time management necessitate simply jumping in and handling those things that beg for your attention? Not exactly . . . Often, you have to slow down in order to speed up.

By slowing down, you give yourself a chance to collect your thoughts, form a more coherent plan, perhaps take a deep breath or drink some water, and then tackle the project anew. Knowing where items are located puts you in charge and provides freedom to concentrate on creative, fulfilling, or necessary tasks. Part 2 of this book offers many tips on getting organized.

Managing Your Time

Managing your time better at work is the second of four components that contributes to your ability to get things done. You've read much about time management before you picked up this book. The great secret to time management, and perhaps you were the last on your block to be told, is that to speed up—operate at a productive pace and get a lot of the things done—often you first need to slow down and consider how to best proceed.

Minutes Add Up to Years

Have you ever contemplated how much time you have in your whole life, and how much time you've spent on various activities?

Suppose you graduated from college at the age of 22, and in the course of your life expect to work about 48 years, bringing you to age 70. In a 48 year career, on any given day, often it seems we don't value, or perhaps recognize, how small amounts of time add up. Hence, we do not sufficiently value our time.

As explained in *The Smart Guide to Winning Back Your Time*, any activity in which you engage for only 30 minutes a day in the course of your 48-year work life will take one solid year of your life!

Factoid

Benjamin Franklin once said "Time is money." In this world, minutes and even seconds count. The key currency of life, to many people, is time.

If you read junk mail, for 30 minutes on average each day, then in the course of 48 years you've spent the equivalent of one solid year, nonstop, reading junk mail. What a waste!

The time in your career is being drained on frivolous activity; the cumulative impact of engaging in minutia is monumental; your precious years are being consumed. This is time the universe will not hand back to you.

What do you need to stop doing because it takes up valuable time in your life? Here are some suggestions:

➤ Stop reading junk mail because it's addressed to you. Stop reading unsolicited email messages, jokes, and crazy schemes zapped over to you.
➤ Stop allowing drop-in visitors with no useful agenda.
➤ Stop handling tasks that should be delegated or outsourced.
➤ Stop saying "yes" to many requests

Interruptions and Plaguing Time Wasters

The top time wasters for career professionals on a daily, weekly, and yearly basis change little. Lack of direction, shifting objectives, and inadequate planning that leads to crisis management is high on the list. Equally troubling these days, as we've discussed, is the frequency of interruptions via the cell phone and other electronic gadgetry.

As one person commented to me, "I can't tell you how often I've had a conversation interrupted because someone's phone had buzzed with an incoming email, for which the person stopped our conversation to reply . . . People seem compelled to be reachable at all times."

Some people are plagued with the inability to say "no" and otherwise show lack of discipline in approaching vital tasks that they wish to get done. Certainly the lack of organization has manifested in cluttered desks and cabinets, in piles growing around the room, and in misplaced items.

Some people are ineffective at delegating and are steeped in the "Promethean" urge to take care of everything by themselves. Attempting to tackle a great deal might be admirable, but seeking to do too much all the time is simply foolish. It leads to more errors, frustration, and the injudicious allocation of resources. Fortunately, prudent time management principles are presented throughout this book.

The Difference Between Efficiency and Effectiveness

The third and fourth components of getting things done are improving efficiency and becoming more effective.

Misunderstood Terminology

Efficiency and effectiveness are terms that are often misunderstood. Some people think that they are synonymous, and freely substitute one for the other. Actually, they represent two different concepts which work best in concert with each other.

If you run an automated car wash business, on any given day, you want to send as many cars through the wash tunnel as practical (efficient). At the same time, each car's exterior needs to be completely, expertly washed (effective).

Word Power

Think of efficiency as taking the right approach to a job, doing it quickly with few or no errors, generating results with little or no wasted effort. Effectiveness by contrast, means undertaking the right task, with the goal of producing a desired, worthwhile effect.

It's no advantage to offer a complete wash so slowly that you only handled a few cars a day (inefficient). Likewise, it would be deleterious to long-term business to have the fastest car wash in town, but the cars aren't washed well (ineffective). In this case, efficiency and effectiveness, as so often happens, are intertwined.

Improving Your Efficiency

So, a quick review: efficiency can be described as doing a job correctly, and effectiveness can be described as performing the right job. Efficiency is the measure of productivity, how swiftly you can accomplish something.

The following is a list of efficiency-related activities:

➤ Establish a routine of departing the house easily in the morning.
➤ Set out your clothes, work materials, or briefcase the night before.
➤ Respond to overnight communications (phone messages, TMs, faxes, and emails) before mid-morning.
➤ Be professional but succinct on the phone.
➤ Type email responses correctly on the first try by being clear and concise.
➤ Minimize break time. Don't lose productivity when a co-worker happens to drops by. Instead stop at a natural breaking point such as when work is completed.
➤ Use spare time during the day to complete smaller tasks.
➤ Bring a bag lunch and eat at your desk, but recognize that sometimes you need to step away to be refreshed.
➤ Handle tasks in a circular route, for example, from your starting point, plan your route so as to not back track.
➤ Delay tasks that can wait, for example, instead of tackling any project as soon as it crosses your desk, defer less vital ones to a later date, yet allow enough time to be thorough.
➤ Update files as a part of a daily routine, for example, discard notes and papers that are no longer germane to your current projects.
➤ Assemble meeting notes and conduct or attend meetings on time.
➤ Stick to daily agendas as closely as possible.
➤ Straighten up after completing a task instead of letting things pile up.
➤ Maintain flagging energy in the late afternoon by having a mid-afternoon snack or by consciously tackling more taxing tasks before lunch.
➤ Finish up as many things as possible before departing for the day.
➤ Exercise right after work, before you go home.

Effectiveness Is Mandatory

In the quest to get things done, many career professionals are able to display high levels of efficiency in dispatching this task and that; however, the more compelling issue is whether or not they are embarking on the right task. Are they sensibly devoting their time and attention to tackling the key task or project?

On a daily basis, recognize that while efficiency is desirable and admirable, effectiveness is mandatory.

Unfortunately, the present day workplace, as it has evolved, often conveys that motion and activity are more important than closure and results. As a result, you see people dashing about like chickens about to lose their heads.

Those who develop a solid reputation for getting things done, particularly those who aspire to leadership, learn how to master the nuances. They understand that it's one thing to produce, say, a new software program, debug it, and ship it to users, and another thing for the software to be effective in the market.

To become a get-things-done type of career professional, make the commitment to perform your work efficiently while supporting the over-arching quest to attain objectives effectively. Shield yourself from information and communication overload, and focus on results.

When Pure Efficiency Equals Effectiveness

Oddly, efficiency in itself sometimes is all that's needed for effectiveness. For many years, I heard the stories about Chamra Tasmala (name changed to protect the wealthy), a neighbor of mine in Chapel Hill. She allegedly was a superstar real estate agent. I read that she had won an award for selling or renting $18 million worth of commercial property over so many years. My quick calculation showed that she was earning $400,000+ annually.

As time passed, I was considering relocating my office. I called Chamra, who identified several properties that potentially met my criteria.

I was eager to visit sites with Chamra because I was interested to see what she had found for me and to witness first-hand a legendary real estate agent in action.

Chamra was presentable, neither striking nor decrepit. She exuded some measure of success—nice car, no flashy jewelry, and the minimum trappings of fashion. I thought "she probably has an engaging, interactive style"; perhaps her persuasive skills coupled with direct eye contact were enough to make anyone think she had found the location that smartly suited your needs.

To my amazement, she didn't come close to impressing me with her interpersonal or selling skills. Her style consisted of opening the door, showing me around, and saying, "Here's the reception area, here's the bathroom, here's the kitchenette. Well, what do you think?" I kept saying to myself, "There's got to be more to her than this."

Where were the keen insights? The witticisms? The extra touches? The connection with my investment dreams? All were glaringly absent. She didn't possess any special skills. She never called me by name. I felt I was with a first-time agent who was unprepared and in a hurry. Her efforts seemed bare-bones.

She had mastered the critical issue in her industry, however, which was to find many prospects and show many properties. In essence, she played the numbers game and played it well. I thought of all those agents, not merely in real estate, in many other businesses, who earn their living by generating prospects, selling them a product, and earning a commission.

I also thought of all the books, articles, and everything else that's been written on "what you need to know and do" to be successful in such a business. Then, in the span of but a few minutes, Chamra's approach to real estate thoroughly trivialized the importance of these criteria. Focusing on a few critical elements made all the difference for Chamra.

As a top commercial real estate agent she was living proof that traditional success advice wasn't essential for success. I began to understand that the essence of success in most industries is misunderstood by most. All the guidance given by all the schlockmeisters was hardly necessary.

Word Power
A schlockmeister is a slang term which refers to people who have all sorts of advice to give, some of it questionable, on all sorts of topics.

Efficiency Alone Is Often Insufficient

Simply being efficient, in and of itself, usually does not add up to effectiveness.

➤   In a manufacturing concern, a product manager might be predisposed to ship a volume of products (efficiency) while a marketing manager is concerned with how customers rate the product (effectiveness).

➤   A human resources manager might be attuned to how well people are fulfilling the roles(effectiveness), while a shift supervisor is more concerned with not exceeding his quarter budget for labor (efficiency).

You might be proficient at knocking off one task after another on your to-do list. When you focus more on effectiveness, plowing through your list takes a backseat to strategizing

Coming Undone
It's possible to be efficient to the point of losing effectiveness, i.e. win the battle but lose the war. An efficient person is predisposed to staying busy, while the effective person keeps the desired ends in mind.

how to best handle the key items on the list. Some items, perhaps, can be delegated, some deferred. Two items might be combined, and so on.

If you're in sales and you're making calls on prospects daily, being efficient would entail calling on as many as you can. Being effective would mean concentrating more time and energy on higher potential prospects and probing for their underlying objectives.

Some professionals proceed as if they can handle everything as long as they stay focused. This is seen in the sales manager who seeks to increase his department's quarterly volume by 12 percent, inspire his territory managers each day, enroll in an evening course at a local university, spend more time with his wife and kids, rise to a position of leadership in his professional society, and maintain peak fitness.

Such professionals harbor the notion that if they can find a way to work more efficiently, they'll be able to "get it all done." So, they race through some tasks as fast as possible, slow down a bit for others, rarely pause and reflect, and remain in that mode for hours, days, or weeks.

When doing things rapidly doesn't seem to be enough, such managers stay on the job longer each day. To be sure, at times it makes sense to work in a long day. When weekly work hours start to stack up and cut into one's personal time, stress, anxiety, and exhaustion are all but predictable. The stakes seemingly increase as one's perspective decreases.

Remember, an over-emphasis on efficiency, often characterized by attempting to handle too much at once, can lead to burnout.

Coming Undone

Some managers fall into the "I must do it all" trap because they don't trust others. Some have no inkling of how to delegate effectively (See Chapter 21). Others succumb because they see coworkers all around them putting in exorbitantly long hours. Hence they believe that this is the only way to approach one's work and get things done.

Efficiency is wonderful, especially when handling routine tasks or, in the case of Chamra, when you can make numbers work in your favor. Efficiency is more desirable when it's combined with effectiveness.

Becoming More Effective

Some people mistakenly equate multi-tasking with effectiveness, but multi-tasking is an attempt to be ever-more efficient, and the price can climb too high (see Chapter 15).

The ability to stay organized and to manage your own time is critical if you are managing others. For indeed, if you cannot stay organized or manage your own time, how can you possibly manage other people?

The effective manager is interested in how his staff proceeds through their day as well as how they harness their ideas and insights, their knowledge and wisdom, and their energy and enthusiasm. This is the manager who is focused on achieving powerful results and recognizes that sometimes the path to such results involves starts and stops, twists and turns, reformulation and reconfiguration.

The following is a list of effectiveness-related activities:

- ➤ Staying on target.
- ➤ Focusing on the big picture.
- ➤ Matching customer needs with products and services.
- ➤ Getting feedback from customers.
- ➤ Making mid-course adjustments.
- ➤ Minimizing error rates.
- ➤ Striving for results.
- ➤ Establishing repeat customers.
- ➤ Building word of mouth.
- ➤ Engendering client referrals.
- ➤ Aligning goals with priorities.
- ➤ Meeting organizational objectives.
- ➤ Staying true to the mission.
- ➤ Aspiring to market leadership.

Effective managers are open to the ideas of bosses, coaches, mentors, coworkers, or subordinates. They know that no one has a monopoly on good ideas. They're willing to study case histories, examine what other people have tried, and learn what worked well and what didn't work so well. They've heard the expression "An ounce of prevention is worth a pound of cure." They're willing to question their own activities, modify plans, and adjust to changing situations.

Effective managers take the time to re-evaluate, and regard re-evaluation as a key element on the road to getting things done. Effective managers can do great things for themselves and for their respective organizations. Effective leaders can do great things for their society. Effective workers can do great things on the job.

Dyna Moe

Productive managers understand the power of germination, how taking a few minutes break here and there often yields fresh insights that simply weren't available a few minutes before.

Helpful Insights for Getting Things Done

Part 2
Helpful Insights for Getting Things Done

This part of the book contains three chapters, and each offers insights and perspectives to aid you on the path to getting things done. The first covers topics such as the importance of environment, why good ideas are like slippery fish, giving yourself the edge, and harnessing your passion. The next makes the bold assertion that whatever energizes you dramatically increases your ability to get things done, whereas whatever zaps your energy dramatically decreases your ability to get things done. The last discusses how what you do at home, and even how you arrive at work, can impact your ability to succeed.

CHAPTER 3

Traits of the High Achiever

In This Chapter:

➤ Who becomes successful and why
➤ Resiliency through trying times
➤ Being productive in an ever-changing environment
➤ Passion and getting things done

The rich get richer and the healthy tend to stay healthy even at advanced ages. As we'll explore in this chapter, the best at getting things done learn from the best. The adept get more adept.

Early on, by luck or circumstance, budding high achievers recognize the importance of associating with and learning from fellow high achievers. Further, they read biographies of people from the last century like Edison, Disney, and Curie, as well as Hewlett, Packard, Grove, Gates, Jobs, and the current throng of digital and broadband pioneers.

Top Achievers Have the Right Mix

Top-achieving individuals have the requisite energy to succeed, but it's not frantic energy. These trailblazers face the onslaught of information and communication overload much like any other career professional. In both thought and deed, however, they are not inclined to rush around the office, wolf down sandwiches, or jam-pack their schedule to fill every minute. They develop a form of "relaxed" energy that allows them to maintain stamina, concentrate on complex problems, focus on the matter at hand, and get things done.

Dyna Moe

Top achievers have the ability to both stand out and fit in. They understand the importance of being "artful," personable motivators, and good communicators. They seem to intuitively understand or discover how to combine efficiency and effectiveness.

The Courage to Act

Deborah Benton, author of *Lions Don't Need to Roar*, has observed many hundreds of CEOs, COOs, and company presidents with an eye on what enables them to get so much done.

She finds that while it's essential to be competent in one's position, inspire confidence in others, act accordingly at business functions, and become adept at maneuvering within the firm. In business, unlike politics, "empty suits" don't make it to the top, or anywhere near there.

Benton says top executives "are not magical, blessed, or dramatically different from you or me. They simply have skills and outlooks that the rest of us don't have, but can get," and so can you, such as taking calculated risks and enhancing their "people" skills.

Taking Calculated Risks

Top achievers understand that staying put can be risky, so they take decisive action. In the book, *Surfacing the Edge of Chaos: The Laws of Nature and the New Laws of Business*, the authors argue that "equilibrium is a precursor to death."

The people who get things done have the guts to speak in front of others, take calculated risks—realizing that the experience will be invaluable—and make that phone call that others would rather avoid. Benton knows of executive managers who have called individuals months after they were fired from their firm to "see how they were doing." One company executive remarked that when he evaluated a job candidate, he would become leery if the candidate appeared to be

Dyna Moe

The notion of taking calculated risks runs deep among the get-it-done types who are adept at assessing a situation and will go out on a limb to optimize its potential.

too good. "If I see no failures, I assume he's had it too easy." Could this mean that, on the path to accomplishing a lot, now and then you're going to have some failures? Absolutely.

Top Achievers Know that People Count

A popular stereotype holds that high-achievers tend to be stodgy types. However, Benton finds the situation to be the opposite. Get-things-done type executives laugh and smile often, are fond of telling relevant stories, and know how and when to physically touch others. They're well-skilled in how to ask for favors and they realize how important that makes others feel.

Regardless of how high-tech society becomes, people make deals, make products, and provide services. As we'll cover in Part 6, pacesetters learn the essential elements about interacting with people that many others never do. A veteran manager in one manufacturing company allocates a portion of his day to making personal contact with the people who report to him and the buyers in client companies. He cares, and he wants his employees to care, about their company and customers.

Achievers Read Others

Get-things-done types in larger organizations learn to "read" others in great detail and to pay attention to others' needs. By "observing aggressively" anyone can learn to read people, and by reading people, work better with them. Meeting those needs enables successful people to negotiate deals skillfully, manage employees responsibly with the least amount of stress and resistance, gain information, or enlist people to support their cause. The crucial characteristic required in this process is that of "aggressive observation."

When two people meet, aggressive observation requires that a person take action, listen carefully to the content of the conversation, and watch for signals in body language.

Word Power

Aggressive observation, a phrase coined by the late Mark McCormack, author of *Staying Street Smart in the Internet Age*, requires working with people face-to-face whenever possible because what you observe about a person is far more revealing than what you hear or read.

The Brilliance of Resilience

One of the widely observed traits that high achievers possess is resilience. Accomplishing big things at work, or even winning a long-term personal struggle, requires resilience that is

Word Power

Resilience entails adopting behaviors to meet challenges, but it is more than enduring a challenging situation or overcoming an ordeal. It means having the ability to come back even stronger than before.

demonstrated through patience, alertness, and steadfastness. These behaviors set the stage for adaptation and action.

Why is resilience fundamental to dealing with upheaval in our professional or personal lives? Because those who have resilience flourish!

Resilient people are able to establish a balance—they believe they'll succeed; they sharpen their focus on the tasks at hand, they stay loose, and they roll with the punches. They maintain orderliness and self-awareness largely to avoid becoming overwhelmed and confused.

While resilient individuals are as vulnerable to the anxieties of change as anyone else, they're able to regain balance quickly, stay physically and emotionally healthy, and remain productive when confronted by confusing or gloomy situations.

Recognizing that Setbacks are not Forever

When nothing is working, resilient individuals still manage to figure out how to land back on track. They apply such ingenuity to daily tasks, long term projects, group or team relations, and problems with the boss. If they lose a client, they're willing to rigorously assess why. If something's going wrong on a project, they jump in to see why. They consider the possibilities, then take each one and follow it through for any insights that emerge.

Resilient people are adept at managing sudden, significant, and complex change with minimum dysfunctional behavior. Their capability can be a marvel to behold.

Factoid

Ghandi said, "Be the change that you wish to see in the world." So, by identifying, observing, and then incorporating the behaviors of resilient people, it's possible to change your own behavior to better deal with the world around and within you.

Rather than shrink from controversy, they're more likely to dive into the fray. They take a stand-up role, admitting where and when they were wrong, if that be the case. They assess the choices they made that lead to a result and what other choices they could make to achieve a more desirable outcome.

When they find themselves boxed in on all sides, they don't despair or feel sorry for themselves, at least not for long. They're willing to record their feelings, brainstorm, or even rearrange the file cabinet, knowing that such activities can be therapeutic. Perhaps most vital, they determine what they can accomplish right now, today, since getting things done, in and of itself, generally proves to be an uplifting experience, however small the deed.

Who in your workplace is great at getting things done, seems to roll with the punches, and doesn't come unglued in the face of setbacks? That's the person to emulate.

Realizing That Arrangements Are Temporary

While resilient types have or develop flexibility and know when to roll with the punches, often they are above average at overcoming attachment to a place, a piece of equipment, a method, or even a business philosophy. They seem to understand that, particularly in the workplace, virtually all arrangements are temporary. For example, your office or work space, the equipment you use, the people to whom you report, the people who report to you, the customers or clients your company serves, the products or services you offer, even the methods of operation, eventually, are all subject to change.

As a lot, resilient individuals don't seem to be as flustered by bends in the road. If they're thwarted in some project area, they make forward progress in other areas. They use what they have to attain what they want.

Don't Let Good Ideas Slip Away

High achievers tend to record or write down their plans and ideas. They understand that, as the late Earl Nightingale once said, "Ideas are like slippery fish." Nightingale was a soldier stationed on the U.S.S. Maine when it was attacked by the Japanese in Pearl Harbor. Later he became a high-achieving sales professional, motivational speaker, and audio pioneer. He co-founded the Nightingale-Conant Company, in its day, a leader of self-help recordings.

Word Power

Singularities are one-time events in the universe, or in terms of your own thinking, one time events in your brain. You have to make the most of them.

Nightingale knew that if you wanted make a dramatic improvement in your productivity, if you didn't act on the thought, you'd probably end up just working the same old way. Most ideas that slip away will not come back.

You rarely experience the same moment of brilliant inspiration twice. Such moments are what Professor Stephen Hawking refers to as singularities.

Use Your Passion as the Driving Force

Some high achievers tap their passions as the driving force to get things done, particularly when working with others. Many organizations, including yours, have the same basic equipment, technology, resources, and even expertise among their employees.

So what makes one company or one branch more productive than another? A growing number of human resource professionals point to the passion that prevails within the organization.

Passion in the Workplace

In his book, *The Passion Plan at Work*, Richard Chang cites six tangible benefits that an organization can derive as a result of the passion that its managers imbue upon the staff.

1. Attracting the right type of employee. —"The passion-driven organization appeals to the superstars of the job market." says Chang.
2. Direction and focus. —Passion can define the direction the business takes whether at the regional, local, or branch level. The passion of your particular business, office, or store is the filter with which all decisions are made.
3. Energy. —When a manager is passionate about the company, about his work, and about his employees, everyone benefits. Staff can become supercharged. Daily, an extra level of energy can empower the company and often make a huge difference between getting the job done and performing with distinction.
4. Loyalty. —Relationships with employees that are built on passion have a higher probability of succeeding. It's shown repeatedly that money is no substitute for the connection a manager can make with his staff, more so with a young staff.
5. Unity. —When managers, team leaders, and employees share a common passion, they stand on common ground. "They are connected on a deeper level to achieving the organization's objectives," says Chang. Each incident and each day might not go smoothly—this is not to say there won't be some friction here and there—but overall passion is a unifying element for which there is little substitute.
6. Heightened performance. —Passion helps drive improvements in both quality and quantity of work that staff will perform. "If passion is alive and well at work," says Chang, "your company has a clear advantage over its competitors."

On an individual basis, many managers can muster significant levels of passion when it comes to facing competition, meeting a sales quota, or some short-term campaign. The passion discussed here, though, involves making a leap from being a reason-based manager to one who is also a passion-driven manager, not that anything is wrong with reason.

Often, managers lose touch with the passions that they once drew upon to energize themselves and those around them. Chang says when you re-clarify what you want to achieve and find that your purpose is in alignment with your core passions, it will become a sustaining element of your work.

Influencing with Passion

Be on the lookout for what Chang calls "purpose by default." If your purpose fails to reflect your true, underlying passion, this can lead to a lack of focus and less-than-desirable performance on the part of you and your staff.

Once your passion begins to take effect, you might find it easier to influence staff who wish to be involved with the energy that derives from your passion. Go ahead, ride the wave: with seemingly little effort, take-charge types with positive infectious attitudes can amass support from others.

Stick close to your passion. You might have abandoned it once before—it's too easy to retreat to totally reason-based management. Use your passion to help others latch on to your ideas and aspirations. Stay close to your passion and diligently seek to preserve it.

Coming Undone

Be careful: any changes you introduce could confuse others. Staff might not be able to accept or benefit from new approaches if you spring things on them too quickly.

 Manage Energy, Not Time

This chapter emphasizes that how you manage yourself and your energy level says much about how productive you will be with your time. An energetic you is a more effective you. Unfortunately, messages everywhere lure us towards energy-zapping temptations. Energy zappers come in many forms: getting too little sleep, drinking the wrong beverages, eating the wrong foods, and lying or sitting too much.

Let's examine each of these four areas with a focus on what you can do to ensure that your propensity for high productivity hovers at a desirable level.

The Power of Sleep

It's a widespread ritual to plop down in front of the TV or surf the web for at least 30 to 60 minutes before going to bed. You worked a long hard day, handled lots of responsibilities at home, and now feel that you deserve to sit and relax. Alas studies show rather than calming people down before they retire, TV actually stirs them up.

Before the television era, more people would actually read before going to bed. Many people today read a little before conking for the night but usually the reading follows a stint of late-night TV. Regardless of how you feel as your head hits the pillow, if you unwittingly stimulate yourself through TV, your nervous system will respond accordingly. You can't fool it.

Coming Undone

Most of the shows you watch, whether sitcoms, dramas, reality shows, sports, movies, documentaries, talk shows, or news tends to arouse, not calm, your nervous system. Rather than going to bed in a subdued state, ready for deep reverie, your nervous system might be working overtime to calm you down as a result of the added stimuli you heaped upon it before retiring.

Getting Ready for Bed

A survey sponsored by one bed manufacturer revealed that adults engage in a wide variety of activities before getting ready for bed. In order, such activities include:

Watching TV, web surfing	75%
Securing the home	59%
Reading	53%
Setting the alarm clock	50%
Praying or meditating	43%
Checking on children	33%
Snacking	32%
Listening to the radio	26%
Exercising	20%
Drinking a nightcap	13%

Note: these numbers add up to far more than 100 percent since
many people engage in two or more activities before retiring.

Coming Undone

Drinking a nightcap is not recommended for anyone. A glass of wine or other alcoholic beverage will help induce sleep, but the effects are temporary. Alcohol dries out your system and contributes to waking sooner than you'd prefer.

Most of these activities are not conducive to sleep. Securing the house makes good sense, as does checking on the children, setting the alarm clock, and praying or meditating.

Listening to the radio, and surfing the Internet are probably harmless from the standpoint of inducing sleep depending upon what stations or what web sites you patronize. Certainly some people like to listen to a favorite show or visit a favorite website.

Contemplating the list from top to bottom, as many as half of the activities that adults engage in during their pre-bedtime ritual do not support sufficient deep, restful, undisturbed sleep. A Prevention Magazine survey showed that 40 percent of U.S. adults "suffer from stress every day of their lives and find they can sleep no more than six hours a night."

In a *Time* Magazine feature titled, "Drowsy America," the director of Stanford University's sleep center concluded most adults "no longer know what it feels like to be fully alert." The National Sleep Foundation found that almost 68 percent of adults are getting too little sleep, and 58 percent suffer from some type of insomnia at least once a week. These people are not simply a little groggy or sluggish, but walking around as if in a stupor. This situation represents a cultural dilemma, but not one to which you need fall prey.

As a get-things-done type of professional, you've already discovered that when you short change your sleep too often, your mind and body simply don't respond near optimal capability. What you do at night significantly affects your ability to get things done the next day.

Most experts agree that three to four hours of sleep once a week won't cause any long-term problems. You might feel awful the next day, but you can recover somewhat by going to bed earlier the next evening, or napping if that is an option for you. You might have to force yourself to jump into bed at 8:30 or 9:00 on evenings when you'd rather be up and about, but do it—your body will thank you.

If you're missing out on more than ten hours a week, decide to catch up on your sleep now before you further diminish your capabilities. Recovery could take a month or more but it will be worth it.

Factoid

Your immune system and mental skills decline when you habitually have less sleep than you need.

Don't Fight the System

In *The Organic Clock*, author Kenneth Rose observes that each part and function of your body has its own timing. A heartbeat, breathing, speaking, and even hiccupping have their own rhythm. If you sleep too little (or too much!), you disrupt internal cycles . . . that required millions of years to evolve.

Rose observes that each of your body's functions is reset every 24 hours, which parallels the natural daily light cycle. Every essence of your being is subject to this circadian rhythm, which is the daily cycle of activity in living organisms. Altering that rhythm for a prolonged period is contrary to your own physiology. It's like being at war with yourself!

In his book, *The 24-Hour Society*, Martin Moore-Ede observes that certain times of the day are important to sleep through, such as between 2:00 a.m. and 5:00 a.m. when human physiology is at its lowest level of alertness. Highest alertness, by the way, is between 9:00 a.m. and noon, and also from 4:00 to 8:00 p.m.

If you're short on sleep one particular day, light exercise such as stretching or a brief walk works well, perking up your energy level perhaps for an hour or two. If you have the opportunity to nap, that would help as well.

Factoid

Your alertness will vary according to hours of consecutive work, hours of work in the preceding week, your regular hours, any monotony you face on the job, the timing and duration of naps you take, lighting, sound, aroma, temperature, and cumulative sleep deprivation, among other factors.

All About Napping

Napping can increase your alertness for the rest of the day. Some people nap easily; others can't seem to nap at all. You already know which camp you fall into. Here are facts about napping:

➤   The best nap time is between 2 and 3 p.m. Any later and your nap might be too deep and interfere with your nightly sleep.

➤   Your quality of sleep will be higher and the immediate benefits more apparent if you nap in a bed or cot versus a chair.

➤   You might feel a little groggy for a few minutes after a nap. This gradually subsides.

➤   Short naps are more productive than long naps. A short nap will leave you refreshed; a long nap might interfere with your nightly sleep. Naps of 20 minutes or less can help avoid REM sleep, a stage where you're likely to wake up and remain groggy.

➤   To derive the most from your nap, ensure that phones or other gadgets won't disturb you. Post a "Do Not Disturb" sign if that will help.

Even with all that said, naps are not a good substitute for regularly getting the right amount of sleep.

What You Eat Is How You Think

Eating nutritiously and at the right times can benefit your attitude and capability at work. For many of us, however, heeding the need for balanced meals is yesterday's news and yesterday's discipline. Since Ray Kroc opened the first McDonald's in 1955, society has become a "fast food culture" ad nauseam. Family and work demands have kept fast food restaurants in business and despite all the scary headlines in recent years, many people still have poor diets and poor eating habits.

To get back on track, start with a good breakfast. Studies show that people who skip breakfast are missing on an important source of energy for their day—and therefore have less energy than those who eat breakfast. People who skip their morning meal also tend to have a higher proportion of fat to other substances in the body. So take the extra ten minutes, and fuel your body in the morning. Your body will thank you.

Don't skip any meals. If you skip a meal, the ensuing hunger and lowered blood sugar can make you tired. It can also make you want to eat a huge meal later, and you will end up consuming a large quantity of unhealthy food to satisfy your hunger instead of eating two smaller, more reasonable meals. This will make you feel tired and sluggish afterward and, if you make a habit of it, gain weight.

Dyna Moe

Have a good breakfast every morning! People who skip breakfast are not as mentally sharp, have less physical energy, and tend to put on weight more easily than those who take the time for for this important and first meal of the day.

Hydrate or Die

Nutritionist David Meinz says that every chemical reaction occurring in your body, including all that goes on during the work day, involves water. Your productivity at work is directly linked to your degree of hydration. The brain itself is 75 percent water. Our thirst mechanisms lag behind our true need for water, so even a 2 percent reduction in the amount of body water renders a pronounced lack of productivity. A 5 percent reduction in our body's water supply yields decreased mental functioning.

Eight cups of water a day is still the standard, but most people wait until their thirst reminds them. Drink before you're thirsty. After a hard work out, your body needs 24 hours to regain the proper water supply. If you regularly work out, you are constantly in need of more water than you think.

Factoid

Air-conditioned rooms usually have some humidity added, but heated rooms generally are dry. So, drink more when you stay in heated rooms for prolonged periods. Women are at risk for de-hydration since they have a lower water content due to a smaller lean muscle mass than men.

Regardless of what you're working on, keep water nearby and take several sips when you can. From the standpoint of getting more done, it is better to pee often than to experience even mild dehydration. Don't wait until you know you're thirsty. Thirst is actually your body's alert that you're dehydrated. So drink up.

Circulation: Work Out to Work Better

Television and computers and other information and entertainment delivery systems have made our society a sedentary one, and our bodies pay the price. In the past few decades an alarming percentage of adults from industrialized nations have become overweight, if not obese. Exercise-deficiency is the major culprit. Exercise gives us more energy, makes us healthier, and boosts self-confidence.

You need some type of exercise every day. Walking 10,000 steps—about an hour for most people—is ideal. If you can't exercise for more than a few minutes at least do something. If you work in a high-rise building, take the stairs when you're heading down and when you're only going up one floor or two.

Seek little ways all day long for a few moments of exercise. For example, park your car a block or two away from a store you're going to. If you're in a mall parking lot, park at the far end of the lot and walk the two to three blocks. If you use public transportation, leave the bus or subway one stop or a few blocks before you normally would, and walk the rest of the way.

No matter how demanding your schedule, make time for leisure. Especially in our supercharged, rushed society, leisure is a vital component of our lives. Creating free time for hobbies and activities is essential to keeping our lives in balance and avoiding burn out in our primary preoccupations. Fortunately, there are more activities to choose from than you will ever be able to perform, let alone perform well, in a single lifetime.

The activities you choose can help you to be energetic, alert, and more productive on the job.

CHAPTER 5

Accomplishment Is Personal

In This Chapter:

➤ Leadership begins at home
➤ Morning has broken
➤ Right time and right mood traps
➤ Energy from small maneuvers

This chapter explains how what you do at home impacts productivity at work. To make yourself ultra-productive at work, make your home life a sanctuary.

Lead at Home, Succeed at Work

Increasingly, it can be argued that one's home life is more stressful than one's work life. High achievers and those who realize the importance of managing their energy as well as their time, acknowledge the importance of balancing work- and domestic-related issues.

At work, for all the demands and pressures, some semblance of order exists. You report to someone, others might report to you. There are meetings, agendas, goals, and objectives. You're assigned specific responsibilities and are expected to meet them within a given time frame. Your compensation and continued employment depend upon your ability to deliver on a regular basis. This regimentation, though challenging, also offers some comfort.

Is any of the above true at home? Home environments tend to have less structure. Whether you're part of a family, live with a significant other, or live alone, your home environment might contribute to your sense of fatigue, indirection, and low energy at work. Too much clutter, distractions, responsibilities, and items competing for your time and attention, and too little order could well result in a tired, discombobulated, unfocused you.

Take control of your home environment, recognizing that your ability to get things done at work is partially dependent upon it. Begin with how you depart your home each morning.

Leave in the Morning with Grace and Ease

If leaving the house each morning represents a time-pressured, hectic routine for you, then you'll might find it more difficult to handle challenges in the office. As you learned in Chapter 4, as in the case of watching television before retiring, your nervous system has to deal with everything that you feed it.

If you live in a major metropolitan area and you're a good distance from your workplace, you might be battling the crowds every morning. Or your morning commute might otherwise be out of your control.

Certainly, you can attempt to arise and depart before the masses, or after them. You might not have leeway as to when you must arrive at work. Hence, make your journey as pleasant as possible. If you drive, then ensure that you have music or programs that soothe and inspire you.

Coming Undone

If you've left yourself too little time; haven't placed important items by the door the night before; gulp down highly sugared, caffeinated, or fat-laden food products; and then fight your way through the masses to arrive at your place of work; be prepared for what might turn into at least 30 to 60 minutes before you finally "calm down" and can begin to focus on accomplishing worth-while tasks.

Take Steps the Night Before

If you awaken by alarm clock then, by definition, you didn't get enough sleep. Determine at which hour you can retire and easily awake on your own without the aid of an alarm. If you need eight hours, then obviously to arise at six you'll have to retire by ten.

Coming Undone

If you're going to bed at 11 or 11:30, and waking up by alarm, you can slug through the day and perhaps, succeed in the short term. In the long term, too little catches up to you and mutes your effectiveness.

If it helps, lay out your next day's clothes the night before. Have nutritious food ready. Eating junk at home or eating too quickly will not give you the fuel you need to accomplish one thing after another at work. You'll run out of gas too soon and then seek quick and easy stimulants . . . did someone say caffeine? . . . to keep you going. This is no way to work, no way to treat your body, and no way to proceed on your life's journey.

Arrive Ready, Progress Steady

When you arrive in the morning, particularly if you're there before the rest of the staff, you have a good opportunity for structuring your day. Envision how you would like your day to go. Review your appointment calendar and plot the few critical elements that will make your day a success. Keep flat surfaces clear when you can.

If you work at home, after everyone else has departed, take a few minutes for the same type of contemplation. If you have young children or other household occupants, carving out a few minutes for yourself early in the morning is even more crucial. How would you like your day to unfold? What are the critical tasks you wish to complete?

Learn Your Productivity Cycle

At all times, the person who best knows how to keep you productive is *you*. As often as possible, you want to work with your internal rhythm so that you generate the best of yourself while minimizing any stress or anxiety you might otherwise experience.

If you've been seated, for example, at your desk for twenty minutes or so, it's wise to stand up and stretch, even if only for a few seconds. Your veins need this, so does your heart.

Physiologically, your body offers the cues you need at precisely the right moment. It's counter-productive to ignore your body's message to you that says it's time to stand up, to stretch, to take a drink, or what have you.

Dyna Moe
Any time you're at your desk and you feel the urge to stand up, stand up!

Mapping Out Daily Performance Ability

Rarely does your body temperature maintain a steady 98.6 degrees Fahrenheit. Body temperature fluctuates over the course of a day in a pattern controlled by the brain. Your body's performance ability for physical coordination, memory, and alertness is optimal when your body temperature is sufficiently high. As temperature decreases you performance ability tends to decrease.

John Poppy, a health writer makes the following recommendations for undertaking work-related activities, given your body's natural capacities at different points in the day:

10 a.m.	*Mental skills begin to rise. From now to noon is the best time to attack a challenging project or to make that pitch for a raise.*
Noon.	*Brain power starts to dip. Contrary to popular belief, this "post-lunch dip" probably can't be entirely blamed on your midday meal but scientists are not sure what prompts it. Here the dip comes even though temperature is still curving upward.*
3 p.m.	*Alertness rises. Whatever the reason for the noon dip, it loosens its grip and your mental acuity and efficiency return.*
4 to 5 p.m.	*Best time for exercise. Muscle tone is at its peak at this time of the day. For many people, late afternoon is the ideal time for exercise.*
8 p.m.	*Last call for alcohol . . . if you want to sleep soundly during the night.*

Based on the above 10 a.m to noon and 3 p.m. to 4 p.m. are the best times to exercise your brain, and 4 p.m. to 5p.m. is the best time to workout.

Tackling the Day's Toughest Task

Suppose you approach the end of your workday and realize that you didn't tend to the most difficult tasks. The solution? You're likely to accomplish more of what's on your daily task list if you start with the hardest tasks. Thereafter, moving on to the easy tasks seems like a downhill bike ride.

Researchers agree that you are best able to perform your hard tasks well if you do so in the morning. Dr. Norbert Myslinski, a neuroscience professor at the University of Maryland, found that cortisol peaks around the time you wake up. Cortisol increases your blood-sugar level, enabling you to energetically handle tasks through their completion.

Tackling tough tasks in the morning generally enhances your confidence level. By increasing productivity at the beginning of your day, you are motivated to perform better and accomplish more throughout the rest of your afternoon and evening.

Word Power

Cortisol is a naturally occurring stress hormone that affects your ability to respond to challenges or perceived dangers you face.

As your workday winds down, seek to tie up loose ends. Can you put away several file folders? Can you return the one key phone call? Can you assemble tomorrow's project notes? Can you discard junk mail and other unnecessary documents?

As we'll explore in Chapter 16 and 17, the more small tasks you complete before departing, the more focused and energized you'll be when you return the next day, especially to a more visually appealing, clear and clean environment conducive to greater productivity.

Energy from Switching Tasks

You can gain from switching tasks. Even the most mundane tasks, if approached correctly, can help to maintain your energy level.

Dyna Moe

Task switching can't be employed all the time for all types of assignments, but it works well when you can mix the mundane in with the tasks that are a little more challenging.

After school, my daughter used to help me in my office. By giving her bite-sized portions of tasks and rotating the tasks, she was able to continue for an hour or more, well past her normal 18 to 20 minutes when tedium set in. This process works as well for adults.

Suppose you're faced with an assignment you'd rather handle. Instead of tackling the assignment for a straight 60-minute period, if you were to proceed for 10 minutes then to turn to something else of a shorter nature, then return to the first assignment, and likewise turn to something else, you can maintain productivity, reasonably high spirits, and energy for what comes next. Because you proceed methodically, in a controlled manner, you avoid the perils of multi-tasking. (See Chapter 15.)

What about Handling Errands?

Everyone has errands to handle—the professional and personal variety. How and when you handle errands makes a huge difference in your energy level and impacts your performance at work.

IDIOTWE is an acronym for I'll Do It On The Weekend. Weekends, if you haven't already discovered, are when everyone else is seeking to do their errands! I suggest using Monday or Tuesday to handle errands and avoid the IDIOTWE syndrome.

The following is particularly useful for entrepreneurs:

➤ If starting from home, prepare for multiple stops in a circular route. List your stops in order on a Post-It note and affix to your car dashboard or radio.

➤ To ward off parking woes, stockpile plenty of quarters.

➤ Keep a file folder, envelope, or pouch in your briefcase for the various receipts, tickets, and sales slips that you will need or will be collecting.

➤ Keep the passenger side of your car clear for the new buys and pick-ups.

➤ Shop by mail. There's no need to pick up stamps at the post office when you can order them by mail or online and have them delivered to you.

Give yourself credit for the smallest of tasks, such as dropping off an item for a client, depositing a check, returning rental equipment, and so on. As often as possible, however, use retained help to take care of these items instead of doing them yourself.

Coming Undone

Cease and desist if you run into undue delays, traffic backups, or long lines. Chances are when you handle errands at a different time, delays will be less.

Forsake "Right Time" or "Right Mood" Traps

How many of us, in attempting to get things done, wait for the right time or the right mood instead of making that break, taking that calculated risk that would propel us faster and further?

When I was 26 I moved down from Connecticut to Washington, D.C., the big city. I was excited about my new job. That first day at work went by like a dream. When I left in the evening, I headed up the road to pull onto M Street so I could cross the Key Bridge and go home to Virginia.

Alas, there was no break in the traffic. I couldn't even pull onto the road. I sat there and after six minutes, still no break in the traffic and no opportunity for me to pull onto the major road that lead across the bridge.

I decided to head back down the road, drive all the way around, and try another road where there's a traffic light. That way at least I got onto M Street, even though I was much further back than where I started.

The next day I headed into work again, everything was going well, and I was enthusiastic. I was excited to be there. At night I left work, pulled up to the road to turn onto M Street, and saw another endless sea of traffic.

I thought to myself, "This will *not* become a nightly ordeal. I'm going to drive home, and the Key Bridge is my route across."

So, I waited for a minute, two minutes, three minutes, and finally I simply pulled into traffic. I made my own break. I reached home and felt like I had achieved a great victory.

Sometimes the critical step we need to take does not need to be a large one. For example: Forsaking the "right mood" trap can be more insidious than forsaking the "right time" trap. Many professionals wait until they are "in the mood," to take action. In doing this, they run the risk of being in the right mood at the wrong time or not at all!

Are you among the portion of the population who happens to "never be in the mood"?" Setting a standard for yourself might help overcome the dilemma of not being in the right mood. Let's take writing, for example, since many people face the task with little enthusiasm. Consider a professional writer. Suppose the writer maintains a daily writing quota of so many words per day. This quota helps generate a desired level of output, whether or not the writer "feels like it." On occasion, a writer's daily output might be sub-par but is counterbalanced on days when the writing output surpasses expectations.

You too could be productive when you are "in the mood" to tackle something, making it more vital to focus your efforts when you are in a less-than-enthusiastic mood. By tackling something, regardless of your mood, you're further ahead than if you do nothing. You might not complete a task on your first attempt, but it's to your benefit to at least start.

Hereafter, when it comes to getting things done, have the mental clarity and emotional strength to ignore your mood. Stop waiting until you "feel like proceeding." Instead, move forward based upon your professionalism or personal quest for results.

Dyna Moe

Forcing yourself to produce so many words per day accomplishes little if you generate low quality writing. However, in the case of writers who set a word quota, many edit their works by days end. Thus, what they write is seemingly effective, potent, and on the mark from one day to the next.

Being in the Zone

In, *Breathing Space: Living and Working at a Comfortable Pace in a Sped up Society*, I discuss time warps which occur when you're not conscious of your output or responsiveness in relationship to fixed time intervals, such as an hour. You can increase the likelihood of experiencing a favorable time warp effect by removing yourself from a time-measured environment, such as by hiding the clock.

Other people have other names that they use for what I call time warps. Some people call it being in the zone. Some call it being on a roll.

Regardless of what you call it, it is useful to know how to consistently benefit from time warps. Here's an exercise to help you create an environment in which you do your best work:

1. Think back to when you were highly productive:
   Where were you?
   What time of day was it?
   Was anyone else around?
   What was the temperature?
   What was the lighting?
   What resources were available?

2. Think about yourself at that time:
   What were you wearing?
   What did you consume the night before?
   How long did you sleep the night before?
   How did you feel?
   What was your level of fitness?
   What did you eat that morning?

3. Think about the time of day and week:
   What time of day was it?
   What day of the week was it?
   What had transpired earlier?
   What was forthcoming?

4. Think about the tools available:
   Were you using a computer, tablet, or smart phone?
   Were you using other equipment?
   Did you have a pen or pencil?
   Did you have a blank pad?
   Were you online?
   Were other resources available?
   Were periodicals, books, or directories present?

5. Consider other factors that were present:
   Did you have a view?

Were you in a comfortable chair?
Were you at a desk or at a table?
Were you in a moving vehicle, i.e., a plane or a train?
Was there quiet or soothing background noise?
What color were the walls surrounding you?
Were you in a room with rugs?
Could you hear others?
Was water nearby?
Were you near the bathrooms?
Were you near the coffee machine?

As you recall the situation when you were in a time warp, circle each item above that was present or was a factor at this time. New insights might emerge.

If you can, recall a second time in which you achieved a time warp and run through each of the questions above once again. What items have now been marked or circled twice?

If you have the momentum, use this list for a third or fourth time in which you were highly productive. You might see a strong pattern emerge. You'll uncover the specifics as to what factors were present at those times when you were highly productive.

Your goal is now to emulate the scenario to increase your probability of achieving similarly pleasing results. I've used this technique to isolate those factors that are present when I've given dynamite, rousing keynote presentations—the kind that the audience members remember long after the event. To the best of my ability, I seek to ensure that future speaking engagements have all of the key factors present. And you know what? A large percentage of the time, it works!

Master Your Immediate Environment

Take charge of your immediate environment as often as practical. You might find low productivity stems from the feeling of not being in control. When you creatively carve out sanctuaries for yourself, they give you the quiet you need to do quality work and serve as a reminder that you're in charge of your career.

Dyna Moe
Taking control of your immediate environment enables you to derive the best from yourself, to work with your internal rhythms, and to more easily and effortlessly produce desirable results.

High Energy When Working with Your Computer

Whether you work with a desktop, notebook, tablet, smart phone, or some combination thereof, it's easy to fall into unproductive, energy-draining, customs and postures. This is especially so when you sit for prolonged periods, fixated on a screen.

Here are exercises to keep you on a more energetic keel:

➤   To experience an energy boost, breathe in slowly through your nose, and hold your breath two seconds and then exhale through your mouth. Repeat this often.

➤   To loosen up your shoulders and upper torso, using a wide circular motion, roll your shoulders forward four or five times. Then roll your shoulders in reverse.

➤   To stretch your neck, turn your head slowly from side to side and look over each shoulder. Count to three and then repeat the exercise several more times.

➤   To stretch your back, while seated (and with no one looking!), slowly bend your upper body between your knees. Hold this position for a few seconds, then sit up and relax. Repeat this exercise a few more times.

➤   To stretch the muscles in your forearms and give your wrists some relief, hold your arms straight out in front of you and raise and lower your hands bending them at your wrists. Repeat this several times.

➤   To give your upper back and shoulder blades some relief, fold your arms in front of you, raise them up to your shoulders, and then bring your elbows straight back. Hold this for several seconds. Repeat several times.

➤   To relax your fingers and hands and make them feel more nimble, make a tight fist with your hands and hold it for several seconds. Then, spread your fingers as far as you can and hold for another five seconds. Repeat this exercise several times.

Better Eye Health at Your PC

Electronic monitors and screens are comprised of pixels, dots of light that are bright at the center and dimmer at their borders. It is hard to read such screens for a prolonged period because your eyes have nothing to "lock onto."

Factoid

Gazing at a screen for long periods of time, day after day, quickly adds up to eye strain, which directly contributes to a drop in energy. Eye strain is rampant among career professionals. One government study estimates 91 percent of people who use a computer for more than three hours daily, experience eye strain at one time or another.

Common ailments people experience when looking at a monitor for extended periods include headaches, itching or burning eyes, blurry vision, fatigue, aching shoulders, and an aching neck.

Here are exercises to minimize or even ward off eye-strain associated with too much time in front of a monitor:

➤   Reduce any glare from the walls surrounding you, especially if it reflects back onto your screen.

➤   Seek to match the brightness of your room to that of your monitor.

➤   Refocus your eyes on distant objects every few minutes, then turn back to your monitor. Also blink often!

At least once every twenty minutes, stretch or drink some water. That way you can be at your best nearly all day.

Workplace Organizational Issues

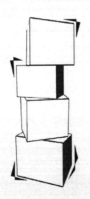

Part 3
Workplace Organizational Issues

Thus far, we've eased you into the get-things-done frame of mind. In this part of the book comes observations and suggestions that require a little more work on your part!

To get things done, often you have to get your act together, and that means dealing with workplace organizational issues, including your desk, your office, the paperwork all around you, your computer, the web, and email. All these arenas require some type of order so that you will be able to work comfortably, find things when you need them, and be in command of your resources.

CHAPTER 6

Your Desk, Your Office, Your Career

In This Chapter:

➤ Your work environment
➤ Rule your desk
➤ A new set of commandments
➤ Love your surroundings

Your productive work life is finite. You will work for so many years at such and such a pace and then, one day, that will end. When it comes to getting more done, taking control of your immediate environment works wonders.

This chapter is all about the direct connection between how you manage your desk and office and how that ultimately impacts your long-term career achievements.

Filing and Organizing Effectively

Much of getting things done boils down to how well you're able to retrieve what you need, and that means mastering the ability to file.

Filing is a non-glamorous procedure for becoming and staying organized. Filing involves allocating information and materials into their best home, for now. What do you need to be a good filer for hard copy items? Clear objectives and the space to put a chair in front of a filing cabinet.

If you fear that filing means you're becoming a caretaker, remind yourself you are taking care of items that you deem to be important. If something isn't important, don't save it. If it is important, file it with gusto.

Conditioning your environment is a crucial step in organizing and filing effectively. This means that you arrange, stock, and maintain such spaces to support your efforts. For example, organizing a desk drawer initially takes time and could be slow going. Thereafter, finding what you want in the desk drawer is simpler and faster.

If you avoid organizing the drawer all together, always have things strewn about, and go on a "hunt" each time you need to find something, in little ways, you're hampering your productivity rather than devising a system that will support you every time.

Managing the Beforehand

With the vacant space you have created, you now have a clearing for the items that you'll be receiving. These include new policy memos, articles you want to save, meeting notes, and other printed information that you want to review at a later date. The items could be different for each person.

The important point in an over-information society is to take control in advance, *manage the beforehand,* as opposed to *dealing with the aftermath* of receiving too much information.

Once you develop the habit of clearing space in all the compartments of your life—your desk, your car, your closets, etc.—you accomplish many things: you demonstrate to yourself that you do have enough space to manage your career and conduct your affairs, and you keep in a ready state to handle what is next rather than trying to figure out where to store things or how to create ad hoc piles.

The table below presents eight typical mis-management scenarios in the left column and corresponding preventative measures in the right column.

Word Power
Managing the beforehand means to prepare for something in advance of a need, such as to prepare your files in anticipation of new items that will arrive. Rather than having files and cabinets filled to their brims with information, strip them of all excess materials so that you have some vacant space.

Dealing With the Aftermath	Managing the Beforehand
Not knowing where to put things and hence creating ad hoc piles on your desk and around your office.	Creating space in advance of the arrival of new information or items in your life.
Returning to your office from a meeting lugging mounds of new information.	Returning from a meeting with a thin, highly potent file of key ideas.

Panicking when a key employee calls in sick one morning and no one else is prepared to handle the job.	Having already cross-trained your staff so they can fill in on short notice or have good relations with temps!
Leaving for work in the morning in a mad rush, forgetting things and feeling stressed to start the day.	Leaving with grace and ease because you assembled everything by the door or in your car the night before.
Heading into the city without the quarters and dimes needed for parking meters and pay phones.	Having at least 50 dimes and 40 quarters (a roll of each) safely and subtly stashed in your car.
Being totally surprised when your primary customers change their focus and hence what's important to them.	Not being surprised that your customers change focus, since you subscribe to their key publications.
Having a pile of magazines and other publications stack up because you can't keep up with them, nor identify relevant articles or information.	Having no piles because you've dropped most subscriptions, and you quickly strip those you receive to a few relevant pages before recycling them.
Pretending that the six things currently competing for your attention are there because that's the way it is in your office or line of work, or with your boss.	Remembering that typically you're in charge of your situation. Putting systems in place that limit the number of things competing for your attention.

Conditioning Your Office

The quality and ambience of your work space works best when it demonstrates the quality and ambience of your life or how you would like your life to be.

Conditioning your work environment—coordinating the arrangement of physical spaces in your career in an anticipatory, supportive manner, works well on many levels. You can apply the principles to your entire office. Whether yours is a corporate or home office, you can discover how to gain greater balance. Obviously, you will have more leeway if you are self-employed, or the "boss," but the principles work much the same.

If you need them, room dividers and sound barriers are available in a variety of shapes and sizes and can support any existing sound barriers. The gentle, rhythmic "white noise" of a small fan's motor serves as a sound buffer to many of the sounds that might distract you. Maybe you want a couch for quick cat naps during the day.

The table below presents examples of working in an un-conditioned environment followed by corresponding antidotes.

Unconditioned Environment	Conditioned Environment
Being inundated by junk mail on a daily basis at work and not liking it.	Rarely receiving junk mail because you prevent your name from being entered on lists.
Being embarrassed all afternoon because at lunch you spilled ketchup on your white dress shirt.	Not experiencing embarrassment because you always keep an extra shirt stowed in your office.
Being interrupted by all manner of phone calls and text messages all day long.	Scheduling concentration time and being away from the phone.

Your other environments, including your car, briefcase, and work space, each have a pronounced impact on how you get things done. To ensure that your home environment supports your sense of balance, don't allow ad hoc outposts to build up: Take the trip receipts out of the folder right after the trip. Adopt supportive docking and unloading techniques. Always transport important paper items, such as mail, office work, tax receipts, warranties, and other purchased items to their final destinations: bring them to your administrative outpost for processing and integration into your organization system.

The more you are able to keep flat surfaces clear—your desk, tables, shelves—the greater your ability to manage the flow of items in your career, deal with them capably, and move forward. You experience a sense of balance.

Factoid
The London subway system was experiencing a growing problem of unwanted vandals and thieves in their tunnels. So they devised a plan to play classical music and opera, such as Vivaldi, Mozart, and Pavarotti in the effort to make unwelcome visitors uncomfortable with the subway environment. Studies have shown that this type of music is unfamiliar and unacceptable to the thugs who hang out in the subway. Making them miserable with music they don't enjoy will drive them away.

The 10 Commandments of Deskmanship

Keeping in control of your desk is divine. Speaking of which, if Moses climbed to the top of Mount Sinai today, considering all the desks that are disorganized, here's what he might bring back:

1. Thou shalt clear thy desk every night. Yes, every night.
2. Thou shalt continually refine what goes on thy desktop.
3. Thou shalt not use thy desktop as a filing cabinet.
4. Thou shalt predetermine what belongs inside thy desk.
5. Thou shalt keep 20 percent of the drawer space vacant.
6. Thou shalt furnish thy surrounding office to support thy desk.
7. Thou shalt take comfort when at thy desk.
8. Thou shalt keep clean thy desk and thy surrounding area.
9. Thou shalt leave thy desk periodically.
10. Thou shalt honor thy desk as thyself.

It's Divine to Refine

Let me expound upon a couple of the essentials:

➤ Furnish thy surrounding office to support thy desk with familiar and comfort inducing objects, for example, plants, pictures, slogans, and anything that supports your efforts.

➤ Clear thy desk every night. Yes, every night. This forces you, the next morning, to start on those things that are important and not to continue with what happens to be cluttering your desktop.

➤ Keep clean thy desk and thy surrounding area. This is crucial if only to maintain the perception of being in control. Also, take comfort when at thy desk, in other words, your desk should be a comfortable place for you, not a war zone.

➤ Continually refine what goes on thy desktop. What you used to keep on your desk because it was convenient and useful might no longer be so. Also, continually assess different items that support your desktop arrangement, such as computer trays, hanging lamps, and swivel mechanisms to conveniently move equipment as needed.

Factoid

Researchers at the University of Texas conducted a study that found people with cluttered offices accomplish little, are less efficient, less organized, and less imaginative than people with clean offices.

Always remember, keep 20 percent of thy drawer space vacant —in an information-overload society, your desk will not serve you if all available compartments are filled to the brim. Cut back now and acknowledge what is coming, i.e. manage the beforehand to stay in control.

The Perils of a Messy Desk

In the over-information era, your desk needs to be a comfortable place for you. What does it say if your desk is continually a mess? Beyond the logistical problems of not being able to find things, a messy desk sends the wrong message to those who might otherwise include you on big, important projects!

Personal organization is fundamental in the quest to get things done and disorganization is costly. A cluttered desk reflects poorly on one's efficiency and capacity for clear thinking. If you want to stifle your career, having a messy desk will help.

When your desk is a mess, it appears that you're not in control, whether or not you actually are!

A messy desk suggests you can't handle your responsibilities. When a supervisor is delegating assignments, you might be passed over out of the supervisor's concern that the assignment will go into one of your piles and never find its way out.

In working others, appearance matters and the appearance of your desk is as vital as appearing professional in formal business meetings. Besides doing good work, to make a positive impression on co-workers and bosses, take control of your desk and office environment.

Dyna Moe
If your situation appears hopeless, at the least establish a drawer where you can temporarily house what you want out of sight, and keep the drawer closed.

Getting Things Done with Grace

I often have readers and audience participants ask me questions about taking control of their work environment. What is the issue behind such queries? How to get things done throughout the day with greater grace and ease.

Q: "I may be responsible for how organized I am each day, but I don't feel that way. There are things that I have to do that seem to throw everything off. How do I increase my feeling of control and sense of responsibility for how my space is arranged?"

A: Begin to recognize behavior that you practice that is comfortable but outmoded and time consuming; ceremoniously (but not strategically) arranging the items on your desk, over-surfing the web, and dozens of other habits qualify here.

Q: "Many days I am in control for at least most of the morning, sometimes even into the afternoon, but then all of the sudden, like a train derailment, everything seems disorganized and out of control."

A: Take mental pauses throughout the day, particularly as new developments occur. The best laid plans often go astray, and those who are able to maintain order know when to let go of one activity and redirect their focus towards another.

    Being in control often is more related to how you feel about a situation than the presence of evidence. Ten minutes before the end of the day, if your boss springs a one-hour assignment on you to be done immediately, you can regard this as a major intrusion in your day and an affront, or you can see it as a professional challenge or an opportunity to demonstrate your overall value to your company.

    Make a note of the times you have taken on such challenges and bring them up particularly at raise times. Also, before, during, and after handling the late assignment thrown on your lap, keep considering the many benefits of completing it. These include learning something new, practicing maintaining grace under fire, and serving as a reminder for you to discuss this type of situation with your boss so that it doesn't happen too often.

Q: How do I determine what items I need on or around my desk?

A: Surround yourself with what supports you! When deciding whether to have a particular item in your office, ask yourself, "Does this item deserve prime real estate?" This includes those gifts from family and friends. In most cases, hold on to the love and let the gift go!

    Create a signature environment to project who you are. Allow for a lot of open space and keep it simple. If it helps, make a list of everything you might want to be surrounded by while working.

Q: Are there any early warning signs that indicate when I'm heading for disorganization?

A: Anytime you start stacking horizontal piles on your desk indicates that you are operating in a malfunctioned mode. If you find yourself perpetually five to ten minutes late for meetings and always handling activities up to the last minute before turning your attention to what is next, you're leaving yourself wide open for some anxious moments.

Coming Undone

If you don't give yourself enough space—physical space—to handle a task, you are likely to feel at least bit disorganized.

If it helps, for each item that crosses your desk, ask these fundamental questions:

➤   Why did I receive it? Should I have received this?
➤   What's the issue behind the document?
➤   Why keep this? (Is it vital? If it will be replaced soon, I don't need it.)
➤   How else can this be handled? Can I delegate it?
➤   What will happen if I don't handle this?

At every juncture, avoid playing the victim, believing that circumstances of others cause you to be disorganized while not acknowledging your participation and willingness to be a victim. Take ownership; that is, lay claim and accept responsibility for what occurs in your career. You'll go further and faster, and you'll get more done.

The table that follows serves as a quick guide to keeping your desk and office in order.

Items	Feel Free to Toss or Recycle if . . .	Feel Free to Retain if . . .
Business cards, assorted notes:	You have many cards and never call anyone, or you can't recall someone or his goods or services	You can compress and file them, and know you will use the information.
Paper, files, documents:	They're old, outdated, un-informative; they've been transferred to disk; or they no longer cover your derriere.	It's your duty to retain them, you refer to them of-ten, they have future value, or they simply comfort you.

Reports, magazines:	They're outdated or stacking up; you think you need them to keep up; or you fear there'll be a quiz	They're vital to your career or well-being, you choose to retain them, or there will be a quiz.
Books, guides directories:	You've copied, scanned, or made notes on the key pages; they're obsolete or have updated versions or are easily available on the web..	They're part of a life collection, you refer to them monthly, they have sentimental value, or you simply want them.
CDs, cassettes, videos, and A/V:	You never play them or, if so, they don't evoke any memories. They play poorly. They take up valuable space.	You play them, you like them, and you couldn't bear to part with them. They're keepsakes.
Outdated office equipment:	You can donate or sell it; it's collecting dust, or takes up space.	It serves a purpose, can be revitalized, or adds to the decor.
Mementos, memorabilia:	They no longer hold meaning, you have many similar items, you don't have room, or you've changed.	They still evoke strong memories, you will hand them down someday, or they look good on display.
Gifts, cards, presents:	They're unwanted, never in use, or the bestowers won't know or care that you tossed them.	You use them often, are glad you have them, or are saving them for some special reason.

High Accomplishment Through Shelf Management

Shelf management and self-management are not dis-similar! Your shelves are generally home to items you'll probably use in the next two weeks, items too big for your filing cabinet (or collections of such items), current projects that you'd rather not file, and supplies (that ought to go in supply cabinets).

It makes sense to shelve the following: items that you might use within a week or two including reference books, directories, books, phone books, manuals, instruction guides, and large magazines.

Items that are too large to put in a file cabinet might include books, large reports, and any item that is part of a series. If you're working on a task or project that requires a variety of materials and they can be neatly housed on your shelves, go ahead—as long as the project has an end, and these items don't linger there forever.

What doesn't go on your shelves? Anything that belongs in a supply cabinet! Now you know.

CHAPTER 7

 **Paper Plagues**

> ## In This Chapter:
>
> ➤ Paper offenses
> ➤ Forms beyond reason
> ➤ Merging and purging
> ➤ Quiet contemplation works wonders

This chapter discusses why, amazingly, paper still plagues us and what to do about it.

Even with the dominance of the Internet and smart phones, when we discuss information deluge, paper remains a culprit. In the United States, we have the lowest postal rates in the world, which contributes to a huge direct mail industry. We also have the greatest amount of paper-generating equipment per capita, laser printers, personal computers, and personal copiers. We nearly paper each other into oblivion.

Increasingly, the sheer volume of paper that we all face is, in and of itself, an impediment to productivity as well as to staying organized.

Pounded by Paper

As a speaker I've had the opportunity to take many cruises and have seen as many as 45 countries. On your first day before you're fully settled, pieces of paper are placed in your cabin related to tours available, sales in the gift shop, daily activities, and what to wear.

Under Your Door While You're Asleep

That night someone will slip more pieces of paper under your cabin door while you're sleeping. There will be a sale offering an inch of gold. Drinks in the bar will be half off. One of the shore excursions will have been cancelled, and another one will have been added. By the next morning there will be at least three more pages in your life, even on cruises that feature information on designated TV channels available in all cabins.

Each day will continue the same way. In as few as ten days, without trying you'll have 70+ pages, just like at work. This was supposed to be your vacation! You thought you could escape information overload! Instead, you're papered to death.

School Papers

When my daughter entered high school, I attended parents' night. I met each of her teachers, going from class to class, as she does during the day. In the first class, the science teacher handed us a syllabus, a reading list, a list of rules and regulations, another page with his website and homework for the next several months, and other sheets related to the class.

Before I left, I had seven sheets in all.

In the next class, I received another nine sheets. Thereafter, the teachers gave me seven to nine sheets per class. I left that evening with 50 sheets of paper, when receiving maybe two or three had been my expectation.

When I arrived home, I said to my daughter, "Look at this! I attended parent's night for freshmen and ended up with 50 pieces of paper! Here, you take these. I've already been to high school. I graduated. I can prove it."

How about your workplace? Despite the cyberworld or, as some say, because of it, a preponderance of paper plagues each of us.

Factoid

The United States consumes more paper per person than any other country on earth. By some estimates, the typical U.S. office worker consumes 40 sheets a day or 8,000 a year.

Another Form to Fill Out

A stifling array of government laws and regulations hampers business, allowing the United States to support 70 percent of the world's lawyers, observed Barry Howard Minkin in *EconoQuake*.

It is crucial for you, a mere pawn in the game of rules and regulations, policies and procedures, to keep your own systems as uncomplicated as possible. It won't be easy; there is a pervasive tendency among organizations and individuals to over-complicate things. You can see its effects every time you have to fill out some new form at work.

Are such forms getting any easier to fill out each year, despite many organizations' commitment to streamlining information, or are they becoming more difficult and involved? Have you bought any office equipment recently? Are there more forms, or fewer?

Some companies have double the number of approval and reporting forms that they had ten years ago.

If you're an entrepreneur, or if you supervise others, think about the last time you tried to fire someone. Is it getting harder or easier from the standpoint of completing paperwork?

Examine Your Own Forms

Examine the forms in your organization, department, or venture, and then re-examine them. What can be eliminated? Here are potential benefits you might experience from combining two or more forms into one or eliminating a single form:

➤ Reduced paper consumption: Less ordering, fewer costs, less receiving, less handling, and less storing

➤ Reduced printing and associated costs: Less retrieving, less printer use, less electricity, and lower cartridge and toner costs (or lower outside costs if purchased from a printer or forms vendor)

➤ Reduced need for storage: Less collecting, less transporting, less storage space used, less employee time used.

Any way the wind the blows, when you successfully reduce or eliminate forms multiple benefits accrue.

Coming Undone

Often, in the business world, if you can create a new reporting form, you do. Thereafter, it becomes difficult to eliminate. If anything, such forms grow longer, more complicated, and more time-intensive.

Rule Paper Before It Rules You

Don't pitch everything coming in, but recognize that problems begin when you allow even one unnecessary piece of paper to enter your office. Every unneeded page diminishes your ability to stay organized.

Each day, fight to keep your desk clear. In the evening, after you've cleared your desk, acknowledge yourself for what you accomplished that day. As you learned in Chapter 6, if you keep the spaces of your life clear, especially flat spaces like the tops of your desk and filing cabinet and the corners and windowsills around the room, control of your time and control of your life tends to follow.

Never Volunteer to Be Inundated

Sometimes the piles of paper and documents, that thwart our ability to remain organized, arrive by our own invitation! I was phoned one afternoon by a marketing representative from a well-established investment company. With such calls, after a couple lines of their spiel I find a polite way to quickly end the conversation.

This particular caller seemed to be different, so I listened a bit longer. He discussed his company's various investment options. He offered to send a brochure that listed the 35 different investment vehicles available, plus his company's annual report, and a prospectus.

"Wait a moment," I said. "I have no interest in reading about 35 different investment options. Please, do us both a favor and confine your information to a single page on the three best options you think would be right for me." I told him I wasn't going to read his firm's annual report, hence no reason to send it. If I liked what he sent me on the single page, I could always request the annual report at another time.

I explained further that while I have an MBA, and previously earned the certified management consultant (CMC) designation, "I loath reading prospectuses, so please don't send that either."

As our conversation drew to a close I repeated to him that I only wanted to see a single page with the three investments he thought were best for me. If he wanted to send one other slim brochure that contained data on his company's financial standing, that would be okay. Seemingly he agreed to send only those two items.

Several days passed, and I forgot about the call. In Monday's mail, I noticed a thick package from his investment firm. Uh-oh. I opened it and saw everything I had asked him not to send. I took the assemblage and with one flick of my wrists, sought to tear it in half, but it was too thick. I quickly tossed it, and you can rest assured that I did not become a client.

Never volunteer to be inundated. If that agent had sent me what I asked for, who knows, I might have made his day.

Take In and Retain Less, Starting Now

People make excuses at work all the time about why they are overloaded with paper. Someone else is forcing them to receive more periodicals and subscriptions than they can handle or is forcing them to put their names on more mailing lists. No one is doing this to you—you are doing it to yourself.

Factoid

Wired Magazine featured an article that stated "clutter is among the lowest forms of spatial organization."

A pile simply allowed to stack up contains items that, if not retrieved, will lose their previous usefulness. Massive clutter lacks geometry. Stuff that is haphazardly strewn across one space has little—if any—value where it currently lies. What's more, it diminishes the value of the space it occupies, ultimately offering the perpetrator less value, less freedom, less control, and greater poverty."

Curiously, the more information we attempt to consume, the more we seek to acquire. We're like information switchboards, marveling at how much we can keep our fingers on. To ensure no dull moments, we open up yet another piece of junk mail or we look at yet another non-essential bulletin.

Accumulations, by their nature, steal your time. First you receive them, then place them somewhere, look at them, move them, arrange them, perhaps file some items and discard others, move things again, and then put up your hands and fall into despair.

How would your career proceed if you merged and purged on a regular basis, as these items came across your desk? You'd likely have more time and ultimately get things done.

Word Power

To merge and purge is to discard what you do not need, while combining like items or information that you deem as worth retaining.

The Surge to Merge and Purge

In the course of a workday, week, month, and year, you encounter memos, magazines, calendars, promotional items, reports, faxes, newspapers, newsletters, bulletins, and all manner of sundries. Right now you're hanging on to too much paper and that is slowing you down on your path to getting things done.

Grasp the information that impacts your career, stay on top of that, and have the strength to leave the rest behind. Not to suggest that you ignore things willy-nilly, but make conscious choices about where to give your time and attention. Most of what competes for your attention needs to be ignored.

To stay organized and get things done, I advocate that you take in even *less* paper and less information than you currently do. Actively choose where you will give your time and attention.

Don't be concerned that you'll miss some vital information. The redundancy in our information channels increases the probability that you won't miss major developments that merit your attention.

What to Do with All the Paper

At work when you receive a magazine or other periodical, even one that you actually want, do you need the whole magazine?

Continually strip down magazines to the basic elements relevant to you. Pull out the few articles that matter, and recycle the rest. Streamline the information you receive regardless of how big and thick the item. You can probably pare a 250-page book down to the eight or ten key pages in less than ten minutes.

When confronted by a large packet of information, I swiftly break it down to the few pages that appear most useful. I use the edge of a ruler to deftly and neatly extract only the bits of information from each page that I need, then quickly assemble such tidbits on the copier and create a one-or two-sheet composite of what might have been many, many more pages. This affords quicker review in the future, keeps my files leaner and more targeted, and is anxiety-reducing.

Streamline the Information Mine

Organizing your desk, updating your lists, re-arranging files, answering mail, and handling paper helps in feeling and being in control. Then, like clockwork, more "attention grabbers" will arrive. Email requests appear and require effort. Mail arrives presenting something worth your attention. The phone rings. Suddenly, that newfound sense of order seems to evaporate.

Each of us encounters waves of "attention grabbers" throughout the day that render our sense of order and control futile. Yet, simple ways to stay in control exist in spite of the obstacles.

As piles on your desk mount up, the task of dealing with them soon becomes overwhelming, at least mentally. "How am I going to deal with that information?" When you keep them to a minimum, they seem manageable. Perception is an important tool. When you believe you're on top, you tend to act accordingly. It's not merely positive thinking—a positive chain reaction occurs.

Dyna Moe

Strip arriving mail down immediately, discover what parts are vital, and what can be tossed or recycled. When you receive a large packet of information, immediately extract the key pages, paragraphs, or contact information.

Remember: to help stay organized, reduce voluminous materials to the slimmest, most potent file folders or packets that still retain the essence of what you need to have for the task or project at hand.

Depart from Extraneous Mailing Lists

It's a wonderful morning when you open up your mailbox, and see only six pieces of mail, instead of 18 pieces of mail and 12 of them junk. Develop a standard letter, sticker, or stamper that you mail back to the other party: "Please take me off your list."

The myth of "handling each piece of paper once" and others like gives way to the reality that most pieces of paper should never cross your desk at all.

A vital part of reducing correspondence and paperwork is to remove your name from junk mail rolls. Write to the DMA or register online at www.dmachoice.org/static/about_dma.php and ask to have your name removed from their lists. This will reduce your junk mail by 40 percent for nearly six months after which time write them another letter requesting the same thing.

Mail Preference Service
Consumer Assistance
Direct Marketing Association
P.O. Box 282
Carmel, NY 10512

Engage in Quiet Contemplation

It is helpful to schedule time to peruse the material you've retained, in a quiet place away from phone and email. Your concentration powers will be at their best. You'll be able to

Dyna Moe

Clearing out what you don't need to retain is good housekeeping as well a vital discipline among those who win the paper war. Merging and purging is essential because even with all the new technological tools, paper will continue to proliferate in the foreseeable future.

zip through the folder at a quicker pace than if you attempt to on the fly. As you review the items, pare them down further.

Instead of a two-page article, perhaps you need only one key paragraph. Instead of a flyer or brochure listing some offer, maybe you only need the toll-free 800 number or URL. Simply log in the important information on a palm top, note pad, or pocket dictator and then chuck all the pages. Hence, you are lighter, freer, and able to handle whatever else comes into your work area. In a single file or two, you have the essence of what you need or want to pursue.

The Best Times to Merge and Purge

In the course of your year and career, when are the best times to merge and purge what you've retained? Here are some suggestions:

➤   As you approach New Year's day. When the end of the year approaches I find it easy to rip into files and chuck half or more the stuff I know I'm never going to use again. I clear more room in my files, enabling me to be more organized, and ready to face other things that compete for my attention.

➤   Spring cleaning. This has tradition-ally been a time for clearing out the old and making room for the new. The arrival of fall works as well, to-ward the end of the summer around Labor Day. Having the crisp, cool air return is a stimulant for getting your desk, office, home, and car back into top condition.

Dyna Moe

Approaching a birthday is a good time, particularly age 30, 40, 50, 60, or 70. If you're about to hit 40, for example, this is one of the opportune times in your career and life to let go of the stuff you no longer need. Age 35, 45, 55, 65, and 75 also work well!

➤ Whenever you move offices or work locations. There's no sense in hauling stuff to your new location if you're never going to use it. Make give-aways to co-workers if appropriate and helpful, but don't transport items that you can do without to a new location.

➤ Obviously when you change jobs or careers, you'll clean out your desk and office or work station. Again, don't make the mistake of carting unnecessary paper, documents, and files with you that are best recycled and out of your life.

When is a good time to regain control? The answer is *whenever* the spirit moves. Merge and purge. You don't need to wait. Begin to sense the power inherent in regaining control of your files, your possessions, and your career.

Operation Clean Sweep

In This Chapter:

➤ Important versus urgent
➤ Where and when considerations
➤ Pile it up as high as it will go
➤ Act, file, toss, or delegate

Thus far in Part 3, we've covered the mechanics of organizing your desk and office, and of handling paper. In this chapter, we turn to a way to quickly breakdown the recurring accumulations that cover your desk, hamper your productivity, and certainly diminish your sense of control. I call the procedure "Operation Clean Sweep."

To make the procedure work best, we first need to classify what the paper, documents, messages, piles, and accumulations represent: tasks and projects of wide-ranging importance and varying urgency.

Importance and Urgency

The work of the late Steven Covey and his approach to handling important and urgent tasks has been given much attention. The basic concept is that everything that you want and need to handle falls into one of four quadrants:

The Four Task Quadrants

1) Urgent and Important: act now	2) Important and not Urgent: choose when
3) Urgent and not Important: assign it	4) Not Important and not Urgent: Forsake it

Important and not Urgent

Ideally, you want to devote the brunt of your time and energy to Quadrant 2 types of tasks: important and not urgent. Type 2 tasks include:

➤   long term planning

➤   the big picture focus on the direction of your career

➤   key company projects

➤   maintaining a harmonious team

When you're able to concentrate your efforts into important but not urgent tasks, many of the other things that you need to get done at work fall into line. Having a smoothly functioning team translates to less time having to put out fires and, hopefully, fewer crises.

Dyna Moe

Taking a big-picture look at important projects enables you to identify potential obstacles in advance, again helping you to avoid crisis management.

Important and Urgent

At first, it seems odd that merely important issues generally outrank important and urgent issues represented by Quadrant 1. Important and urgent certainly need to be addressed right away. They could involve:

➤ tending to the budget
➤ conducting meetings
➤ conducting and attending appointments

Understandably, items that are important and urgent are more likely to demand your attention. Important and urgent tasks don't tend to go away, they'll always be with you. However, your ability to focus on purely important tasks, (Quadrant 2) eases the burdens you face in regards to important and urgent tasks (Quadrant 1).

Urgent and Not Important

Quadrant 3 represents urgent but not important tasks which can include:

➤ returning phone calls
➤ addressing email
➤ filling in time sheets

Here, you might be able to efficiently dispatch such tasks because you have handled them before. You know the routine and completing them speedily is desirable. No need to worry about effectiveness for many urgent but not important tasks.

Not Important and Not Urgent

Quadrant 4, not important and not urgent, often represents trivial activities. Many of the web sites we visit, and much of the mail and email we dwell upon do not merit the time or attention we devote to them. Some of the reading we undertake at the office falls into this category as well. Sometimes we delude ourselves into saying that this or that is vital to our overall understanding of the customer, the market, the industry, or society at large. Minimize how much time you spend on the non-important and non-urgent, while recognizing that occasionally we all dip into this realm and it does help to fulfill some basic human needs, such as providing escapism and mental vacations.

Coming Undone

The paradox of addressing important but not urgent tasks is that often they have no specific deadline or the completion date is sometime in the distant future. So, it can be easy to give them no attention. Then, when that future does arrive, one ends up resorting to crisis management to accomplish the task.

Many of the crises you face and deadlines you fail to meet are a result of something being important, not urgent. The wise manager understands the necessity of carving out the short-term portion of long-term tasks and addressing those short-term activities on a regular basis. I'll explain this in greater detail in Chapter 11 on creating the super to-do list.

Avoiding the Urgency Trap: Assessing Tasks as they Emerge

The proliferation of office technology has a profound effect on our sense of urgency. Suppose one morning you receive an overnight package. You're probably willing to devote your attention to that package more readily than others you receive via first-class or even priority mail. You receive an email message from another customer.

Which form of communication merits your attention first? Whatever your answer, recognize that the form of technology employed does not equate to the importance of the messages' content.

The typical response is to address the latest communication, independent of its importance. Hence, the email would trump the overnight package. Watch out! Managing by email is an insidious trap. Remember to continually assessing what is important, versus what is important and urgent, versus what is merely urgent.

The Highest and Best Use of Your Time

Allen Lakein, in his classic book *How to Take Control of Your Time and Your Life*, suggests monitoring yourself by determining, "What is the highest and best use of my time?" If you fail to consciously assess how you are allocating your time, then you will disproportionately skew towards the urgent, independent of its importance.

In the short run, skewing towards the urgent can be okay. If this is a long-term habit, you will become more and more adept at handling the minuscule, while

Dyna Moe

If you've have been the kind of person to throw your time or energy at everything, all day long, week after week, you'll find that taking a more structured approach can yield tremendous benefits in as little as a few weeks, depending on the project!

failing to accomplish the grand achievements that you seek to accomplish . . . the same achievements that your boss and others will notice. Higher-level achievements are what count with your boss and are typically goals set for your performance reviews.

Developing the discipline and ultimately the habit of focusing on important but not urgent tasks followed by important and urgent tasks pays off faster than you think.

Stop and Consider

If you're the type of person who arrives at the office and jumps right in, perhaps you need to take a few minutes to:

- ➤ pause and reflect on how you'd like your day to proceed
- ➤ contemplate which tasks to handle and in what order
- ➤ consider who you'll be meeting and the results you seek
- ➤ determine how you choose to feel throughout the day

Rather than check email right away, curb your raging inclination and simply sit there. Take out a pen, or your keyboard, and capture your thoughts.

The five minutes or so that you invest in simply pausing and reflecting, repeated each morning for several weeks, can have a profound impact on your ability to get things done. I've employed it and found the benefits to be enormous.

As time passes and you permit yourself such intervals at other times throughout the day, you might surprise yourself as you ascend to a new and uninterrupted level of accomplishment. You might unwittingly improve both your efficiency and effectiveness.

Handling Tasks Based on "Where and When" Criterion

David Allen, in *Getting Things Done*, says that attempting to address tasks and projects based on important and urgent criterion is not always the best way to proceed. He overlays the important and urgent approach with a mild adaptation: tackling tasks and projects based on when and where it is most appropriate to handle them.

For example, all the things you need to do at the copier, at the phone, or via email, in Allen's approach, are best handled in clusters. I agree, as long as you don't become obsessive, hence deciding to address all email during the same interval or to make all phone calls during the same interval. Otherwise, "where and when" considerations done can be most worthwhile in getting more.

Important and Urgent: Preparing for Operation Clean Sweep

Now that you understand the distinction of important and urgent tasks, we're ready to discuss the all-time desk-clearing, energizing, get-it done technique: Operation Clean Sweep.

Accumulations cost you double—you don't take action on them and you keep confronting them. To handle the array of items competing for your attention, and to balance big goals with the daily grind, collect everything on your desk and elsewhere that might need attention.

Have you collected everything? Stack it high in a temporary pile—the higher the better. This gives you a much clearer idea of what you've allowed to accumulate. Within a span of thirty minutes or less, you're going to rip through this collection of breathing space-threatening items. Without hesitation or sentiment, you'll allocate each item to one of four designations: "Act-on-it" Items, "File-it" Items, "Toss-it" Items, or "Delegate-it" Items.

Coming Undone

Don't attempt Operation Clean Sweep when you are weary or otherwise not fully alert because this procedure will seem overwhelming.

Top-of-the-Pile Decisions

How do you handle each piece of paper, document, or artifact currently at the top of the pile? As you confront each top-of-the-pile item, quickly decide what to do with it. There are four categories for dealing with the top of the pile items including act-on-it items, file-it items, toss-it items, and delegate-it items.

If you are unsure of any particular item, you may place it at the bottom of the large stack, but only once for each item. On the second encounter, you have to deal with it.

Act-on-it Items

Ideally, only a fraction of what makes your clean sweep pile will actually end up in the act-on-it category. These are the handful of things that are important, or important and urgent, and those that you otherwise deem appropriate for addressing soon. You can collect these items in a file folder if that's convenient, or if the tasks represent something on your screen, then list or file them in order of when you wish to tackle them.

File-it Items

Many items in your clean sweep pile are best filed rather than acted upon. Some items require no action. Such items represent information you wish to retain and hence go into a file. Remember, filing, a non-glamorous tool of organization, supports you because that which you file presumably has future value.

Many people have 43 rotating tickler files that they label with the 12 months and 31 days (to accommodate the longest months). Tickler files automatically remind you of when you need to deal with a particular task that does not have to be handled today. So, when a task comes your way, you can place it in the tickler file for the appropriate future date. Then each day of the month, you check your tickler file to identify the tasks that need to be handled or at least initiated.

If you receive something on the third day of the month but don't have to deal with it until the 24th, put it in the file marked the 22nd. Or, to give yourself some extra time, put it in the file marked the 20th.

The monthly files and 31-day tickler files aid you in staying organized and reducing office clutter. Also, when you view something several days or weeks after first filing it, you could have greater objectivity and a new chance to act, file, toss, or delegate it.

If you maintain a tickler file, then you could place the item in that file near the date when it makes sense to take action. It might make sense to add the item to the long-term portion of your super to-do list. In any case, the item is off your desk and out of your mind for the time being, and can be handled at a more suitable time.

> **Dyna Moe**
> This system of using tickler files works well with smaller and recurring tasks that you'd prefer to not bother including on a to-do list or as part of an electronic calendar or scheduler.

For those items that can be handled another day, simply slip them into a daily or monthly tickler file. If the materials are too big to go into the tickler file, put a project note in the file, and neatly house the materials in another location, but away from your desk.

Toss-it Items

Prior to filing any particular item, assess whether or not it should be filed at all! Much of what we file, represents information crutches: stuff we're never going to use again but somehow it makes us feel comfortable if we retain it.

Many documents we save represent old or obsolete information that has already been updated or can quickly be found someplace on the web if we need it. So, items that make your toss-it category should add up quickly. Ideally, your toss-it items will represent the largest of accumulations.

If you have trouble tossing any particular item, sometimes it helps to identify other people within your office who might benefit from the item. If you find someone else who would be grateful for receiving what to you represents nothing new or vital to you, it's a lot easier to part with the item.

Delegate-it Items

As you continue with Operation Clean Sweep, seek out those items that can be delegated. The more items you can delegate (see Chapter 21), the clearer and cleaner you keep your desk and work environment, and the more energized and focused you could remain on other, more important tasks.

If it helps, with a pencil and Post-it pad, mark the items with the names of those to whom you will be delegating.

Clear and Clean and Ready for Action

Once your Operation Clean Sweep pile is down to nothing—and I mean nothing—immediately delegate the tasks that you have identified as suitable for delegation. Toss or donate that which you do not need to retain, and file those things that are most suitable for filing at that particular time. What's left are the handful of items that you need or want to act upon: the important and the important and urgent tasks you face today, this week, this month and on a periodic basis.

Word power
When something is done on a periodic basis that means it is done from time to time, and at least often enough to avoid potential hazards.

To Review: thirty minutes and, poof, the mess is gone. Starting with the act-on-it items, estimate how long it will take to complete each item. Add all your estimates and multiply that number by 1.5 (to account for your optimism or naivety!).

As the number of task hours before you climbs, as it could, you can see dramatically that there is no point continuing as you have. So, become meaner and leaner, and more focused. What else can you chuck? What can be combined, ignored, delayed, delegated, done in multiples, farmed out, automated, or systemized?

Dyna Moe
As each new day or period of high anxiety over all the tasks you face ensues, repeat Operation Clean Sweep and remember to include the items in that day's tickler file.

Anti-Pile Behavior

The best of all worlds, in terms of controlling your sacred turf, is to engage in a routine that heads off piles before they even begin. For example, as soon as the mail arrives open it—over a wastebasket. Constantly be on the lookout to reduce key data and vital information to its least voluminous form.

Whenever you see a pile starting to form—not only those on your desk—on top of the filing cabinet, around the corners of your room, and covering flat surfaces and ledges, break it up.

Whenever you find folders and tasks mounting up on all sides of you, remember how they got there, and that you are in charge of them, not vice versa.

Nothing will move you along as fast and as focused as Operation Clean Sweep. You'll find yourself dropping non-important, non-urgent tasks.

After you've identified the most important project or task, begin working on it to its completion. If you can't complete it because it requires input from others, or for some other reason, proceed with it as far as you can go. Then go on to the next item.

Trouble Getting Started?

If your desk is such a mess that you don't know where to start, first re-read Chapter 6! Otherwise a quick step would be to round up all the pens and pencils that populate your desk, from the far corners to those that are right in front of you. Put them in a pencil holder or pencil can or whatever you want to call your container.

Next, grab all the Post-it pads, small notes, and scraps of paper that contain some type of vital information, be it an address, a phone number, a website, or what have you. Decide here and now to do the following:

a) enter the information on your hard drive in a folder that is typically designed to be a catch-all for such tidbits of information, or

b) lay down these Post-it pads and scraps of information on the copier to create one or two collective pages to be neatly filed, or folded and parked in the corner of your desk for quick reference. (Clue: If you have all such tidbits in one place, you have a better chance of finding and using them as needed.) Ideally, you don't let such tidbits pile up to begin with; however, human nature being what it is, you are probably going to keep doing this.

Now collect all the papers, documents, and file folders on your desk. Also gather any books, reports, or other large documents, and place them on appropriate shelves. If you need specific pages from such documents, copy them on a copier, put those pages in the appropriate file folder, and put the books, documents, and reports on shelves or appropriate file folders.

Factoid

Time test show that people can clear up and re-organize a desk top in a matter of minutes when they put their minds to it.

If you have trouble getting started, schedule your session in your appointment book or calendar as you would any other vital obligation.

Wait! Scheduling *Operation Clean Sweep*? Won't that represent another burden in a long line of tasks you face? Actually scheduling such time increases the probability of your success!

Formally scheduling Operation Clean Sweep sessions to stay organized automatically raises the status of the procedure.

File with Style

As you begin to allocate the top-of-the-pile items during Operation Clean Sweep, once again you'll find yourself doing significant filing. As we've discussed, in this information overload era, filing is essential.

What you file, given that you've made good choices about what to retain, supports your career. The goal of filing is to be able to withdraw what you need when you need it (whether it's on a hard drive or in filing cabinet). The basic tools for effective hard copy filing are a wastebasket, file folders and labels, a marker, and a chair.

I file for several hours once a week. To file intelligently, acquire colored file folders, colored file tabs, and dots. You can set up a system similar to what you would see in a dentist's office with visible, color-coded files. You could have everything related to clients in red files, and everything related to marketing in green, and so on.

The more files you have, the more difficult it is to find any particular file. You are better off with a handful of large files than many small files; this way, you have a much greater chance of choosing the right file.

Found in 60 Seconds

Generally, if you can't find an item in about 60 seconds, you're not organized. This could seem like a stern standard, but how long should it take you to open up a file cabinet, flip through a couple of files, and find exactly what you're seeking? Organized managers don't required more than about 60 seconds.

Reaching this hallowed state won't happen over night, especially if you haven't given your files supreme attention in recent weeks or months. But cut yourself some slack, you can make it.

You'll probably have to expend the equivalence of three weekends, or about six days, metered out a half day at a time. If the prospects of killing a half a day doing nothing but organizing is going to throw you out of whack, then come in on a Saturday morning when no one is around, and you can work undisturbed.

Periodically, sort through your files, look for outdated items, and chuck them. Make it fun. Pare down those files until you have only the essence. Regardless of your particular inclination towards organizing (some people enjoy it), practically speaking, you have little choice. When others are counting on you, you need to have your materials in order and easily retrievable.

Coming Undone

Disorganization can cost you the trust and confidence of those to whom you report and those who report to you. If you have a reputation for mislaying what others have given to you, they begin to change their behavior around you, and not in ways that would please you.

Creative Filing

Be creative when you file. Feel free to experiment—create files that say, "Check in one month," "Check next year," or "I don't know where to file this." Feel good about your style of filing.

You might establish a "rainy day" file. You would include handwritten notes from other people, pictures, memos, and anything else that helps brighten your day. It could include performance appraisals, evaluations from presentations you have made, or simply your bosses' handwritten words or praise accompanying something that you have submitted. Anything and everything that lifts your spirits is fair game for this file.

In closing, if you can't find what you have, your files are of no value. When you're in control of your information and files, you're able to retrieve items easily, and use them to get things done. The information your files contain, appropriately used, equals power!

 # Email as an Organizing Tool

---

In This Chapter:

➤ Does email dictate your day
➤ Why email is addictive
➤ Ground rules and common sense
➤ Take an email vacation

This chapter takes a firm stance about email, text messaging, and instant messaging: they are tools and, as such, should be treated as tools.

We Manage our Tools, They Don't Manage Us

In preparation for my presentation to an annual convention of commercial printers, I visited the office of one of the larger printers in my area. I had an appointment with the vice president of operations. He made an observation I've never forgotten and that I seek to practice every day. His observation has tremendous implications regarding getting things done: don't let email dictate your day.

The savvy executive talked about the people on his staff who receive email in the morning and let it rule the rest of their day. Vital messages you receive in the course of the day or a week merit a significant allocation of resources. When your time and efforts are driven by email, however, as opposed to what you've listed to accomplish (the subject of Chapter 11), the type of tasks you'll complete will likely be different, lesser in magnitude, and less satisfying than those you achieve when you stick to the items and the course you've plotted.

Email is a tool, something like mail, something like the phone.

Email and instant messaging take the place of face-to-face communication, special deliveries, occasional meetings, and verbally conversing with others. All of those benefits, as convenient and critical as they are, do not offer a substitute for you taking control of your activities, time, and day.

So much has been written but so great is the problem about the crushing burden of email with which managers contend every single workday and then some. To glean the advice of someone who provides solutions to executives in a broad swath of industries and occupations, I turned to one of North America's foremost experts on getting more done via email, Wayne McKinnon.

Wayne's pearls of email management wisdom extend throughout this chapter. As you proceed, notice the ways in which skillfully managing your incoming email parallels managing your desk and office—act, file, toss, or delegate—via Operation Clean Sweep (discussed in the previous chapter).

The Wisdom of Managing Your Messages

Wayne observes that most people have a hard enough time managing the stacks of paper on their desk, let alone the piles of information in their computers.

Keeping the number of stored messages to a minimum saves time.

If you have to sort through hundreds of messages each time you seek information, your search will be inefficient. Many stored messages become redundant once you receive a more recent message.

It's easier to clean things up as you go along than to face the daunting task of tackling a mountain of unsorted messages.

Read Your Email in the Morning

By getting an early start, you can arrive at work relaxed and ready to take on the day. Spend your first quiet moments before the day piles up doing the necessary things—plan your day before the hectic pace takes over.

For some people an efficient start includes checking their voicemail, email, and text messages. Perhaps your daily plan depends on the email you receive. Depending on the nature of your work, you might check email once at the start of the day, or only after all of your other tasks are complete.

Your answer will depend greatly on how strategic email is to your job function. If you are in a support role and your email indicates that you have a fire to extinguish, then by all means make checking your email a morning priority. But don't waste your most productive time of the day checking discretionary messages. Focus on the vital ones when they need your attention.

Assign and Delegate Tasks Before You Respond

If you begin your day by reading new mail, delegate what you can. You might find that others can handle the tasks better, or provide you with useful information to help you

Factoid

Surveys show that most people simply want a reliable answer to their email questions . . . and they are not concerned if their reply comes from someone who was assigned the task of answering.

respond. Where appropriate, ask the person to whom you delegate the message to respond directly to the original sender, with a cc to yourself. This saves time and keeps you from being an email bottleneck.

You have to do the remaining tasks, but is today the best day or should they be scheduled for another time? If you have an integrated contact manager, you can prioritize and schedule your tasks all in one place. If not, enter your tasks in your daybook, calendar, or personal information manager.

Save Most Replies 'Til Later

Once you have collected the necessary details, and received answers from those you have delegated the tasks to, you are ready to respond. Your goal is to reply to everyone who emailed you that day by closing time, or at least before the next morning, when they'll likely sort through their email.

If you're completely swamped, respond with a standard reply stating that you have received the message and it will be X hours or days before you can reply in detail.

Not all messages are equal, so mark your messages with the proper priority. Messages from customers and your boss generally are important and could be urgent. Peruse those messages before the rest of your in-box. Since many email systems allow you to mark an urgency level on the messages you send, encourage your colleagues and any staff to use this feature appropriately.

Rules of Email Engagement

After clearing out the spam and junk, resist the temptation to read all of your remaining messages. Information messages from listservs and other sources could be worth retaining, but these can be read when you choose. They can be stored for later reading or for reference.

With messages containing a common thread, read the latest first. You might not need to read the earlier messages at all.

Dyna Moe

Be creative when it comes to establishing electronic file folders that serve as holding bins. You can create files based on the project name, a team member name, the client or customer name, and so on. You can also create files for the day of the week, the weeks in a month, and the months in a year. It takes less than 30 minutes to set up this file system and the dividends pay off, over and over again.

Create folders on your computer for each of your projects. Move all correspondence into the appropriate folders. If a response is part of a project, move the message to the appropriate project folder to have both sides of the conversation on file for future reference.

When the project is over, you can delete the folder, combine it with something else, extract relevant parts, or archive it.

Set a Time Limit

If email is not a business-critical application for you, in other words if you're not hired specifically to handle email, don't let it distract you from your work. Determine what times of the day are your most productive and make this an email blackout period.

If you typically run out of steam at 3:00 in the afternoon, schedule half an hour or so then to review your messages. Stick to the time limit you have chosen. Without time limits, you could spend an entire day sorting and reading the in-box on your desk.

By quickly sorting discretionary mail into one pile, you can simply throw it all away if you run out of time. If you have been out of the office for a while, scan your messages and read the newest ones first. If you see more than one message from an individual, the most recent likely contains more information, or tells you that they have already received the answer they need.

Some companies discourage the use of email during certain hours in an effort to encourage employees to talk again!

Set Aside Items You Receive

Do you regularly read the messages that people copy to you for your reference? If your in-box is jam packed with cc'd items that you can't seem to tackle, you could miss some of the important messages sent directly to you.

If you subscribe to mailing lists, ensure that your email service allows you to automatically sort and store messages in specific folders. You can set up your rules to recognize the subject of the message and automatically file appropriate messages. You might never look at these items, but they are filed for future reference if you ever need them. If you have an automatic rule that sorts messages based on the subject, be aware that if the subject line is not exactly the same for each message, your rule will not work.

Dyna Moe
Email comes in waves, all day long. Most of it is junk, but much of it requires attention. To engender a feeling of accomplishment and completion, and at the same time actually get many things done, maintain zero email in your *in-box*. It sounds difficult, but in practice is easy. There's no justification for having a huge number of emails build up in your in-box and a great case for maintaining zero or close to zero mail in the in-box.

The same can be said for the *sent* box. Once you've sent an email to someone, simply allocate it to one of the types of folders previously discussed.

Keeping it Moving

Set up a rule to automatically move material—newsletters, for example—to appropriate folders. Begin by moving new messages to a subfolder titled "Newly Arrived."

At the end of, say, each week, move unread items from "Newly Arrived" to a subfolder called "Recent," and move the items in "Recent" to a third folder called "Remove."

If you decide that any information more than a month old can be discarded, then every month delete the entire contents of the "Remove" folder . . . without reading a single message! Once this folder is empty, move the contents of

Coming Undone
Information that you can't bring yourself to delete, can go in your "Archive" folder. Make the title of that folder today's date. Promise yourself that if the file is still there at this time next month, or next year you will throw it out without opening it. Be careful: You will sabotage your plan if you even peek at its contents.

the "Recent" folder to the "Remove" folder, and move the "Newly Arrived" to the "Recent" folder.

Any time during the week you can read the contents of any of these folders, keeping in mind that at the end of the cycle it's time to throw away the contents of the "Remove" folder without looking at it.

You Can't Read Them All!

If you receive relatively few email messages daily, the following is likely not a problem for you. If you're swamped, attempting to keep up is useless. Be selective about which information items you read. Remove yourself from mailing lists that you don't actually read. If you have an assistant, prepare a list of criteria so that he or she evaluate whether or not you need to personally respond to each message.

Don't jeopardize your time, income, or sanity by becoming a full time message handler and personal advisor to the world. Some people will take everything you give them and then ask for more.

By answering their questions, you invite them to ask again. If you find that your willingness to help is being taken advantage of, refer the offender to a book or other resource.

Make your response brief. In seeking to be polite, we often send the message that we would be happy to keep helping. This example shows a polite but conclusive response to a request for help:

Q: Hi! Could you tell me how to do ABC?

A: Please refer to page 10 of your user manual.

If you have to respond to the same question repeatedly, save the response and re-use it the next time you need to answer that question again. Better yet, post the response in a public area such as your website. You can build a list of frequently asked questions (FAQ) where others can find their answers.

Decide and Move On

Make decisions based on the subject line! Most times, you can make filing or action decisions based on the subject. This is more crucial when you are traveling, since email via smart phone lets you view the headers even before downloading the messages.

Use previews to sort and delete, and resist the temptation to read! If you're swamped with email, quickly scan your messages. If the subject line does not provide enough detail, the preview function provided by many email programs allows you to see the first few lines of text without opening the message.

Dyna Moe

Be sure to write informative subject lines yourself. If your message requests action, mention that right at the top, so your reader doesn't have to wade through the message to prioritize it. If everyone you communicate with uses this procedure, you won't need to read most messages past the header—you'll see it's not critical information.

Filter out the Junk

Email software offers filtering systems. By setting up specific rules, you can automatically sort, respond to, and delete messages. If you receive junk mail from a particular address, set up a filter that will file or delete any message they send to you. You already know this but are you using your filter to best advantage? Largely for review, here are basic examples of what filters can do for you:

➤   Maintain a list of your top-priority contacts, and move all else out of your in-box.
➤   Weed out unwelcome known addresses.
➤   Filter based on message text. (Seek common phrases).
➤   Find what works for you depending on the types of messages you receive.

Give Yourself a Break

Internet addiction is characterized by incessant web surfing, obsessively checking and rechecking email for new messages, or by refusing to be away from online connections, so as to always be wired and available to others.

As you read in Chapter 1, information and communication overload is a sociocultural phenomenon impacting virtually every adult in society. This phenomenon has reached pathological proportions for many individuals. I hope you're not among them.

Email can be addictive. It is gratifying to receive thanks for a job well done or for information you forward to someone else.

Dyna Moe

Incessant means "without ceasing," or more commonly, "without interruption."

For people working from home, email could be the primary vehicle for contact with the outside world. For their corporate counterparts, it can be an escape from the office while still at one's desk.

These little gratifications throughout the day can be addictive. Like a kid waiting for a letter from your pen pal, you anxiously await a new email message . . . from anyone!

Sure, many people need to check in regularly for messages so that they can reply in a timely manner, but for email addicts, checking email one more time is not unlike popping one more quarter in a slot machine or video game.

If you are starving for attention or gratification, sometimes it's best to give in. Pick up the telephone and complete an entire conversation in minutes instead of dragging it out over days. Once satisfied, move on and finish some tasks.

Take an "Email Vacation"

Many tasks require concentration. When you're in a state of "flow," you can accomplish your work more easily. If your email system automatically notifies you of each incoming message, turn that feature off when you don't want to be distracted, which ideally is much of the time. Email is supposed to be unobtrusive, so why do you let it interrupt you when you're rolling?

Many people find that checking email is a good way to wind down before leaving the office. Others find it a predictable way to raise their stress level. If you find that work has taken over your life, a few evenings per week, cut yourself loose and enjoy some down-time away from email and other forms of communication.

Dyna Moe

Schedule your email reviews. Plan your day in constructive blocks of time dictated by the type of tasks you have for that day or week. Even huge projects can be broken down into smaller tasks that will give you a sense of accomplishment. Allow yourself to check your email only after you have completed a task.

CHAPTER 10

 # The Hard Drive for High Productivity

In This Chapter:

➤ The rise of electronic addiction
➤ Don't fight the system
➤ Hand held and powerful

In Part 3's first four chapters, we addressed organizational issues related to your desk, files, shelves, and office; paper and correspondence; important versus urgent criteria; and email. In this chapter, we turn to the issue of organizing information, per se, as in what to do with all this stuff?! What do we make of it? How can we classify information and benefit from it?

The Rise of Electronic Addiction

Electronic addiction—the overarching desire to stay connected and seemingly on top of things, be in control, and be in the driver's seat—is rampant among career professionals.

In our over-information society, where people are bombarded on a daily basis with more information than they can comfortably ingest, oddly enough, they often go out of their way to take in more than they know they can handle!

The Internet has both elevated and exacerbated our ability to quickly gather information. Enter a few key words, and voila, hundreds if not thousands of hits appear. As one observer said, "the Internet is so big, powerful, and pointless that for some people it is a complete substitute for life."

The quest to stay on top of it all, however, is not solely related to online and voice communications. People sign up for more catalogues, more brochures, and more information coming their way.

With the flood of email in everyone's in-boxes, along with the abundance of informative and entertaining Internet sites, on top of all the printed information that comes one's way, is being deluged equated with being alive? "I'm overwhelmed by information, therefore I am."

In 1844 Henry David Thoreau succinctly summarized his approach to a satisfying life: simplify, simplify, simplify. Today, it appears that we can't follow even one third of his advice.

A Little Bit Can Go a Long Way Towards Wisdom

By continually assessing the information you encounter, staying organized, and applying what you've learned or know, you can become more valuable in the work place, accomplish more, and rise faster and further in your career.

Here is a basic classification system for the progression to knowledge and even wisdom:

➤ The lowest level of input is bits, single packets of information that essentially say yes or no, left or right, on or off. In combination, bits add up to data. Mostly, this distinction doesn't affect you.

➤ Data are raw numbers in chart form, equations, lists, and so on. Ideally, they are readily observable, objective, and understandable. When worked upon, data can have value.

➤ One step up from data is information. As used in this classification system, information is the manipulation of data, analysis, interpretation, and reporting. For example, every article that you come across in magazines and newspapers contains information. Some even share knowledge or convey wisdom (see below). Article, document, and book authors draw upon data or observable phenomena, make conclusions, and offer commentary.

➤ When information is added to experience and viewed with reflection, depending upon whose brain is in the driver's seat, it can yield knowledge. Think of knowledge as the product of lots of information that somebody gathered, pondered, and drew conclusions from. Knowledgeable people in your profession, not by coincidence, tend

Dyna Moe

Comparing knowledge with others makes one valuable both within an organization and with clients and customers. Knowledgeable salespeople, all other things being equal, have the best chance of achieving desirable.

to read considerably, organize their notes, develop original thoughts, and then draw conclusions from what they have ingested.

➤ When new knowledge is gathered and added to one's existing knowledge, wisdom becomes possible. This is as true for organizations as it is for individuals.

Wisdom comes slowly, sometimes only after years of accumulated knowledge. In your career, it's easy to become snarled by the glut of data and information. It could be temporarily satisfying to read everything that crosses your desk, download files, subscribe to publications, and so on. Indeed, much new knowledge can be generated from such efforts.

Wisdom, in an age where too much information confronts each of us, can come from the ability to recognize broad-based patterns and long-term trends rather than being caught up in short-term phenomena and fads.

Dyna Moe

As you draw upon your own accumulated knowledge and the wisdom that you develop, you'll be less prone to ever accelerating flows of information, save time, get more done, and be more valuable to those around you.

Jumping in Versus Establishing Control

Here is some organizing wisdom to which we can all relate. How often have you slugged your way through new software without bothering to read even the summary card of instructions? You learn enough to be proficient, but you never master the program. You undertake trial and error approaches to getting things done.

Sometimes things work on the first couple go-rounds. Buoyed by a few successes, trial and error becomes your method of operation.

Coming Undone

In our culture people often work 50 to 55 hours a week for 40 hours' pay. Many "throw their time" at problems as opposed to establishing control over the immediate environment and thereby devising useful systems for accomplishment.

Too often, however, you're frustrated and stymied. You spend endless hours going down wrong paths, experiencing more errors for your trials, and still you have no intention or even notion of actually reading the directions.

You fail to take the time to devise a system, which, initially, makes for slow going, but ultimately yields increased time savings with each deployment. Many of the systems that we could devise to make us more productive and avoid throwing our time at a problem, simply involves taking an organized or more methodical approach to learning.

Learn a System or Devise a System

Submitting a monthly report that requires consistent headings and format is best facilitated by learning your word processing software's style management function. That takes time and effort but represents a viable approach to accomplishing what you need to do.

Refusing to learn the style function and manually formatting each month's report is analogous to throwing your time at a problem.

You'll finish the report, but the ten to 15 minutes you lose each time in preparing it has a cumulative impact. Add this behavior and resulting time loss to all the other ways that you throw your time at problems rather than devising or taking advantage of pre-established systems.

It becomes clear that the time cost of getting things done, for you, is much higher than it needs to be. This cost, in turn, exacerbates other time pressures you experience when getting other things done. You're on a downward cycle that knows no end.

You remain at work longer, enjoy your work less, and wonder why others are surpassing you. You don't seem to be completing the critical tasks and have little hope of tackling larger, longer-term challenges.

Minor Changes, Major Results

Along your career path, how you previously got things done or what worked yesterday will have less value with each passing day. You certainly want some stability, but don't fear change or close yourself off to it.

Peter and Rosemary Grant, Princeton University biologists, spent decades in the footsteps of Charles Darwin, studying mate selection. Cactus finches, for example, breed based on what nature provides for them. In 1977 they only had a few seeds left from the year before, as a drought devastated the landscape. Breeding was down. As a result, the next generation, actually evolved larger, blunter beaks.

Six years later, there was a surplus of seeds along with heavy rains. The finches bred profusely.

In 1985, there was another drought, leaving only small seeds on the ground. These seeds favored smaller, quicker birds with thin beaks. The Grants came to an astounding conclusion: even the most minor changes in the environment, such as an increase or decrease in rain or rising temperatures, can have a huge impact on the course of evolution.

In many respects, the same holds true for your career: even minor changes in how you manage your environment (i.e., organize your desk, your office, your time, your approach to learning) can yield great payoffs.

A Simple System and You're Welcome to It

Options abound when you install new software. Toggle this on, toggle this off, choose this, elect that, ignore this, make this your default, customize this, ignore that. So many options, so little time!

Sure, some people understand these things and they're usually under 20 years old. If you were born before the personal computer came along, however, then it's not as likely that it will become second nature to you. With this as a backdrop, the real issue becomes, how much time do you want to waste in your life and in your career fiddling with such stuff?

I am among those who won't read the instruction manual or card. In fact, I refuse to open an instruction book, and I refuse to look at the laminated instruction card that comes with so many products today. I choose to spend *zero* seconds juggling with hardware or software instructions and spend the brunt of my time getting things done that I seek to accomplish.

Factoid

Thomas A. Edison, on accomplishment: "Hell, there are no rules here— we're trying to accomplish something."

Help Is at Hand

I bring in a junior instructor, a web guru, or a PC specialist, individuals who know the Internet like the backs of their hands, students who major in computer science. I find them by posting on job sites of local colleges.

Item by item, function by function, we review what I ought to be able to do with the equipment and what I want to complete as a result of being able to use the equipment. Then, we codify everything. Gadget by gadget, item by item, function by function, we list the instructions that I need to know.

Word Power

When you codify something, you organize it into a system such as a body of laws or instructions.

We review the instructions until I have it down cold. It's called "Jeff-proofing," (instead of calling it idiot-proofing).

After my guru departs, I have the sacred set of instructions. And you can do the same.

Now and then, yes, I still run astray. No problem, I'll park that one for now. At the next opportunity my guru makes the necessary modifications to the instructions. Sometimes, it's simply a word change, "enter" versus "click" versus "return."

By and by, we hone and refine any instructions that require modifications. No endless bouts with instruction manuals for me.

Dyna Moe

The larger your organization, the greater the chance someone can help you. So strike up a business relationship: they help you with all things technical and you help them with some skill you can teach which they wish to master. Or you pay them!

Creating a Computer and Software Instruction File

I haven't opened a computer or software instruction booklet in more than ten years. Yet, I know exactly how to operate my hardware and software to accomplish what I choose to accomplish.

I've learned the importance of creating one master file, alphabetical by topic, of all the instructions that I need. Whether I learn these instructions on my own, attend a training session, or am told specifically by a computer guru "how to do it," everything I might need to refer to is housed in one ever-growing file.

Currently my instruction file is 26 pages, but it wouldn't matter if it were doubled in length. I can find what I need in a hurry. Whether it's how to use the print screen function, the actual specifications for each of the computers that I own, how to access the server to make changes to my website, or how to synchronize the database on my main computer with my networked computers, I have all instructions boiled down to the essence in this single, amply backed-up file.

When I learn a new routine or way to do something, I immediately codify the procedure and save it in my instruction file.

Over the years, I've had different computer gurus instruct me. As one departs and another arrives, the new one is always ably aided by my instruction file. Using the word-search function, we can quickly find any topic or set of instructions.

What Can Go Wrong Will

With any tool of productivity, over-use as well as mis-use can diminish, not enhance, your productivity.

Anytime you enter incorrect data, it will give you incorrect data until you fix it—the old garbage in garbage out problem, except this time you could be relying heavily on the garbage.

Dyna Moe

What does portable computing power add to your life? More organization, reminders, less clutter, and, perhaps, peace of mind. Until such devices can decode your brain waves, however, any time your priorities or your schedule changes, add the information to your system. Your schedule is up to you, and your effectiveness is up to you.

Becoming More Efficient in the Workplace

Part 4
Becoming More Efficient in the Workplace

In this fourth part of the book, four chapters help you become more efficient in getting things done in both the short and long term, and in particular stay in control on the bigger and more involved tasks and projects you face.

CHAPTER 11

From Your Head to the Page

In This Chapter:

➤ Keeping it all straight
➤ To-do lists forever
➤ One giant list for everything
➤ Short circuits with the shock

This chapter presents a guide on making the kind of lists that will help you to stay organized and productive.

Once upon a time the typical worker sweated a little more, but was anxious a little less. Actual physical work would tax one's muscles but would not contribute to the mounting form of stress that builds up when handling office work. When you could easily see what you had done, say, moved all the boxes from this side of the room to that side of the room, there was less of a chance of misunderstanding how much you had accomplished.

The Best Chance to Keep it Straight

In days of yore, the factory whistle at 5 p.m. signaled the end of the workday. Today's work is linked to a never-ending stream of information and communication, much of which needs to be addressed. Often little barrier exists between professional tasks and personal tasks, and it's hard sometimes to differentiate when you're work day is actually "done."

What signals the end today? Virtually nothing. With so many items begging for your attention and your unvoiced disposition to attend to them, the state of being overwhelmed never seems to subside. Considering everything on your plate, how are you going to keep it all straight?

To-do Lists: Virtually Universal

As I speak at conferences and conventions, it never ceases to amaze me: to this day, people are always asking me about to-do lists. Do they need to have one? How do they best maintain them?

Can you name anyone in the workaday world who doesn't use some form of a to-do list as a primary tool for getting things done?

I don't believe there is a tactic as appealing or that proves to be as useful as a classic to-do list. It seems the more you do, the more you need them.

The more responsibility you have at work, the more you need to write down and codify everything you need to address. Especially when you have two or more people reporting to you, too much is floating in your head.

Except for the brief tasks that confront you, for which it makes sense to take care of them on the spot without entering them on a to-do list, all else needs to be recorded in one way or another.

Count on this: the to-do list is not going to go away soon (nor should it). The human brain, the wonderful contraption that it is, has trouble retaining lists, specific sequences, and minute detail. If you doubt this, recite the sequence of digits of the two credit cards you use most often.

Dyna Moe

It's a semi-bonus anytime you can knock out something without it having to make your to-do list, but the brunt of the tasks and projects that you face, being longer and more involved, don't fall into that category.

A Quintessential Tool

In this era of unprecedented, non-stop bombardment of information and communication, to-do lists have become a quintessential tool in furthering our careers. They help shape what we do, when we do it, and even how we do it. A career professional without a to-do list is worse off than a ship without a rudder. At least the crew might be able to conjure up some makeshift means of navigation.

Proceeding without a to-do list is a recipe for going over the rapids. You could recall some things that you need to address, but you'd forget others for days, or forever. Items screaming for your attention, the urgent, would keep jumping up to the front of the line, squeezing out the *important* and the *important and urgent*. Worse, the *unimportant and not urgent* would too often see the light of day!

What's more, the items that you do not finish, incompletions, have a way of reverberating in your head (see Chapter 16), coming back to you over and over, hence magnifying and multiplying themselves.

Log it In

Since the number of responsibilities, tasks, and projects that you face exceeds what you can cognitively monitor, you have to get it all down on paper, disk, or microchip. Otherwise, you'll face mounting forms of anxiety that can lead to trouble.

One of your primary tasks is to log in everything that you want to accomplish. If you don't, you're liable to receive intermittent alerts from your brain all day and night.

Dyna Moe

To be in control of your career and your life, to handle your tasks and responsibilities, and to maintain your sanity, employ to-do lists with the enthusiasm of a crow in a cornfield.

To-do List, a Brief History

Who knows when the first to-do list was constructed. It might have happened in the caves of France along with those early drawings depicting "the hunt." Soon after human kind gravitated towards carving massages into the barks of trees, logs, and stone slates, somebody somewhere probably recorded a list of stuff they wanted to complete:

➤ Hunt the mastodon
➤ Gather firewood
➤ Make new war-clubs
➤ Repair bow-and-arrow
➤ Grab woman by hair and drag back to cave . . .

Paper Proves Handy for Making Notes

Invented in China in 105 A.D., paper proved to be handy for making notes. Early forms of to-do lists flourished after this invention. By the height of early Greek civilization, and certainly by the time the Romans ruled the Western world, making lists was a common practice.

Flash-forward a millennium and a half and you have Martin Luther nailing his 95 theses to a church door in Wittenburg. Okay, they were more like grievances but, inverted, could be seen as a grand to-do list containing all kinds of changes that this protestor felt that were necessary in the church.

Word Power

Theses, as used here, refers to strongly suggested reforms —items that needed to be changed.

The To-do List as Near Art Form

Two centuries later, Ben Franklin published gazettes and almanacs, turned the to-do list into a near art form. Let's see:

➤   Start the first public library
➤   Perfect bifocal lenses
➤   Launch first volunteer fire department
➤   Discover electricity
➤   Acquire a printing press, publish a gazette
➤   Write Poor Richard's Almanac
➤   Invent the Franklin stove
➤   Become Governor of Pennsylvania
➤   Help draft and sign the Declaration of Independence
➤   Raise funds in France for the Revolutionary War
➤   Sign the U.S. Constitution
➤   Live to a ripe old age

Quills gave way to pens, and ratty paper gave way to smooth sheets, 500 to a ream. Here and abroad, the world of to-do list makers were on an upward trajectory.

Aided by manual typewriters, then IBM Selectrics, then Lexigraphs, then computers, along with copiers, fax machines, and printers, the to-do list as notation of desired personal and professional accomplishments became the most ubiquitous productivity tool in the world, and with Post-its we don't even need tape or a nail!

> **Dyna Moe**
> Documenting all that you want to get done—from this afternoon's tasks, to forthcoming trips, to long term goals, to retirement—puts you on the path to greater control and accomplish-

To-Do Lists Rule

Among career professionals, do you know anyone who proceeds throughout the workday and week without some written or recorded compilation of what they want, need, or have been told to get done? To-do lists appear in notebooks, on notepads, on single sheets of paper, on Post-it pads, and on every type of screen imaginable.

They're transmitted via disk and email, and copied in duplicate and triplicate. They're posted here, there, and everywhere.

People carry them in their front pocket, back pocket, purses, briefcases, billfolds, satchels, and everything in between.

People are forever updating, merging, losing, rewriting, and becoming frustrated by to-do lists. Many people have more than one to-do list! They have one for a particular project, one for recurring items, one for longer-term distant types of objectives, and so on.

Utility Over the Top

When you maintain a to-do list, and any of its kin such as an appointment schedule, or plain old rosters of stuff that you need or want to get done, you accomplish several things:

➤ You have a document you can review, amend, or update, as well as print, copy and bring with you.

➤ You free your mind from having to dwell on such items. You take comfort knowing that you've put it on paper.

➤ You more likely take an organized approach to handling tasks and responsibilities. You can rank, schedule, rearrange, and even eliminate them when you've either accomplished the task or the situation has changed.

➤ You enjoy the satisfaction of crossing tasks off your list when you have accomplished them.

Independent of how much you rely upon to-do lists, if you've gone months or years with too much dancing in your head, it could be hard to recall when your mind was last free and clear. A cluttered mind is a terrible thing, as is a cluttered desk, office, and email inbox.

Dyna Moe

A free and clear state is a license to create, perform, and achieve—like a person giving a speech who is no longer concerned about the preparation, rehearsal, and coaching, and is now simply in a pure delivery state.

Getting Clear about Your Task List

To establish a viable to-do list, transfer everything from your head to the page. Whether you use a simple pad and paper, a smart phone, a tablet, a notebook or desktop computer, or something else, once you've listed everything that you want or need to accomplish, your anxiety level diminishes.

What are the processes for collecting everything floating around in your world, desk, office, home, car, briefcase, and wallet, as well as your head? I prefer to use my cell phone recorder and transcriber function to both quickly generate and save lists. You could use whatever tool you find to be convenient.

Aligning Your World

You might need to tap a variety of source materials: lists, rosters, notes, business cards, outlines, phone messages, etc. You alone are responsible for generating this grand compilation, for initiating and maintaining the pipeline of source materials that ultimately will be organized

Coming Undone

If you haven't aligned your life with the implements that would enable you to capture what you want to record or what you want or need to add to your compilation, then you're not serious in your approach to getting things done. You'll get some things done, tasks that are easier to recall, and you'll bypass others, those that momentarily crept into your consciousness and then crept out.

and captured on your to-do list. This massive undertaking requires setting up your various environments to support this effort.

Collecting Bins

Many people find it convenient to maintain a catch-all folder in their briefcases or desk drawers so that all the notes, lists, receipts, article clippings, business card, and announcements can be temporarily housed. Then when you return from travel or from a nearby meeting, you can quickly allocate the items in the folder.

From Making Lists to Taking Action

You've undertaken the exercise of listing what you want to get done, but *how* and *when*?

Smaller, less critical tasks are easier to tackle than larger, more intricate tasks. Regardless of the size of the project, if you break it into steps and have a clear and bite-sized task before you, you can build momentum more easily than you imagined.

Divide and Conquer

For each item that makes your list, go ahead and record a first, second, and even third step as to how you'll realize its accomplishment. For a small project, the steps could be as simple as visiting a website, calling for information, or walking over to the file cabinet. By perpetually having a next step ready, then a next and a next, none of the items on your list need linger. Certainly, you don't want to bite off more than you can chew by engaging in too many first steps on too many projects at once. However, identifying a few first steps for projects is sufficient to start you rolling.

Once you're comfortable with the sequence of steps you've plotted for the various projects before you, reinforce your progress by further honing and refining your environment to support your various quests. For example, set up a 12 month and 31 day tickler file system (explained in Chapter 8) so that you'll have a place to park and locate associated task documents in a timely manner.

Dyna Moe

You can't always proceed on every task project as swiftly as you'd like. Sometimes you have to wait for other people. Or, there are delays in obtaining information, and so on. Fear not, there's always something else you can work on for a while.

You could also group projects and associated steps by where you will actually take action, such as at the copier, storage room, and so on.

You can prepare checklists for recurring tasks such as visiting branch offices, the company library, or select clients.

Physically Arrange Your Spaces

People reflexively put things by the door when they need to take items with them to meetings or with them at the end of the day.

It makes sense to put a small table or set of shelves by your door.

Don't be surprised if you find yourself in need of organizing items from your organization's supply center or office supply stores. Arranging your environment to make you more productive, at first, often leads to the installation of some items and/ or the removal of others.

With all that you want to get done and all that competes for your time and attention, if you're not occasionally shifting things around on your desk, in your files, or on your shelves, then your efforts are suspect.

Word Power
Reflexively has several meanings including automatically, naturally, habitually, or without thinking.

Likewise, as you look around your office and other work spaces, think about how you can arrange them to accommodate the tasks on your list, the steps you've identified, and the associated actions you want to take to further your progress.

When and Where to Tackle Tasks

If you tackle tasks based on when and on where you're going to handle them, your productivity rises. In our daily high-wire balancing act, handling dozens of emails, scads of inter-office messages and phone calls, and "gotta have it now" assignments dropped in your lap, when we group tasks based on when and where types of considerations, we tend to handle the important and the important and urgent items in the mix.

Coming Undone
Getting more done means acknowledging the reality of working and living in an era of information and communication overload. How you've currently set up your desk, files, shelves, and office might be insufficient as the months and years roll on. Getting too comfortable can cost you.

Review Items on Your List and Conquer

As you proceed down your to-do list, stick to the basics: continually peruse your list, cross off what you've completed, add next steps as needed, and consolidate all items.

Now you're cooking. You've written down your to-dos, identified next step activities, and aligned your environment to support your efforts. Continually reviewing your grand list helps you mentally reinforce your commitment to getting those things done.

A few minutes throughout the day works wonders. Also, one good long review (say, every Friday or Monday, if that suits you) is recommended.

I conduct a weekly, hour-long review in a quiet place without my cell phone and where I otherwise won't be disturbed. These precautions give me the best chance to let the ideas on my to-do list linger, which enables me to more fully understand them.

Dyna Moe

Review your to-do list so that your projects and activities stay in mind, but not so much that such reviews become burdensome. If it helps, actually schedule your long review. Perhaps you want to do it on the same day at the same time each week. You'll find that long after, it becomes automatic.

Managing Your To-do List, Long-term Versus Short-term

What if you could maintain a handy to-do list *and* a comprehensive list of everything short and long term, minuscule and grand, now and for a lifetime that you want to get done? The primary dilemma we face each day is balancing short-term versus long-term tasks and activities. My solution to the dilemma is to compile and maintain a super-long to-do list, sometimes eight pages!

I have hundreds of things on my to-do list arranged by major life priorities. How do I keep from (visibly) going crazy? Most of what's on the list are medium- to long-range activities.

Turn to Page One

The first page of my list represents only the short-term activities —the things I've chosen to do now or this week. I continually draw from the eight page list, and move items to the top as it becomes desirable, or necessary, to tackle them.

Mine is a dynamic to-do list containing everything on this earth I want to get done, but at any given time, I only need to look at page one.

All the anxiety about the things you want to get done diminishes once you generate your super to-do list. My list is long, and it will stay long. I am always updating the list and running a new printout, but that's fine. I wouldn't proceed any other way.

I don't worry about items on the list; I can only get so much done in one day or one week. I know that I'll periodically review the entire list, and continually move items from, say, page eight up to the front. Sometimes, I extract a small portion of a long term task and move it to page one.

Suppose you are organized and use lists, but you don't know if a multi-page list is for you. Perhaps with this approach you feel like everything is too planned out. Relax. The items that make your back pages can ably serve as mental place holders -- they might change in many ways, many times, and even be dropped, but for now, at least, you have them all listed in one place.

Not Everything Everyday

The super to-do list enables you to keep an eye on balancing long-term important tasks and projects with short-term important and urgent, and merely urgent tasks and projects. If I'm working on something during the day and an opening appears to tackle something buried on page seven, I'll certainly consider it. Many days, however, I don't look at pages two through eight.

Maintaining a long to-do list helps me to become more proficient in managing long-term or repeated tasks. With long-term projects, I can constantly draw from them those portions that can be handled in the short-term and, so, move them up to page one.

Dyna Moe

Consider using the super long to-do list. At the least, you'll have identified everything you face, and have it all on one gigantic roster. At the most, you'll have a tool that will support you for years to come.

Likewise, if something is a repeat or cyclical project to be addressed every month or every year, I can move the item up to the front page.

Short-circuiting the To-do List

Most people who encounter information worth retaining make a note or add it to a list. The information stays there for days, weeks, or months. On occasion, short-circuit the to-do list and finish some tasks without entering them on your list!

Sometimes a task you want to accomplish is small enough that you can launch right into it. No need to write it down because that would be more work than it's worth.

Since whatever information you encounter usually involves calling or writing to someone else, rather than adding it to your to-do list pick up a recorder and immediately dictate a letter or memo to whomever you need to be in touch with; take action.

When you short-circuit the to-do lists on some tasks, and you're on a roll, you begin to knock out other smaller tasks that might be on your super to-do list. That's fine. Your goal is to get things done, and practically speaking, any technique or strategy that happens to work at any given time is worth pursuing.

CHAPTER 12

Getting Things Done Right Now

> ## In This Chapter:
>
> ➤ Over-preparation and underestimation
> ➤ The costs of tackling projects
> ➤ Productive resources
> ➤ Rewards system to encourage
>   productivity

Beyond composing, maintaining, and implementing to-do lists, this chapter focuses on immediate measures for getting things done that you want to complete today, this hour, or right now!

Two common mistakes to accomplishing short-term tasks are over-preparing and, paradoxically, underestimating what will be necessary to succeed.

The Hazards of Over-preparation

Over-preparation thwarts many would-be get-things-done enthusiasts. Consider the sales professional who makes fewer sales calls per week, because he or she is semi-perpetually preparing to do so. The over-prepared professional means to do well. His anxiety level, however, might prompt him to over-complicate one sub-task after another en route to actually calling on prospects.

On the day he is ready to make a sales call, this is the person who is bound to blow it. He's soooo ready that he has more information than he'll ever be able to succinctly present in the time allotted for the appointment.

Forsake the crutches that seemingly aid but often impede your progress. The crutch that most often impedes many individuals is information. Too often, many people want to have the broad swath of information, data, figures, and statistics all assembled before launching a task.

More data is not always the answer, especially in a society where we're deluged with data. Enough data exists to lead to all answers which inhibits choosing. Forsaking crutches means you will not allow extraneous factors to impede

Coming Undone
Besides hogging the conversation, the over-prepared salesperson could be too quick to respond to the prospect's objections. He could come off as a know-it-all, or unwittingly offend the client by displaying too much zeal.

your progress. If you have five magazine articles that support your argument, having an additional five articles won't make that much of a difference.

Avoiding rounding up resources that, in retrospect, will prove to be only marginally helpful and unnecessarily draw from the time you expend on the task at hand.

Over-preparers have deluded themselves into believing that all the crutches they've assembled will somehow accelerate their progress once they actually launch into a task. Too late, they find that they've allocated their time and energy in the wrong places.

Sum All the Costs

The second common mistake on the path to getting things done is underestimating what's needed to succeed. The antidotes to this pitfall are to sum all costs, and marshal one's resources.

On any project or task, big or small, it pays to forecast the time, energy, dollars, or other resources needed. The paradox faced by otherwise productive professionals is that they underestimate the time needed to complete a task—even short-term tasks. This is the person who is perpetually racing the clock. His to-do list grows longer and longer because he is over-optimistic about how much he can accomplish in an hour, day, or other short time span.

In the information-based society engulfing us, estimating how much time it will take to complete a particular task can be difficult especially for first time tasks.

➤   Who knows how long it's going to take to learn a new software routine?
➤   Who can say precisely how much time it will take to complete a particular form?
➤   How much time will be needed to review a team member's first interim report?
➤   How long will it take to respond to the three critical emails that recently arrived?

Many of the tasks you face on any given day are "first-time" type tasks, and the time to complete them is not clear at the outset. So it's useful to establish benchmarks and set time limits.

Word Power

A benchmark is an indicator or reference point used to compare a current outcome or experience to one previously documented or noted.

Benchmark Your Tasks

Suppose you have to read a team member's eight page report. From past experience, you've found that your reading time is roughly three minutes per page. For effectiveness and efficiency, you'll be reading slowly and carefully, line by line.

For an eight page report, with a benchmark of three minutes per page, you'll need about 24 minutes. With an occasional interruption, a rough spot that could slow you down, or other unforeseen factors, it might be better to make it 28 minutes.

Suppose you have no benchmark for a report of this length or of this nature. How else could you approach the task without underestimating what it would take to get it done? Set a time limit!

You could give yourself 15, 30, or 45 minutes to handle this report. In the case where you've given yourself 15 minutes and you notice, with about three minutes to go, that you're still on page five, you have a good indication that you underestimated the time.

You now re-compute and acknowledge that 25 or 30 minutes might be more realistic. You might not have the extra time to devote to the report right now, but at least you have useful information.

Alternatively, you could greatly increase your reading speed for the last three pages and still finish within 15 minutes, recognizing that you might need to review the last three pages again at some other time.

Take Advantage of a Miscalculation

Suppose you picked 30 minutes as a time limit to review a report for the first time. In this case, you might finish after 24 minutes or 28 minutes and have between two to six minutes to spare. Is that so bad? Actually, that's a nice state of affairs.

Dyna Moe

Ideally, you want to have a little slack at the end of a task. This enables you to collect your thoughts, finish up your notes, and file, return, or otherwise process what you've been working on.

Suppose you allocated 45 minutes, and you finish after 28 minutes? "What *am* I going to do with the extra 17 minutes?" Have there been any days in the past ten years where you couldn't use the 17 minutes "savings"?

Maybe 17 minutes from now you have a meeting, you have to make a phone call, or something else has been scheduled. Those 17 minutes represent prime time to handle smaller things that have accumulated, prepare for what's next, or simply take a mental or physical break.

Word Power

A fudge factor is a numerical adjustment you make to an estimation. In this case, we are applying it to time limits in completing tasks.

The Fudge Factor in Estimating Task Times

Many otherwise competent career professionals often underestimate the time it will take to complete certain tasks. If you estimate that a task will take, say, 24 minutes, then automatically increase your estimate by 50 percent. In other words, allocate 36 minutes for a task you initially estimate to require 24 minutes. Allocate 90 minutes for a task you initially estimate will take 60 minutes, and so on.

Coming Undone

Your might use the 50 percent fudge factor a handful of times, and find that it works reasonably well. Caution: you could slip back to what you've been doing for years, being unwittingly optimistic about the time needed to accomplish short-term tasks.

Forgetting What Works

In time, you might forget about the fudge factor. In the blink of an eye, you'll revert to making estimates that are at or under any previous benchmark, don't represent appropriate time intervals, and don't encompass a fudge factor. In short, you'll be underestimating too many of the tasks you handle in a given day, and hence your day will seem like an endless struggle.

Coming Undone

If you're psychologically beaten by the end of the day, you'll wake up the next day thinking you're already behind, and the next day and the next will proceed much like the previous ones. You'll feel tense, rushed, and unproductive. Yet, none of these feelings need be incurred.

As you saw in Chapter 11, maintaining your buoyancy, feeling good about your accomplishments, and sustaining yourself workday after workday are essential to getting things done.

The notion of summing all costs actually extends to all dollar outlays, and includes the energy you might expend on a project, staff resources, equipment, etc.

All of this leads us to a major approach to avoiding common mistakes: marshaling your resources.

Dyna Moe

In all cases, having a realistic notion of what it will take to accomplish the task will serve you better than learning midstream that you underestimated what it would take.

Marshal Your Resources

Consider your activities when you move to a new town. You obtain local phone books and other directories. You find a doctor, a dentist, and other healthcare providers. You call utility companies to ensure that your services are running the first day you move in. You learn which stores carry the goods you desire.

You meet people at work, in the neighborhood, and around town. Soon, you develop a network of resources that enable you to handle domestic tasks, such as have a well functioning car, have a dental checkup, and so on.

At work, when you assume a new post, you arrive at a desk that is, hopefully, clean and clear. Soon, you'll fill it with files supplies, and personal items. You align your office, cubicle, or work space with items that keep you productive, and ideally, balanced and happy.

Surround Yourself with Key Items

The road to accomplishing both short- and long-term tasks works much the same way. You surround yourself with key items useful in the clutch. For short-term tasks in particular, it makes sense to have adequate supplies. If you're making conference calls, then the equipment, numbers, and pass codes need to be in place.

If you're tackling first-time tasks, marshaling your resources takes on an added level of importance. Which key contacts can give you a crucial bit of advice, the right file, or key phone numbers, on your way to accomplishing something right now?

Get Your Resources Together

Before tackling the next short-term project, flesh out the resources you'll need to successfully handle a short-term task. List what you might need in terms of equipment, supplies, staff help, guidance, money, and time. The more involved the short-term task is, i.e. a half-day or day-long task, the more valuable this exercise becomes.

Variables such as equipment, supplies, staff support, guidance, money, and time might be significant. Making notes about those that will be significant will serve you well, and the added measure of using insight and perspective is invaluable.

Start Simply, Revise Later

Much of the hesitation that occurs before the start of a short-term task is due to erroneous assumptions. For example, if you have to compose a letter or brief report, you might be hung up on starting with that perfect opening sentence or that powerful opening paragraph.

It's often to your advantage to simply start writing and later go back and determine what sentence or paragraph makes for the best lead. Likewise for other tasks you face.

Coming Undone

It might be raining outside. Construction crews might be making noise on the next floor. If you had your way, you'd rather begin on something else. Start on the task anyway.

If helpful, take a small step for openers, such as opening up a file folder, making a phone call, arranging a meeting, or finding a website. The strange and wondrous human brain likes to continue progressing on the same path it's already on.

One minute of activity in pursuit of a task helps lead to the next minute and the next. For most short-term tasks, the fact that you did start clears the hurdle on the path to completion.

Tap the Power of Immersion

Develop a skill that is becoming rare among professionals today: practice the art of doing one thing at a time and become immersed in that task. When you put all your energy and concentration into one task, great things will result.

Fight the tendency to multi-task. It seems easy enough, but the practice of doing one thing at a time, today, rubs against the grain of society, which delivers the message that you need to do many things at once to be more productive.

Dyna Moe

Allow yourself to become immersed. In doing so, you can mow down five to even ten minor tasks that loomed large collectively as hours or days passed without you tending to them.

Even for tasks that take five minutes or less, you can achieve great productivity by immersing yourself in the pursuit. The impetus and joy of getting *one* thing done, and done well, can carry you to the next task, and the next, and the next.

Giving your total attention to the task at hand yields benefits that might not otherwise be achievable. Step away from your online connections. Close your door. Focus your efforts and reap the rewards!

Create a Rewards System

Much of behavioral psychology can be explained by the simple phrase "Behavior that is rewarded is repeated," even when you reward yourself for your own behavior. To accomplish things right here, right now, identify a "reward" in advance that you'll allow yourself for completing a desired task.

The reward could be as simple as making a phone call, taking a stroll around the block, checking email, having

Factoid

Aubrey Daniels, Ph.D. in his book *Bringing Out the Best in People*, calls scheduling a reward following a good performance the "Grandma Principle." As Grandma would say, you don't get to eat your ice cream until you eat your spinach!

a cup of herbal tea, summing your earnings for the last quarter, or any other small, favorable event.

If you're facing an unpleasant task, follow that up with something you enjoy doing, instead of the other way around.

Dyna Moe

It's possible that you're one of those few diligent types who are able to receive a reward first and then make good on the silent, unarticulated promise to yourself, go ahead and complete the task that remained to be done. For most people, however, life doesn't seem to work this way.

Instrumental Temptations

Previous generations of career professionals faced temptations and distractions, but nothing from yesteryear rivals the power, lure, and availability of the Internet. It's always there, it's always on, and meanwhile you've got tasks to accomplish.

If you are subject to temptations, and who isn't, find a way to include them into your rewards system. Rather than succumbing to such distractions, you enjoy them periodically throughout the day in small measures not detrimental to your productivity or long-term career prospects. Otherwise is to flirt with disaster.

Thereafter, you go from hour to hour, day to day, week to week, without getting the small things done and having them build up, each one looming larger than they actually are, while impeding your progress on longer term projects and tasks.

Dyna Moe

If surfing the Internet is one of your temptations, then make it part of your rewards system, to maintain a modicum of control.

The Long and Winding Road to Long Term Tasks

Even if you maintain a super to-do list with a large, long-term portion, you'll find it challenging to maintain vigilance on long-term tasks. Accomplishing long-term tasks requires a different approach, execution, and set of behaviors than accomplishing tasks of a shorter term nature. Chapters 13 and 14 will help you with larger, longer term challenges.

CHAPTER 13

Accomplishing Longer-Term Tasks

In This Chapter:

➤ Win more battles with clarity
➤ Charting your path
➤ Software to keep you in control
➤ Keeping up

This chapter offers strategies for approaching problems, followed by a discussion of project-management tools including time lines, flow charts, and other visual aids. These tools provide both a viable means of tracking productivity and progress.

Problem Solving by Clarifying the Challenges

From presidents, prime ministers, and heads of state; to CEOs and COOs, one's reputation is largely defined by the longer-term tasks and projects completed. You can mess-up here and there on the smaller stuff, as long as you tackle and resolve bigger issues and challenges.

You first arrive at a new position and problems await. You might be hired to tackle specific issues and the direction of your course is pre-established. Other times your focus on getting things done is based on the course you set, and how you respond.

In August 1981, 13,000 of the nearly 17,000 U.S. air traffic controllers went on strike. This caused a near panic throughout the nation's transportation network. Managers worked overtime to handle most air traffic control shifts themselves. The airlines took it hard and could only operate at 70 percent of capacity.

The air traffic controllers all belonged to the Professional Air Traffic Controllers Association (PATCO). The organization felt reasonably confident that the strike would work—their members would win the concessions they were seeking. They knew that such a strike, if prolonged, would do damage to the U.S. economy.

By striking, PATCO's members had defied federal law, which prohibited strikes by government employees. Every air traffic controller was required by law to take an oath not to strike when they were first hired.

At the time, President Reagan had a choice; he could have backed down and allowed PATCO workers to dictate on what terms his administration could negotiate. Or, he could stand his ground and bolster his credibility in following through on his verbal promises. This was no easy decision, but Reagan saw his options and contemplated the consequences and their implications.

The strike was illegal and, to Reagan, coercive. These federal workers were hired to serve a mission. Their actions put the government, airline industry, and nation's transportation system under duress.

Reagan stated, "There is no right to strike against the public safety by anybody, anywhere, any time." With the support of the Secretary of Transportation, Reagan gave the controllers 48 hours to return to their posts. Most disobeyed and 48 hours later found themselves unemployed.

Firing thousands of air traffic controllers was a bold and decisive move. Reagan knew, however, that if he gave in to this group, in time, his administration would have to continually bargain with

Dyna Moe

The PATCO strike was a stern and rigorous early test of Reagan's administrative capabilities and he was not going to stand down. All the while, the Soviets were watching. Years later, in his memoirs, Reagan said that the decision he made "convinced people, who might have thought otherwise, that I meant what I said."

different groups. Rather than bargain with PATCO leaders, the administration hired more controllers, increased the overtime of those who were still on-board, and made do with available resources until the situation calmed down.

Certainly if there had been a single commercial airline mishap during this interval—and fortunately none occurred—Reagan's plan might have backfired.

Specificity Matters When Problem-Solving

The PATCO situation represents a practical application of problem solving by clarifying the challenge. The challenges you face are as likely to come in the form of surprises and emergencies as they are based on your own defined objectives. In any case, when you clarify the challenges confronting you and consider both short- and long-term ramifications, you're in a better position to solve problems.

Henri Poincare, the nineteenth-century French mathematician, devised a four-part strategy for creative problem solving that still has great utility today:

1. preparation
2. incubation
3. illumination
4. translation (application)

Poincare said that preparation is the first step: you immerse yourself in a problem and collect all relevant information. Depending on how big the problem and the resources available to you, preparation could last a few minutes, several hours, several days, or many weeks.

Coming Undone

If you skip the incubation step in creative problem- solving and immediately try to devise solutions, you might be successful, but sometimes you miss out on more innovative or unique solutions.

The next step is incubation. After gathering the most relevant data and framing the problem to the best of your ability, you clear your mind through meditation, going for a walk, even taking a bath—whatever works for you. Let the problem simmer.

The third step is illumination. After immersing yourself in the problem, collecting all the relevant information that you can, framing the problem, and allowing the situation to simmer for a while, invariably a solution comes to mind. The most creative people of Poincare's day couldn't say why but, at this point, feasible ideas sprang forth.

Illumination leads directly to step four: translation. Apply your potential solution, make observations, make calculations if applicable, and determine if you have a practical solution. If not, try a second solution, then a third and so forth, until one of them proves to be a true and winning answer.

Tools to Stay in Control

For much of what you wish to accomplish, or challenges or problems you need to resolve, particularly those that represent longer-term tasks, a variety of leadership and management tools can help guide you every step of the way. The bigger the project, and the more steps, dollars, people, and interplay between players, the greater the need for specification.

The tools discussed in this chapter are tested and proven. We'll review them in their most basic forms so that you'll have a clear understanding as to how to employ them. Each tool is available in analog (a wall chart) or digital (software package). Happily, you probably have some experience with each of them in one form or another. So, the following need not be foreign to you.

Dyna Moe

Plans can change, contingencies arise, roadblocks emerge, and course alteration might be necessary. Still, as you initially plot your path and as you proceed along it, specificity matters.

Gantt or Milestone Charts

The Gantt chart or "milestone" chart is a basic tool for staying in control on your path to getting things done and one with which you probably have some familiarity. Gantt charts help you to both plan and monitor tasks and projects.

Word Power

A Gantt chart basically is a bar chart that aids in planning and scheduling, with activities or tasks shown graphically as bars or line segments with specific time frames.

You update the chart as you make progress on each task. You can determine whether tasks are on schedule, ahead of schedule, or behind schedule by comparing your actual progress to where you're supposed to be based on the chart. An example will make this easy to understand.

Map It Out

Suppose you've established, or been handed, a goal of increasing your company's visibility in the marketplace over the next five months. To support that objective you've identified five activities:

➤ Finishing the XYZ project for release to the trade press.
➤ Getting an article published in a key industry journal that highlights your firm.
➤ Completing a pilot program for employing interns.
➤ Establishing an 800-number hotline program so that clients can call any time.
➤ Hosting a local forum where subject matter experts discuss critical issues in your industry.

All of these activities are to occur within the next five months. How can you best allocate your energy and resources to accomplish all of the above, thereby increasing your company's visibility?

What You Need To Do and When

Map out what you need to do and when, on a Gantt chart such as the one that follows, to gain a clear, graphic representation of the sequence and time lines for each of the five activities.

Activity:	Month 1	Month 2	Month 3	Month 4	Month 5
1. XYZ project	Bxxxx	xxxxxxxx	xxxxC		
2. Article published	Bx	xxxx	xxxx	xC	
3. Intern program		Bxx x	xx xxx	xxC	
4. Hotline program			Bxxxxx xxxC		
5. Local forum		Bxx	xx	xxxxxxx	xxxxC

The most basic information is easily conveyed in the chart above, including activity, sequence (1 to 5), begin, progression (x's extending month to month), and completion time.

In developing a pilot program for interns, for example, you plot several intervals because the action required is not continuous.

Use Symbols for Added Meaning

At your discretion, employ whatever symbols add detail to and clarify your chart. For example . . .

➤ numbers could refer to chart footnotes.
➤ a dotted line can denote germination.
➤ initials could represent other people involved.

Here is a variation of a Gantt chart that yields a bit more information:

Activity:	Month 1	Month 2	Month 3	Month 4	Month 5
1. XYZ project **JS, CG, IR**	Bxxxx	xxxxxxxx	xxxxC		
2. Article published **JS**	Bx	xxxx	xxxxC		
3. Intern program **JS, FG**	Bxx x	xx xxx	xxC		
4. Hotline program **JS**		Bxxxxx	xxxC		
5. Local forum **JS, BM, IR**		Bxx	xx	xxxxxxx	xxxxC

If you so choose, you could employ colors to indicate progress. For example . . .

➤   green could indicate the start of an activity.
➤   red could indicate a critical phase.
➤   blue could indicate completion of an activity, and so on.

For greater sophistication, you could devise a Gantt or milestone chart for each of the five activities, indicating all of the substeps involved in completing the project. Armed with project planning and scheduling software (discussed shortly), you could plot the time lines for all activities and all substeps on one master chart.

Program Evaluation and Review Technique—PERT

PERT charts, also referred to as network charts or logic diagrams, help you manage projects where scheduling is critical. The PERT highlights tasks and interdependencies between tasks. To employ a PERT you identify the activities you've earmarked as crucial, the order and time line of each activity, and the critical path. This indicates, with a given outcome, whether you then take path "a" or path "b."

PERTs can be intricate, and depending on the outcome of specific activities, you might need to revise the chart to reflect constraints, setbacks, or opportunities.

PERTs are somewhat like Gantts but the sequence of steps you complete for an activity are interdependent. As the chart shows, steps that need to be completed can intersect and

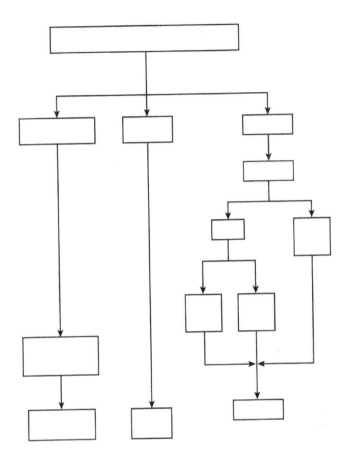

converge at critical junctures. In the case of developing a pilot program for interns, you could:

➤ develop a manual
➤ have several peers make critical reviews
➤ schedule a proofreader
➤ obtain approval from department heads
➤ initiate a test phase
➤ refine the program
➤ re-circulate it for a critical analysis

Dyna Moe

When you're tackling a project with multiple activities involving other people and various resources, PERTs enable you to remain on course, identify critical junctures and potential bottlenecks, and in general, stay on schedule.

To consolidate the inputs of others, some of these tasks have to be completed concurrently before you can proceed.

Flow Charts

You've been exposed to flowcharts since you were young. Your third grade teacher might have drawn a big circle on the board, followed by an arrow that leads to a second circle, or a square or triangle, and then maybe another arrow extending from that figure to a third figure.

Although flowcharts traditionally are used to convey a process, i.e., how something happens, they can be used to help you stay on target and complete a project within specific time lines.

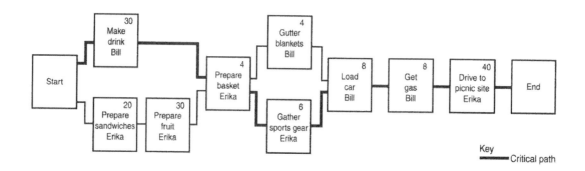

Looking at both the previous PERT example (on successfully completing the pilot intern program) and the flow chart that follows (which includes time lines), you can quickly surmise that the PERT chart and a flow chart have similarities.

As with the other types of charts, you can employ colors on a flow chart as you choose. Also geometric shapes are often employed to convey additional information when constructing flowcharts. For example:

➤   Circle—connecting points
➤   Square—information
➤   Triangle—yes or no decision

Other symbols are often used to convey information as well:

➤   Straight line—direct connection
➤   Squiggly line—interrupted or undefined connection
➤   Broken line—one way or partial connection

For any chart you create, you can devise your own symbols. Initials of another party could represent the need for their input. Stars, X's, check marks, and other symbols can convey other information, as long as you're consistent throughout your chart, and you keep a key handy, so you don't forget what the symbols mean!

Calendar Block Back Method

To get things done based on the time lines you've established, the calendar block back is a viable way to ensure completion. This method involves creating a process to complete your task, using a monthly calendar.

Suppose you are seeking to achieve a 4K increase in salary. From the starting date to the ending date, you would identify the five key subtasks. You would also list the interim steps to attain your specific increase in salary.

Suppose you need to deliver a test program to new employees by the 31st of the month. You decide that you'll need to schedule a conference by the 22nd and the training manual must be critically examined by the 9th, proofread by the 15th, and finalized by the 19th. The month-long plan you have laid out will look like this:

MONTH *March* _____ YEAR _____

SUNDAY	MONDAY	TUESDAY	WEDNESDAY	THURSDAY	FRIDAY	SATURDAY
	1	2	3	4	5	6
7	8	9 *Critical review of Training Manual*	10	11	12	13
14	15 *Proofread Manual*	16	17	18	19 *Assemble Training Manual*	20
21	22 *Schedule Conference*	23	24	25	26	26
28	29	30	31 *Deliver test program for new lines*			

The Calendar Block Back chart is the most basic of all.

You will then fill in this calendar with the activities you're implementing and interim due dates accordingly. Symbols and colors can be used here to organize the process further.

You're doing well when you can track your tasks in reverse and in a manner that reflects your available resources as well as take into account events during the month, such as weekends, holidays, time off, and vacations.

Meanwhile, to tackle life's big challenges, lay out a plan with the end in mind. An example would be reaching retirement at a certain age with X amount of savings.

Suppose you want to have $750,000 in savings by age 65. If you're currently 36, taking into account a certain rate of interest, inflation, and taxes, you can estimate how much money to save per year, and more specifically how much to save each month.

Coming Undone

Plotting too many subgoals and related tasks will make your calendar too difficult to follow. This method works best and can be most useful when you keep it simple and thorough.

If you work in an office where employees, vehicles, or goods need to be scheduled for optimum efficiency, this method isn't news to you. However, this type of calendar plotting works especially well on a personal basis: you are the boss of the calendar. You can shift things around according to your own preferences.

Factoid

Office supply stores offer a variety of wall charts to aid you in getting things done. You can use these supplies to implement a Gantt, PERT, flow chart, or the calendar block back method for plotting and monitoring your progress. Some charts are erasable and can be modified if needed.

Project Managing and Scheduling Made Easy

The job of project managing and scheduling is increasingly easy thanks to ever-more powerful computer software. So, no matter what I describe to you now, it will be quickly superseded. In general however, scheduling software, calendar systems, and other types of project organizers share common principles.

All such software provides calendar systems where you can keep appointments, readily identify schedule conflicts, and be alerted as to when you need to engage in some critical activity.

Project scheduling software allows you to choose the form of chart, be it Gantt, PERT, flow, calendar block back, and so on, that's most convenient for you. Using pull-down menus, familiar icons, and drag and drop techniques, you can cue in the subgoals and associated tasks or activities with them, in the sequence you desire. You can indicate start and stop times or add various other symbols as well as color to give you a vivid portrayal of the time lines you've established and your overall progress.

You can print your charts and calendars to keep with you, and create buzzers, bells, and alarms that remind you to send an email, make a call, and so on.

All the scheduling tools in the world can't ensure that you yourself will remain on schedule. The most critical factor in getting things done is managing yourself. While the scheduling tools can help, you alone have to make critical decisions as to where to proceed, and where to drop back. If you don't keep your charts and data current, or if you attempt to take on too much at once the whole process could become worthless. The tools can help you pinpoint trouble spots, but management is up to you.

CHAPTER 14

Monitoring Longer-Term Tasks and Projects

In This Chapter:

➤ When confidence or optimism hinders efforts

➤ Course correction is the name of the game

➤ Smart managers anticipate

➤ Metrics as progress indicators

This chapter is about how to monitor your progress on longer-term projects so that you are prepared and ready to convert problems into solutions, and how to anticipate potential problems ranging from laissez-fare project management to miscommunication among co-workers.

The greater the deed you seek to accomplish, the more essential to monitor your progress. If you have responsibility for a long-term project that involves different types of resources over a prolonged period, not monitoring your progress is synonymous with failure.

Even if you catch resultant problems in time, you could be scrambling for weeks on end, putting in overtime, and causing others to work longer and harder. You'll get things done, but no one will like you.

Danger Ahead: "Been There, Done That"

Perhaps no phrase in the English language more closely belies the dangers that can befall a veteran manager than "Been there, done that." Projects can exceed budget or the schedule by more than 50 percent because the manager did not monitor sufficiently. From manufacturing, to government, to education, projects (often called programs) can miss the mark because somebody who otherwise should have been in control felt confident in his or her ability to revert to cruise control. And, as discussed in the previous chapter, project management software alone cannot ensure that you'll stay on course.

Coming Undone

If you're brought on to manage a large task or project, consider that there is no "automatic pilot." There is no cruise control you can lock onto and have the project take its course.

In some organizations, a rookie manager with limited experience specifically is sought to work on projects. This person doesn't need to be shorn of unwelcome project management styles, which might include the nonchalance some veteran managers bring to projects resulting from their comfort level in working in project situations.

To Succeed on Tasks Accurate Information is Essential

I once had the assignment of driving from the consulting firm where I was employed in Rockville, Connecticut, up to Bangor, Maine. My boss told me that it would take about three to three and a half hours, this being in pre-GPS days. I had no reason to doubt him. I left at 8:00 a.m. for a noon appointment in Bangor. I figured that with at least a half hour of slack time, it would be no problem. I brought food with me and determined that I'd probably only take one bathroom break along the way.

I'd been on the road already for nearly three hours, and the road signs in New

Dyna Moe

Often we optimistically underestimate the time necessary to complete tasks. When we fail to monitor our progress, which might have identified the earlier miscalculation, we end up feeling intense pressure to be productive. Sometimes, we're given misinformation as to how much time a task will take. Not allowing enough time for a task is a pervasive problem, particularly among otherwise highly competent professionals (see Chapter 12).

Hampshire indicated that Bangor was still another 64 miles to go. In no way would this trip require only three and a half hours driving. I put my foot to the pedal, averaged 75 the rest of the way, fortunately wasn't pulled over, and made the noon meeting with about six minutes to spare. However, I was stressed and anxious the whole way, and wasn't at my best.

My boss wasn't trying to do me wrong, he had inaccurate information and was nonchalant on this aspect of the project. On my part, I should have looked on a mileage chart before leaving and planned my trip accordingly. You can bet that on the way back, I allocated 4 hours and 20 minutes and, as it turned out, arrived about then.

No matter how sophisticated your scheduling might be, if you input faulty data, you can't expect to proceed as planned.

Project management and scheduling tools can only be as good as what you enter into the system. Hence, the ability to reasonably estimate how much time a particular task will take is no small matter.

As you learn to know yourself better and better, you realize allowing somewhat generous time allocations for certain tasks is not going to turn you into a laggard.

Any time you create time-savings through this method, apply it to other things that you want to get done. You'll be as productive as before, but mentally, you'll have set up your day in a manner that enables you to feel less frustrated, more content, more energized, and ready for what comes next.

Course Corrections Are Routine and Vital

In effective project management, veering off course is an everyday event and making course corrections follows closely on its heels!

For example, most passengers aren't aware—and perhaps they're better off not knowing—that the typical airline flight is off course most of the time. The pilot takes off, and plots a course heading. Because of prevailing winds and a host of other factors, the pilot then veers off course by a few degrees, adjusts, and resumes course. A few minutes later, the plane could be off course a few degrees in the other direction.

For the duration of the trip, the plane veers this way and that off the path of the desired course. Through enhanced navigational systems and pilot control, the plane continually readjusts and resumes course.

If the pilot were to announce over the intercom every deviation in course, the passengers would be aghast. They'd lose confidence in the pilot, the crew, and the airline in general. Continual monitoring and adjustments during flights is the norm, however, not the exception.

Eventually, as the plane approaches the destination, course settings become critical and all attention is focused on assuring a safe landing.

Being only a few percent off in the early phases of a project can yield dramatic negative results later. The only productive method that makes sense is continual monitoring of your progress and applying any necessary adjustments along the way.

More Complexity, More Drift?

The more people you manage, the bigger the budget. The more resources involved ,the more interconnectedness. More connections between resources uniformly lead to higher levels of complexity.

Dyna Moe

At every step, ask yourself if you are merely making check marks on charts, or performing high-quality work that will please everyone associated with the project.

Assembling a winning team takes skills, hard work, and a bit of luck (see Chapter 24). As the project moves forward, team members cooperate with one another, ideally, at even higher levels than at the outset of the project, much like a winning baseball team progressing toward the pennant. Efficiencies occur that enable you to save time and resources on some tasks. Team members leave at day's end feeling good about what they've accomplished and looking forward to what comes next.

Help Me Make it Through the Day

In project management, some mornings you think, "How am I going to make it through this day?" Miraculously you do, and then you repeat the process again the next day. Depending on the project, completing everything on time and on budget, and achieving the desired outcome—with nothing extra or spectacular, just a bread and butter performance—will earn you kudos.

Sometimes even though you are up-to-the-minute in terms of your reporting requirements, you don't receive timely feedback that would enable you to better do your job. If this is so, what alternative strategies do you have in place?

➤   Who else can you turn to?
➤   What other resources can you tap?
➤   How can you expedite the feedback process? You need feedback!

Top executives and managers, however, might not give you the in-depth regular feedback that would be so appreciated and helpful to ensure your success. So, proceed as if you alone are responsible for monitoring your own progress. If others are involved, then they could serve as project safeguards. If no one else is involved, then tackle the issue head on.

Reporting results might be a requirement of your position; monitoring progress accurately is crucial. As many project managers have learned, it is easy to become side-tracked in the course of your daily activities. Something comes up that is enticing, but objectively adds little to the overall project.

This is where you have to have the mental and emotional strength to let go of the "nice, but not necessary."

Anticipate Challenges

Consider what roadblocks and barriers loom in the short term. Can you prepare for them? What can you head off today, although it is not at the top of your list, to will ensure smooth operations several weeks or months down the pike? Like the driver barreling down the highway, you still have to pull into the right lane and slow down when your exit is coming up.

Dyna Moe
If you inform others about what's ahead, they'll feel more comfortable with your leadership.

Keep others focused—rven if everyone was on the same page when you started the project, don't count on it staying that way for long. Other people involved in a specific project might think they understand your intentions and goals but what they hear and identify with, via personal perception, might not square up with the reality of the project. To bypass potential hurdles, speak with other participants and seek to understand what each is thinking. Don't allow a miscommunication to derail progress.

Your project plans run the risk of not being read, understood, and followed. Too often, people do not read project reports, or if they do, they do not comprehend them. Some simply circle a few items here and there and feel that they now have the adequate background that they need.

Factoid
Some organizations that have existed for decades post a single mission on the walls and every place in between. Yet, untold numbers of employees cannot state the organization's mission!

Appoint a Project Reviewer

How can you monitor project progress for little or no investment and achieve a great return? Assign a key staff member to do a thorough project review for which he will be thanked profusely, regardless of what shortcomings he might identify.

Alternatively, recruit another project manager within your organization with whom you can make a reciprocal agreement.

Periodically, you monitor progress on his projects, and he monitors progress on yours. Or find an accountability partner, mentor, fellow project manager, or peer who will cooperate with you at scheduled times to co-monitor your progress.

Metrics for Success

Do you find yourself so involved in the nitty gritty that you can't see the proverbial forest for the trees? Don't become caught up in the capability of the technical tools while missing fundamental project issues occurring right before your eyes.

Whenever your monitoring activity uncovers variance between your plan what is actually occurring, you need to take action. Proceeding as scheduled and on budget represents a key indicator of project success, although that alone is not sufficient. Is the desired level of quality, a mark of effectiveness, being met? Are the higher-ups pleased with the project? Will the end-user sing the praises of the organization as a result of the work on this project? These types of feedback indicators are most telling.

Word Power
A metric is anything that serves as a performance measure, a quantifiable indicator used to track and assess performance.

Numbers as Indicators

Sometimes, a simple tally is highly useful in indicating project success. For example, if you are cast to design a new safety program and are running a test case in one of your organization's divisions, the good old "X number of days without an accident" prominently posted can be adequate.

Similarly, if you are working on a new software package counting computer bugs in the program, a reverse metric can be put to good use. Whereas in the above example, a greater number indicates success, a smaller number, hence the reverse metric system, indicates success in the de-bugging software example.

For items not readily countable, create a subjective numeric rating system. For example, when you watch divers in the Olympics plunge into the water, there is no absolute indicator of how good the dive is. Judges hold up their signs saying eight, nine, or ten and through a simple mathematical formula, an overall score for the diver results.

Your team members, as well, can assess project performance for the day on specific tasks or subtasks or on any aspect of the project. If you can capture their attention, and they are willing to participate, top managers, executives, and other stakeholders can do the same. What aspects of the project do you rate? Any issue that is deemed to be of importance.

Dyna Moe
The best rating scales are those that remain simple: such as 1 to 5 or 1 to 10. Never mind this 87.2 stuff.

Metrics of Another Kind

Sometimes symbols can be used in place of numbers. Think of a weather chart, where sunny equals a smiling face, cloudy equals a neutral face, and heavy rain equals a scowling face. In like manner, you can design and post charts that elicit the feedback of project team members, and do so in a non-intrusive, somewhat humorous way.

You can also use a form of questioning to help monitor your progress. For example, how will we know when we have completed Task X to everyone's satisfaction? The answers could be:

➤ When the top boss immediately flashes a big smile upon hearing the news
➤ When the typically hands-on boss, takes a hands-off approach.
➤ When everyone on the project team spontaneously decides to rendezvous after work at the nearest watering hole.
➤ When team members leave for the evening with no take-home work.

These are subjective to be sure, but if indicated in advance of the completion of some task, subtask, or event, they serve as better progress indicators than no pre-established indicators.

The Project Auditor Cometh

For larger and longer-term projects you could be subject to the uneasy experience of having your project audited.

Depending on your project, auditors might examine your records in detail, interview your staff, and interview clients or customers. They might trace the flow of funds, observe and time project management staff, examine equipment, and visit facilities.

After they have completed their efforts, they debrief you as project manager, on their way to producing a written report that will be seen and read by all the people who wouldn't otherwise read your reports.

If you're fortunate, an auditor's report will offer observational gems and lead to key opportunities for progress. If you are unfortunate, the report will slash you to ribbons and you will be spending untold hours seeking to undo its effects. In any case, a project audit is certainly an eye-opener. If you have to endure one, cooperate fully; anything else tends to work against you.

Word Power

An auditor is usually an experienced expert or team of experts who rapidly familiarize themselves with the requirements of your project and what you are seeking to accomplish.

If you are audited, it doesn't necessarily mean that someone above thinks that the project is in trouble. It might be standard fare, or there could be something unique about your project that prompted the process.

Maintaining Momentum on Longer-Term Projects

Here are a handful of other tips for pursuit of the things you want to get done, when tasks could extend over weeks or months:

➤ Monitor some aspect of the project every day, even if it's the smallest of tasks. You'll be amazed at the usefulness that some kind of daily monitoring provides.

➤ Alternate when you'll examine the largest versus the smallest segments of the projects. While it's best to stay focused on the large segments, sometimes you can't make yourself start. At least review something.

Dyna Moe

Make that call or send that email when your monitoring efforts indicate that the help of someone external to the project is crucial to your momentum.

➤ Often unplanned tasks pops up. Look for help along the way. The kinds of assistance you need at various junctures might not have been identified earlier on.

At all times proceed with a "divide and conquer" mentally. No matter how well you've planned and how well you've plotted, monitored and re-planned at various times, certain elements of long-term projects seem rather insurmountable. Break them down into bite-sized tasks.

PART 5

Becoming More Efficient in the Workplace

Part 5
Becoming More Efficient in the Workplace

This part of the book can be summed up by the phrase "Thinking is the best way to travel." These chapters will guide you through the obstacles that block your path on your way to getting things done.

CHAPTER 15

Attempting Too Many Things at Once

In This Chapter:

➤ Multitasking isn't pretty
➤ Multitasking is stressful and counter-productive
➤ Concentration is king
➤ Conquering techno-stress

This chapter focuses on the productivity disruption caused by multi-tasking and misuse of technology, and offers methods to minimize such disruptions.

As we've learned, the tools of technology that surround us aid and abet the inclination to multitask. We work with a computer that can search for information, while running a print job, and while backing up files.

Admiring these characteristics, we attempt to emulate the operating capabilities of our gadgetry. We resonate at a speed which, often, is not internally generated and predictably we experience some degree of technostress.

Word Power
Technostress is everyday stress that is exacerbated by technology, most notably present when we do not rule technology, it rules us.

Are We Doomed to Multitask?

A magnifying glass held up at the proper angle to the sun will quickly burn a whole through a piece of paper. At the same time, no matter how much sun shines through your office window onto your desk, none of those tedious memos are going to catch on fire. In an era of committed multitaskers, concentration and focus are underrated.

Against a back drop of information and communication overload, ever-advancing technology, and more choices than anyone needs or even wants, as described in Chapter 1, seemingly an entire workforce generation multitasks as if this is the way it has always been, needs to be, and always will be.

Multitasking is occasionally helpful and seemingly satisfying but represents a paradoxical impediment to getting things done.

Generally, we feel guilty if we don't multitask! We contemplate our increasing workloads and responsibilities and how they are subject to continual shifts, and justify multi-tasking as a valid response to a world of flux.

Factoid

The term multitasking evolved from the computer industry: performing multiple tasks simultaneously. The early mainframe computers designed with parallel processes is perhaps the prime example of automated multitasking.

We might well be hardwired to continually seek to economize our use of time. Nevertheless, focusing on the task at hand is vital to getting things done, despite the temptation to do otherwise. Whether a handful of tasks confront you, or only one, give all your time, attention, energy, focus, concentration, and effort to the task at hand, and then turn to what's next.

Coming Undone

Multitasking has become a norm giving rise to "continuous partial attention," where nothing gets your true and undivided focus, and everything carries nearly equal weight. We can barely tolerate stillness. For many, silence doesn't appear to be golden, only an unwelcome phenomena that inhibits productivity.

Multi-tasking: Misunderstood, Over-employed, and Undesirable

People likely have always sought to handle many things at once, starting from cave dwellers. Their multitasking effort probably seemed crude by comparison.

Our age old "flight or fight" response to perceived stressors in the environment works well, at intermittent times. The small jolts of concentrated energy and vigilance helps us to safeguard our selves, our loved ones, and our possessions. As a species, however, we do effectively handle continuous streams of two major stress hormones—adrenaline and cortisol—on a daily basis.

Bruce McEwen, Ph.D., professor of neuroscience at Rockefeller University, observed that while we can apparently weather stresses and hormone surges in the short term, about three to 15 days, thereafter chronic stress ensues. The result is a weakened immune system, aggression, anxiety, and a decrease in brain functioning, which results in burnout.

Focus and concentration are your keys for getting things done. Multitasking, as it is popularly understood and practiced, is not your answer. It is expensive in terms of the level of stress induced and the rise in errors, and can actually hamper productivity.

Factoid
Dangerously high levels of cortisol can result in poor sleep patterns and insulin resistance, which can open the door to bad eating habits and weight gain.

Stress, More Mental Effort

You don't have to be a physician to observe the entrenched levels of workplace stress, but physicians themselves are noticing it with alarming regularity. Few patients ever remark that their stress levels are low, while most confess that they're stressed to the max. As multitasking takes hold in the workforce, stress levels are rising.

Here's the unwanted news. Next week, next month, and next year, you'll be asked to do even more without necessarily being given any greater resources. If you work in a government agency or in a nonprofit organization, you might be asked to do more with less.

If your budget or your staff has been reduced, or eliminated, you might be asked to do more with nothing!

Evidence is appearing that multi-tasking contributes to a more stressful workday and life. It dampens our capacity for pleasure. It hounds us long after closing time and can render the benefits of leisure less effective.

Marcel Just, Ph.D., Director of the Scientific Imaging and Brain Research at Carnegie-Mellon, conducted a study in which he asked participants to listen to sentences while comparing two rotating objects. These tasks draw on different areas of the brain, yet participants' ability to engage in visual processing, comparing the two rotating objects, dropped by 29 percent.

Participants' capabilities for auditory processing, listening to the sentence, dropped by 53 percent when engaged in this mild multi-tasking test. Dr. Just remarked that while we certainly can do more than one thing at a time "we are kidding ourselves if we think we can do so without cost."

Factoid

Research conducted at the National Institute of Mental Health confirms that when the brain has to switch back to something, it has to overcome "inhibitions" that it put in place to cease doing the task to begin with. It's as if the brain is taking its foot off the brake peddle.

It Gets Worse: More Errors, Lingering Effects

Multitasking seemingly enables one to save time, but does it? While some people remain relatively unscathed by multitasking, most people suffer in ways they don't understand. Rather than increasing their productivity, multitasking diminishes it. They make more mistakes. They leave too many things undone. Their quality of work is not what it could be.

The list of potential hazards of multitasking is growing. Are you a victim to any of the following:

➤ Suffer gaps in short-term memory?
➤ Experience loss of concentration?
➤ Have problems communicating with co-workers?
➤ Suffer lapses in attentiveness?
➤ Experience stress symptoms such as shortness of breath?

Sometimes your brain can go into a crash mode when multitasking, characterized by being unable to remember what you just said or did, or what you wanted to do next! Such phenomena is called "having a senior moment," by some people, but it's no joke and it doesn't only happen to seniors.

David Meyer, Ph.D., Professor of Psychology Cognition, at the University of Michigan, established a link between chronic high-stress, multi-tasking, and loss of short-term memory. "There is scientific evidence that multitasking is extremely hard for someone to do, and sometimes impossible," he observed. The time lost switching between tasks increases the perceived complexity of the tasks and can result in making a person less efficient than if he had chosen to focus on one task or project at time.

The most difficult type of multitasking occurs when you try to engage the same area of the brain. We encounter this everyday: people who are on the phone, while listening to the radio, surfing the net, or in earshot of someone in the next room.

Whether you attempt to handle conflicting visual-processing tasks or conflicting auditory-processing tasks, you're not going to handle either task as well as you would handle each individually.

Lower-Level Tasks

If the multiple tasks you're juggling are lower-level, such as folding a letter to insert into an envelope while gazing at your computer screen, you'll probably be okay. Both are easy to do, and one requires no heavy mental output (folding a sheet of paper). The more vital the activities you handle simultaneously, especially if they are of equal weight, the more likely you are to run aground.

Longitudinal studies on the effects of multitasking indicate that you can waste so much time backtracking, correcting, or redoing what you've done, that you're better off staying single-focused. That's the key to productivity

Coming Undone

One can improve multitasking capabilities somewhat. Being well-rested helps as does eliminating distractions. Yoga, meditation, and visualization in certain ways each help to improve your mental focus.

Even if you could master the beast, is it worth it? Not so, however temporarily satisfying or momentarily gratifying.

The Pleasure of One Task at a Time

The quickest and easiest way you can diminish the unhealthy chain of events that occur with multitasking is to abandon it, like a smoker who quits smoking for good.

Concentrate on the task at hand. For example, read this sentence without sounds in the room, without snacking on something, and without otherwise diverting your attention. Give yourself the benefit—the pleasure—of doing one thing at a time.

➤ Your attention span will improve.

➤ Your cortisol and adrenaline levels will be more likely to stay in check.

➤ Your immune system will benefit.

➤ Your overall health and peace of mind will likely improve.

When you focus on the matter at hand and achieve homeostasis, the psychological and physiological stability engendered might enable you to become more industrious and more creative.

Think of the times when you were humming along—on a roll -– and while not even trying, new insights, perspectives, and ways of accomplishment came to you, like that!

Only one task at a time can command our sharp attention, and more often than not, those are the times when it seems like you're on a roll. Why? Research indicates that the human brain is unable to process two or more unrelated tasks at the same time. It seems like we can, but actually high-speed task switching occurs.

Word Power

Homeostasis is the balance among elements in a system.

The Rise of Technostress

In Technostress, spouses Larry Rosen, Ph.D and Michelle Weil, Ph.D. observe that technology can help place innovative workers in the driver's seat. It also can create such dependency that you end up questioning your own creativity and capabilities.

Many managers fear that increasing levels of work-related technology will lead to loss of privacy, information inundation, erosion of face-to-face contact, having to continually learn new skills, and being passed over for promotion because others coming up the ladder are more technologically savvy. Larry Rosen and Michelle Weil observe that "technostress is worse on the executive suits."

To keep technology in proper perspective, the authors advise to declare your independence, offering a "Technology Bill of Rights" as follows:

1. I am the boss, not my technology.
2. Technology is available to help me express my creativity.
3. I decide when to use the tools technology provides.
4. I have the right to choose what technology to use and what to put aside.
5. I can use technology to stay connected, informed, and productive, my way.

6.   Technology offers a world of information. I can choose what information is important to me.
7.   Technology will have problems, but I will be prepared to handle them.
8.   Technology can work 24-hour days, but I can choose when to begin and when to stop working.
9.   Technology never needs to rest, but I do.
10.   I can work successfully by enforcing my boundary needs.

Some of the "articles" to this bill of rights are particularly appropriate in the context of getting things done.

You're In Control

Article #3, "I decide when to use the tools technology provides," is worth its weight in microchips. Some people are ruled by their email, having to check it upon arising, throughout the morning, at lunch, throughout the afternoon, as they leave the office, and then even at home a few more times. Worse, they check in the middle of doing some other task that requires steadfast concentration.

It is okay to use checking one's email, or any other brief activity, as a mental break from a rigorous task. The problem with checking email or a cell phone for break time is that you're likely to be exposed to more tasks at an inopportune juncture and not be prepared to address them.

One executive from an Inc. 500 Company (the fastest growing entrepreneurial companies in America) revealed that he permits himself to check email only three times daily: at 10 a.m, 2 p.m., and 4 p.m.

At those intervals, he remarks, he can stay on top of the email communications coming his way, not miss anything, or not have anything become too "old." Hence, he's able to have long stretches free of email throughout the day.

Coming Undone

Constantly checking for messages in the middle of working on something is akin to multi-tasking and you don't have to head down this path.

You Do the Choosing

Article #6 bears scrutiny. "I choose what information is important to me." Consider all the times you've visited the Internet in the past eight years, and all the information you've gleaned. If you're like most career professionals, the sites you regularly visit boil down to a handful—perhaps six or seven.

Sure, if you're going shopping, if you want to find a particular location, if you have keywords to throw into a search engine, you'll visit other sites based on a specific need.

Every now and then, you go where the Web takes you. Otherwise, as a creature of habit, you follow the same routine, visiting the same sites. You might use bots and information services to alert you to news and information based on the topics you've indicated are of interest to you. Do you, however, seek out the alternative viewpoint? For example:

➤ Do you visit sites that explore issues in greater depth?
➤ Do you visit sites from other countries?
➤ Do you use the Web to paint a fuller picture of the knowledge you're seeking on a particular topic or issue?

For many people, much of the time, the answer is no. We gather what we can gather as easily as we can gather it and that becomes the extent of our perspective. Often, this is okay—you don't need a well-rounded, in-depth answer, you simply need quick information.

Those times where greater depth, clarity, and focus are required call for you to invoke article #6 of the Technology Bill of Rights.

Follow the Scout's Motto

Article #7, "Technology will have problems but I will be prepared to handle them," is worth noting. Do you have resources in place if a virus cripples your computer, if your cell phone dies, or if any component of your hardware or software is malfunctioning?

Conscientious motorists belong to auto clubs, have a favorite repair shop, and know a few things about car troubleshooting.

When it comes to computers, conscientious users take precautions.

The greater your reliance on technology, the more adept you need to be, and the more important to have resources and backup systems in place, should problem situations arise.

Rest, Who Needs Rest?

Articles #9 and #10, "Technology never needs to rest, but I do" and "I can work successfully by enforcing my boundary needs," are notable. When I hear someone profess to be available "24/7," or when

Coming Undone
You don't want to be "revving" so fast, handling this and that, that you do not safeguard your work flow. The brief time it takes to make some back-up files and hardcopies can save several hours worth of backtracking if your computer crashes.

people hand me business cards that contain their work phone, cell phone, home phone, and pager number, invisibly I cringe.

Dyna Moe

Unless your job specifically calls for you to be available on selected days around the clock—i.e. you're in law enforcement, national security, healthcare, or emergency services—why make yourself available to everyone at all times?

Will you lose out on a business deal because you're not available at 11 p.m. or 2 a.m.? Even if you do business with people in far corners of the world, do they expect you to be available and conversant at 2 a.m. or 3 a.m? If they do, and if you are, what kind of career is that? It's one thing to handle key tasks; it's another to unwittingly juggle multiple tasks and to surrender your work life and every little intrusion.

CHAPTER 16

Incompletions and Their Hazards

In This Chapter:

- ➤ Undone is no fun
- ➤ Incompletions impact individuals
- ➤ The need for neat endings
- ➤ Self-acknowledgment is vital

This chapter will help you to become a master of completions.

Seeking completions is a powerful way to avoid the onslaught of too much competing for your time and attention, and to stay focused.

"Completion thinking" is a proven approach to continually get things done despite distractions. Fortunately, you are already a master of many aspects of completions. Your arrival at work is a completion. When you turn in a big report, and you know it's ready, that is a completion. If you derive nothing else from this book but guidance on using completions, then you've benefitted greatly.

The Ill-Effects of Incompletions

To get things done, especially long-term projects, it's wise to acknowledge your completions at various milestones. Divide and conquer.

When you leave tasks or activities incomplete, however, you have energy vested in them. A lack of completions at work can leave you feeling exhausted and used! Many people unknowingly create serial incompletions, personally and professionally, task-wise and psychologically. The unhappiest people among us dwell on what is incomplete instead of accurately acknowledging the situation and making new choices about what action to take.

The Age of Incompletions

It is vital to understand the nature of what has become our culture of incompletions.

In many ways, we're living in what I call the age of incompletions and the tendency of people to not complete things, in part, might be traceable to sociocultural developments.

Simply being alive during this age might impede your ability to get things done, particularly to finish one thing after another. This takes a few pages to explain, but if you seek to get more done, understanding this phenomenon will help.

Word Power

A sociocultural development is one, quite simply, that signifies the combination or interaction of social and cultural elements.

1963 was a pivotal year, probably before you were born. In November of that year, President John Kennedy was shot. The mystery surrounding his death was solved completely 30 years later in 1993 and presented in *Case Closed*, by Gerald Posner.

Case Closed, Hardly Anyone Knows

In the book *Case Closed*, investigative reporter Gerald Posner walks the reader through every conceivable detail of the case. He shows conclusively how and why, Lee Harvey Oswald, acting alone, committed the crime. He explains how the "magic bullet" took the angles that ballistics predicted and which has since been confirmed repeatedly with today's high technology equipment.

I read *Case Closed* cover to cover and concur. U.S. News & World Report concluded that Posner's work was so convincing that the magazine would never

Factoid

Noted historian William Manchester, after reading Posner's book, said that he couldn't imagine anyone having any further doubt about the fact that Lee Harvey Oswald, on his own, shot and killed John Fitzgerald Kennedy.

feature another "who shot JFK?" book review again. Yet, more than 20 years after *Case Closed*, new mythology and conspiracy theories about who killed Kennedy are still being be concocted and added to the glut of information you can't use, information which serves no one.

Currently, the "who shot JFK?" industry earns more than $250 million a year, with the potential to go higher, constantly fed by more TV show "investigations," authors, books, and tours.

Misinformation That Won't Die

Don't regard the misinformation surrounding JFK's death lightly. The nature of society changed as nearly an entire generation suspected that a conspiracy, perhaps a government-led conspiracy, might have brought down the leader of the free world, in broad daylight. Who knew what level of cynicism about government, the press, and truth itself would ensue?

Thirty years after JFK's death, in 1993, when Posner assembled irrefutable evidence about the single assassin responsible, hardly anyone knew, or worse, actually cared.

To this day, a majority of the U.S. population still believes that President Kennedy's assassination was the result of some type of conspiracy. The case has been long solved without any sense of national closure.

I submit to you, that the nature of your life was altered, even if you were born well after 1963, as a result of the unreality, misinformation, and cultural incompletion that has glutted society's receptors.

This situation represents more than a mystery for the unin   tially signals the start of Baby Boomers and Gen Xers unwittingly entering the era of incompletions. How has that impacted our psyches?

Aren't we supposed to be able to fully investigate such events, especially those that shook a generation, a nation, and the world? What unrecognized psychological scars has the incompletion of the JFK assassination stamped into our collective cerebrums?

Coming undone

When major cases aren't closed, everyone suffers, even if in small and undistinguishable ways.

From Intelligent Inquiry to Media-Induced Untruthfulness

From 1963, fast forward 14 years to the death of Elvis Presley of Memphis, Tennessee. He died from a self-induced pharmaceutical drug overdose, which resulted in heart failure. The coroners' report reveals this, as does reputable follow-up inquiries and analysis. Still, many people from that era, and many thereafter, think Elvis died as a result of a conspiracy.

Some people believe that Elvis didn't die back then, that he was alive and well for years, and showing up in random locations captured by the ever-present photographers of the *Enquirer, Globe* or *Star*.

Regardless of what you think about Elvis, his death, even amidst the jokes, and everything that's been made about it since then, the pervasive message is that *no case is ever completely solved.*

Everything lingers on and on and on. The results of the 2000 presidential election in Florida, with its endless legal motions, and court appeals has spawned debates, arguments, and accusations that exist to this day and no doubt will linger on for years. No conclusions, consensus, or closure, but endless media coverage. The media wins, the pundits win, one candidate or another wins, but everyone else loses.

All of History Up for Grabs

The contemporary turf wars fought in the age of incompletions, particularly in the political arena, retroactively now extend to virtually everything that ever happened, whether you're assessing U.S. history, the formation of our nation, world history, the origins of Islam, the origins of Christianity, and so forth.

At one time, it was widely held that dropping the atomic bomb on Japan hastened the end of WWII, saved a minimum of 60,000 U.S. troops (who would have been needed to fight a ground war in Japan lasting until at least the spring of 1946), and provided the world with the closure it so sorely needed after six years of global destruction.

In recent years, arguments about the U.S. being overly-aggressive . . . the only nation to ever drop an atomic bomb on another, and the inhumanity of it all, have risen to the forefront of many people's consciousness.

Some people assemble scraps of evidence to "confirm" that there was no need for the United States to have dropped the bomb, as if the casualty rate of invading mainland Japan would have been minimal. Some argue Japan was on its last legs (yet, even after one atomic bomb was dropped it still would not surrender!). Some say that U.S. intentions were racially motivated (although the bomb was originally designed to use on the now-surrendered Germans), the hawks had their way, and so forth.

What had served as closure to the most horrific event the earth had ever witnessed, in which 44,500,000 perished, is now the subject of endless debate in some circles. Not that debate isn't healthy, especially for an action of such magnitude.

When every inch of political terrain is contested everywhere, around the clock, and when all public discourse is subject to interpretation, reinterpretation and revision, and essentially nothing is final, it wears on humanity and notably trickles down to the level of the individual.

History occurs on a macro level, but the age of incompletions leaves its mark on the individual. You, an otherwise confident professional seeking to get things done, have reached adulthood in an era and in a culture where a lack of completions, more often than not, is the norm.

Years ago, I worked for a consulting firm in Washington, D.C. and one of my co-workers was ex-military. He told me that in the Army, when he received complicated directives, he didn't become shook up about it. If he bided his time, something else would replace them. In the work-a-day world, this mentality shows up all the time, but in different forms.

Don't like your boss? Sweat it out for a little while, he or she will be transferred anyway. Prefer to not use the new software? If there are several others who feel the same way, it might be abandoned. The danger to the otherwise competent individual is the daily, pervasive notion that some goals and objectives, entirely worth pursing, on second thought, can be modified or circumvented so as to make their accomplishment far easier and perhaps less impactful . . .

Incompletions in the Air

The socially pervasive de facto acceptance of incompletions, which is in the air and swirls around all around us, has a notable impact.

Think about how you feel when you go to a health club to have a vigorous workout but are surrounded by people who are taking it easy. They engage in long conversations. They half-heartedly step onto the stair climber. They seem content to burn however few calories they will as they wile away the 45 minutes they had initially earmarked for working out. They spend more time at the drink machines than on the treadmill.

Days without End

The neat beginning and closing to the day that was once evident in everyone's lives has dissipated. Television programming is on all hours of the day and night, and hundreds of shows beckon, anytime you want. Add in radio, the Internet, headline news, and there simply is no end. Stores are open 24/7. Traffic is always on the road.

For some, there is no day or night, only dimly lit fluorescent lighting bathing otherwise grey mundane offices. These same offices, as well as our homes, with indoor temperature control, diminish the effect of the seasons. Some people even regard heat or cold upon going outside as a bother, as if nature is supposed to conform to the turn of a thermostat dial.

Breakfast, lunch, and dinner have given way to this era of no designated meal times. We eat what we want, when we want.

Actually, food of all types is available at all times. It's not merely the mixing of breakfast, lunch, and dinner foods with one another. There's no sense of seasonal foods. Summer squash, winter tomatoes—we want everything available all the time.

The Undeniable Impact of Our Surroundings

We are impacted by our surroundings, peers, cultural norms, and what we readily observe. If you're seeking to lose weight and you live in a culture where overweight and obesity are the norm, how much easier is it for you to simply stay where you are or, at best, lose a few pounds, but not nearly what you had originally intended? Recent studies confirm that if your closest friends are overweight, the likelihood is that eventually you will be, too.

The "broken window" phenomenon in sociology holds that if an abandoned building in a neighborhood has a broken window that remains unrepaired, in time, more windows will be broken, until finally all windows will be broken. What's more, the windows of adjoining buildings will be broken. Then, it's possible that the whole neighborhood runs down.

In communities where abandoned buildings are fenced off or remodeled for new industry, where street cleaners keep curbs clean, and where abandoned vehicles are not permitted on front lawns, everyone tends to conform to the standard.

What Surrounds Us, Prevails

We are impacted by our environment to a degree that we are not always aware of on a conscious level. I was waiting in the airport lounge at LaGuardia Airport in New York to board a plane to Los Angeles. You know this scene, right? Bedazzled, razzled, frazzled.

This section of the airport was under construction. The passengers waited in a make-shift lounge. I found the atmosphere to be unduly noisy. People looked upset, anxious, and not the type of group I wanted to fly with.

A miraculous thing happened when we boarded the plane. It was a newer jet. The seat cushions were firm and soft. The rug was clean. The place seemed light and airy, and even cheery!

Everything in the interior of the plane helped to muffle noise.

As the passengers filed in and took their seats, a change came over the entire group.

No longer the unruly, boisterous crowd waiting in the airport lounge, these people now were heading to California. They seemed serene. They were certainly less anxious. There and then, I understood the supreme importance of one's environment.

Surround Yourself to Succeed

As a dedicated career professional who seeks to get things done, to become known for one's accomplishments, and perhaps be regarded as a high achiever, it is vital to take control of your environment, associate with other get-it-done types, and embrace "completion thinking."

It's not mandatory to be in total control of your work space, but it helps. (To make your desk work for you, see Chapter 6.) As you look around your office, what strikes you as incomplete?

➤   Are piles building up in corners around the room?

➤ Are Post-it pads serving as proxy to-do list items adorning your desk and PC monitor?

➤ Do you have stacks of unopened mail?

➤ Is your message light blinking?

Similarly, you can observe your home as well as other areas of your life. When you're honest with yourself, you see visible signs of incompletions all around you.

Considering the larger picture, what is incomplete in your career? Are there key instructions, an agenda, a blueprint, or an action map of some sort that you know is valid and appropriate but you have yet to take action?

➤ Are there vital courses that you need to take?

➤ Are there key people within your industry with whom you haven't initiated contact?

➤ Are there initiatives you have in mind that you've let sit for years?

Yes, there are. Each item represents an incompletion. The path to completions, big and small, is to keep acknowledging yourself whenever you complete something. As we'll discuss in the next chapter, your brain can't tell the difference between something as small as sending out a letter versus completing a major training session.

The brain appreciates closure. By acknowledging yourself for the smaller completions, you pave the way for greater and grander completions.

Completions represent a neat ending to what you've accomplished and a great

Dyna Moe

If you want to finish work each night with a valid sense of accomplishment, give yourself acknowledgment for completing what you did get done. Acknowledging yourself for all that you finished is a sure way of leaving without feeling beaten, and often proves to be uplifting.

beginning for what's next. Giving yourself a completion for a minor task opens the door and sets the stage for tackling something larger. Give yourself a completion and make your day!

CHAPTER 17

All About Completion Thinking

You attained a good sense of the effect of incompletions from the previous chapter. In this chapter, we focus on achieving completions, everywhere, all the time!

Silent Self-acknowledgment for Completions

A completion is more than the accomplishment of a task. As used here, it also means *citing yourself* for what you've gotten done. As I describe, in my book *Breathing Space: Living & Working at a Comfortable Pace in a Sped-Up Society*, those who have mastered completions give themselves quick, silent acknowledgment and then move on . . . "I did a particularly good job here, and it's rewarding to have it done!" They are not obsessive and do not seek completions only for completion's sake.

Achieving completions is energizing because it offers a clean end to activities or even thoughts, and it is a good beginning

Factoid
Completions are useful means for giving your mind and emotions temporary energy breaks. Achieving completions is not synonymous with obsessive behavior or overachieving.

for what's next. Some of the happiest, most productive and prosperous people have developed the habit of achieving one completion after another, acknowledging themselves for their efforts and accomplishments. Yet, to an observer it could look as if there is barely a moment to catch a breath.

Score One for You: Acknowledgment

Completions can be acknowledged when finishing a minor or routine task, or even a daily event, not only for monumental efforts. For example, when you awake each morning, you have completed sleep for that night, whether you slept poorly or well.

Completions can be achieved on multi-year projects or even on activities that last seconds. The table that follows offers a brief list of rapid completions.

Completions	Seconds
Blink of an Eye	0.10
One Human Heart Beat at Rest	0.86
Average Rock Video Scene Change	1.50
Average Doorbell Chime	2.00
Average Television Camera Shot	3.5
Average Embrace Between Spouses	7.0
U.S. Pledge of Allegiance	14.3
The 1989 San Francisco Earthquake	15.0
Phone Pickup after Fourth Ring	18.4
Pro Basketball Shot Clock	24.0
Final Jeopardy Countdown	30.0
Average Teeth-Brushing by Adults	58.0
Kentucky Derby (average length)	62.3
Star Spangled Banner (Marine Band)	101.0
World Record for One-Mile Run	217.3

Whether your completions are large or small, they are vital to acknowledge because they provide a mental and emotional break from what you had been doing. And, they make you feel good!

Achieving completions is energizing because it offers a clean end to activities or even thoughts, and a good beginning for what's next. At home, drying and putting away the dishes, or taking out the garbage, are completions that yield benefits. At work, making copies for the staff meeting or making a key phone call represent completions that also yield the aforementioned benefits.

Completions are somewhat like driving along a mountain highway and stopping periodically at scenic overlooks to enjoy a breath of fresh air, stretch out, acknowledge how far you have come, and establish where you are.

Gathering the Loose Ends

As a holiday or vacation approaches, most career professionals instinctively tie up various loose ends so that they can depart in a more restful state of mind.

When your desk is cleared, files put back in place, and other things tidied up to a respectable degree, your whole countenance brightens, as if a weight has been taken off of your shoulders.

Consider the case of Karla. Karla was an independent health care consultant to several large organizations. For each consulting engagement, she had to prepare and deliver a final report. In previous years, Karla considered it enough to write, proof, and assemble the entire report for on-schedule delivery to the client. She would then handle loose ends several days or weeks after delivering the report, in the midst of other activities.

After learning about the power of completions, Karla included binding the report, producing an attractive cover, and making an early delivery in her schedule. She also updated her hard-copy file, completed a project, cost data, and the invoice. She streamlined her working notes file and chucked anything that was no longer needed. She even called the client one day in advance to alert them that the report was coming.

By viewing all aspects of the engagement as a unit, Karla was able to complete all related activities by the day the report was delivered. Karla was clear mentally and emotionally by the end of day. She felt good about her accomplishment and was energized to start what came next the following morning.

Karla understood that unfinished tasks with one client can mount up and perceptually loom larger than they actually are. She knew that each task in finishing an engagement, like each pile she allowed on her desk, represented unfinished business.

The great change came for Karla when she realized that lack of completions in one aspect of her work impacted her activities in other areas. Conversely, completing one thing after another leads to yet more completions.

Dyna Moe

All around you, every day, you complete things, from the mundane to the magnificent. The great thing about acknowledging your completions is it leads to another completion, and another and yet another.

Incompletions: Frustration, Completions: Invigoration

Have you racked up accumulated incompletions in your career stretching back several years? This could involve everything from keeping all your receipts in your wallet to perpetually allowing piles to build up on your desk.

These types of daily tasks can either drain or energize you. Completing them can make you feel accomplished, while having to postpone them can leave you frustrated. Surprisingly, the order in which you approach tasks can have a dramatic impact on your productivity, energy, and enthusiasm.

Ebbs and Flows

Some tasks are best handled at specific times of the day, and are best avoided at other times. Each person has his own preferences.

To maintain balance, finish your work, benefit from the power of completions, and have a life at the end of the day, ensure that the sequence and the timing of your projects support, rather than impede, the chance that you'll accomplish everything you sought.

If you know you are more adept at one type of task early in the day, schedule accordingly. If you know that on Tuesday, you're better prepared to handle a challenging task than at the end of the week, make plans that take advantage of that knowledge. When you can control the timing of activities, you continually give yourself the best chance to achieve desirable completions.

One Month Campaigns

My friend Allie takes a unique approach to getting things done in his consulting firm. He creates month-long completion campaigns by focus area. During each month of the year, in addition to the normal business transactions and activities that occur, Allie focuses on one major area of the business.

For example, in January the focus might be on the billing system, in February, on office equipment, in March, on insurance, and so on. Within a year, he gives extra attention to 12 focus areas and enjoys a great sense of completion as each month rolls by.

Suppose you're a salaried employee for a large corporation. As a variation to Allie's approach, you could delegate a few weeks out of each month, or all 52 weeks during the year, to serve as time intervals in which you'll focus on one particular aspect of your career or work. For example:

➤ In the first week of January, you review long-term goals.

➤ In the second week, you review the status and value of all your memberships.

➤ In the third week, you consider the publications you currently receive and how that line-up might need to change.

Dyna Moe
Periodically carve out a 30-minute stretch where you devote your attention to how your desk is stocked, the ergonomics of your office set-up, whether your e-mail signature is appropriate, and so on. This will help you stay in control and be better prepared to meet bigger challenges.

The key in each case is comfortably and conveniently fitting such reviews and assessments into your daily or monthly cycle. Thus you're able to maintain your normal work pace and finish other tasks that you've been seeking to accomplish.

Meanwhile, you stay balanced and happy, achieve completions, and handle what's next.

Allowing Completions to Occur

Sometimes all you have to do for a completion to occur is not stand in the way. I purchased a 1983 Ford Thunderbird with 35,000 miles on it. The car was in fantastic shape and, amazingly, cost only $7,000 (a sizeable sum back then, but still a bargain). I drove that car for 18 years, because I practice preventive maintenance.

By the eighteenth year, the car's performance had begun to decline. About once in 25 times, the car would not start properly. I'd have to turn the key 20, sometimes 40 times to make it start. Usually these non-starting sessions would occur right after I had picked up, say, five bags of groceries!

I placed an advertisement but expected few if any calls. I was pleased to receive a call within a matter of days from an elderly gentleman who said that he had worked with cars all his life and would be interested in seeing it.

When the man arrived, I prayed the car would start on the first try. I told him that about one in every 25 times the car would not start. He said no problem! He was good at tinkering with cars, and he'd look into it. When we got into my T-Bird, the car started on the first try and performed like a new vehicle!

I was asking $900, firm, for the car. After a couple of spins around the block, we switched places and he got behind the wheel.

Once again, the car performed admirably, but I figured he'd wanted to think about it and call me later. After a few minutes he said that he'd like to buy it. Lucky me! I figured he'd go back home, and write me a check. Instead he wanted to pull up to a local branch of his bank so that he could withdraw $900 in cash, right now . . .

At that point I was thinking, "He wants to pay in cash. There is a God!" As he waited in line, I was completing the paperwork that would be necessary for the transfer of the vehicle. I had no idea what to do. He walked me through the whole procedure. The fates were smiling on me that day.

We left the bank, got back in the car, and I once again prayed that it would start perfectly. It did. We made our way to the motor vehicle office, less than a quarter mile away. There was no line and we took care of business in a matter of minutes. We went back to the car, which started perfectly, and headed to my house.

I had $900 in my pocket, sold what was increasingly an automobile nightmare, and could now enjoy the next vehicle of my life. I was happy for him.

Some completions occur on their own and your role is to simply be supportive. He had come out of nowhere to remove what was only a scrap of metal for me, paid me cash, and all the while was cheerful about it.

This marvelous sale all took place in one day. But, I could have thwarted it. What if I wasn't ready to see him on the morning he requested? What if I had suggested to the buyer that he think about it, and let me know in the next day or two. What if I hadn't assembled my end of the paperwork? And of course, the one factor out of my control, what if the car didn't start the first time we tried?

In this instance, I arranged my affairs so as to facilitate a completion, even if I had not formally engaged in completion thinking. Later it occurred to me, how often do we engage in non-completion type thinking as well as accompanying behaviors?

Coming Undone

How often do we set ourselves up to have things linger on when a completion was completely within our grasp? It's as if we snatch defeat from the jaws of victory.

Completions happen. Allow them to happen, help them along, acknowledge them, and you'll have more of them in your life, your career, your week, and your day.

The table that follows depicts the non-completion versus completion approach to your day. Hereafter, when you can, proceed more along the lines of column 2 rather than column 1, and you'll be achieving one nice completion after another!

Non-completions	Completions
Awaking in the morning, feeling time pressure, and not looking forward to going to work. Eating in a rush, if at all, and then hustling out the door.	Giving yourself completions for finishing sleep, leisurely eating breakfast to aid digestion, finishing your morning routines, heading to work, and arriving at work.
Turning in your report without making a back-up copy or filing the supporting materials.	Turning in your report, making a back-up copy, and filing the supporting materials, and chucking the excess.
Finishing a major assignment at work without reflection, and instantly tackling another big task.	Finishing a major assignment, getting complete, and then taking a stroll or a minute or so before tackling what's next.
Lingering after a seminar to talk to the speaker, then rushing off and being late for the next seminar, finally finding a seat, catching your breath, and not focusing on the new session for several more minutes.	Choosing to linger after a seminar to talk to the speaker, being glad that you did, walking to the next room, acknowledging yourself for fully attending the first session, finding a seat, and being fully present in the new lecture hall.
Dashing off to your car after work so you can slug your way through the heavy traffic on the long commute. Arriving home, feeling as if you barely have enough energy to eat dinner, watch TV, and go to bed. Being concerned that each day seems to race by and that you're not enjoying enough of what you do.	Ending the day by acknowledging your efforts, walking to your car, while giving yourself a completion for doing so. Confronting heavy traffic, but controlling your environment by playing a CD or reflecting on today. Arriving home and giving yourself a completion. Opting for abundant energy tonight. Retiring pleased with your day.
Looking at your child's schoolwork or artwork in the middle of doing something else, not spending much time on it, offering faint praise, and returning to what you were doing, while conveying the message, "I'm busy."	Suspending what you were doing so you can look at your child's work and offer your complete attention. Acknowledging the child for the effort, offering affection, and suggesting what can be done with the items. Then resuming your prior activity.
Having your 32nd (or 42nd or 52nd!) birthday with little fanfare, wishing it would pass quickly so that you can forget altogether about birthdays.	Approaching your birthday with anticipation, acknowledging your age and accomplishments, and giving yourself a completion. Choosing to have a productive life for your time remaining.

More Completions Through Conscious Choice

Choices are positive affirmations that help you move closer to feeling how you want to feel and to accomplishing what you want to get done. Choices are not synonymous with "positive thinking."

Unlike positive thinking, you make your conscious choices regularly regardless of how you feel at any given moment. The key is to keep making them.

Choices facilitate completions because sometimes components of a task or project are out of our control. To gain a sense of satisfaction and closure, we can rely upon a completion statement such as "I choose to feel complete about this project," when no other form of closure realistically will be possible. This is particularly true in the case when:

➤ your contribution might be one of many to some larger project, or
➤ you work with others by telephone or e-mail and are geographically dispersed.

Complete on Two Fronts

Making choices helps you to become complete when accomplishing something that has both a psychological as well as physical component. Suppose, you have to do something that you've been putting off and you know that when you're finished, you'll have mixed feelings about what transpired.

A prime case is if you have to terminate someone at work. You don't want to be the bad guy, but it is your responsibility, and the situation certainly merits termination.

When you've completed the task, no matter how effective you've been, you still might have psychological ramifications. No matter how good you feel about yourself, how well the day is going, and how appropriate your actions have been, devise a completion statement in the form of conscious choice about how you would like to feel. For example, these kinds of statements are helpful:

➤ I choose to feel complete about the task.
➤ I choose to feel complete about my performance as a manager.
➤ I choose to feel complete about the challenging aspects of my job.

Also, these could prove useful to you:

➤ I choose to maintain balance and composure in the face of job-related challenges.
➤ I choose to take appropriate action for the good of the department or company.
➤ I choose to be a confident decision maker.

Many completion statements in the form of conscious choices also are helpful before having to handle the challenging task. Also, such choices can be applied to other types of challenges that you face throughout the day and week.

The Completion that Keeps On Paying Off

An essential choice you can make continually is to feel worthy and complete. In a variety of situations, affirm to yourself, "I choose to feel worthy and complete." This can help you reduce anxiety, remain calm, and feel more relaxed throughout the day.

When you choose to feel worthy and complete, instantly, you tend to redirect yourself. You recognize that virtually everything you do is based on your choice. You can continue working on a particular task, specifically one that has been assigned to you, and choose to remain productive and balanced.

From Breakdowns to Breakthroughs

Suppose your car breaks down; you're stranded. The tow truck finally arrives and now you're two hours behind schedule. You decide it's going to be a lousy day, and many people might agree with you. Another way to proceed is to be thankful that the delay was only two hours.

If you have work with you, you can stay productive. Give yourself a completion for having handled the morning's mini-ordeal. In this manner, you release the psychic energy that might have been bottled up within you. Once your car is ready, you are energized to reclaim your day.

Here are other examples on how to move from potential breakdown to breakthrough by choosing how you want to feel, acknowledging where you are, and what you want to accomplish:

Breakdown Example 1—New software comes with a huge instruction manual. You plow through it but the going is slow and tedious. You'd rather do things the old way.

Breakthrough: New software will be a challenge to learn. Your investment of a few days will be repaid in your long-term productivity. You attack the project with vigor.

Breakdown Example 2—So many items compete for your attention that you could scream. You can't address them all, and you hardly know where to start. The situation seems to grow worse daily.

Breakthrough: You make tough decisions about what to drop versus

Word Power
Psychic energy is an internal mechanism that arouses someone to take action in pursuit of a desired outcome.

what merits action. You clear out the lesser items and dive headlong into the most vital one.

Breakdown Example 3 (here's a tough one)—You've learned that you're being fired and you're devastated. Thinking about your entire career, it seems like one big failure. You're immobilized.

Breakthrough: You've heard the bad news and are shocked. You have wages and benefits coming and you resolve to make this a time for renewal and redirection.

When you add it all up, at least half of the time you can shift from breakdown to breakthrough by *choosing* how you want to feel, and by acknowledging where you are and what you want to get done.

CHAPTER 18

Put the Pareto Principle to Work

In This Chapter:

➤ Learn the 80-20 rule
➤ Alter your approach to getting things done
➤ Find your own personal leverage
➤ Gain leverage from your resources

You've likely heard of the 80-20 rule. Pareto's observation was so profound that it would be no exaggeration to call him the father of getting things done. In this chapter, we're going to examine the 80-20 rule in ways that might change how you approach tasks or even your career.

Vilfredo Pareto, born in 1848, observed a relationship between effort and result in 1906 that became the basis of the Pareto Principle, or what is now called the 80-20 rule. He observed that 80 percent of the land area in his native Italy was owned by only 20 percent of the population. Later, while he was gardening he realized 20 percent of the peapods he had planted accounted for 80 percent of the harvested peas.

Factoid
The Pareto Principle holds that 80 percent of your actions or efforts contribute to only 20 percent of your actual results, while 20 percent of your action or efforts yield 80 percent of your results.

The Father of Getting Things Done

Vilfredo Pareto maintained that outputs, results, and even rewards come from a small proportion of the efforts or inputs directed towards achieving them, or what productivity experts later called the concentrating on the "vital few" and not the "trivial many." Pareto's observation seemed to hold true whether applied to large institutions or organizations, businesses, or even individuals.

In an accounting firm, 20 percent of the firm's clients provided 80 percent of the firm's revenue. In a hardware store, 20 percent of the floor space allotted to certain products accounted for 80 percent of the business's profits. So, owners and managers of firms large and small found it prudent to continually identify those 20 percent of inputs, be it sales representatives, clients, floor space and so on, which contributed to 80 percent of the business' results.

It also made great sense for firms to identify the 80 percent of sales representatives, clients, or even floor space that yielded relatively poor results: only 20 percent of revenue. In the case of the hardware store, if the manager knew which 20 percent of his goods were generating 80 percent of revenue, he would place those goods where they were most accessible and put all else, still reachable to customers, out of prime foot traffic areas.

The 80-20 Rule and Your Career

Often you hear people lament the lack of time available for every things they want to accomplish. The ability to forsake dwelling on minutia is no small task. For most people, the lack of time is due to their focus on minutia, the 80 percent of activities that yield 20 percent of results.

If you can identify those areas at work that help you to achieve the fastest, easiest, best results, and you have the mental and emotional fortitude to forsake those activities that are not benefitting you to a great degree, you can increase your ability in getting things done. Perhaps the easiest place to start is to rid yourself of the unproductive 80 percent of your activities.

Word Power

Minutia, not to be confused with what fertilizes lawns, is the small stuff of life, considered to be trivial matters.

Alter Your Approach to Your Day

When you apply the Pareto Principle to advancing your career and getting things done, some interesting results turn up. For example, 20 percent of the items you've listed as wanting to accomplish today will likely prove to yield 80 percent of your results towards important tasks and 80 percent of your satisfaction.

As hard as it might be to fathom, 20 percent of your peers at work probably account for 80 percent of the leads, insights, perspectives, and tips that you gain while on the job. They probably also account for 80 percent of your enjoyment in terms of interactions with fellow employees.

If you manage a workflow, are most of your delays attributable to 20 percent of the possible origins of the delay? If so, can

Coming Undone

Is 80 percent of what you write and send to others regarded as drivel? If so, prune your prose and target your messages more precisely. At the same time, be more captivating so that people will begin to develop the habit of noticing, reading, and acting upon what you're sending.

you focus on the same irritating root causes so as to improve your entire system? If you're a customer service manager, are you finding that 80 percent of complaints can be traced to 20 percent of your services? If so, can you improve service delivery in those areas, or eliminate services that are too problematic and not worth the trouble?

It's likely that about 20 percent of the memos you receive account for 80 percent of what you need to heed, whereas 80 percent of memos add up to a heap of garbage. Likewise, consider your own communications to others. If you manage a website, do 80 percent of the site visitors view only 20 percent of your site pages? If so, can you make the entire site more inviting?

Small Shifts, Big Payoffs

Amazingly, perhaps only 20 percent or less of your daily activities account for 80 percent of your results. If so, can you weed out activities that yield so little results that you could skip them all together? As a career professional with an upward career trajectory, you owe it to yourself to make a handful of small shifts in your approach to tasks and projects that you want to accomplish so that you will be continually directing your efforts to high output activities.

Coming Undone

Offering macro effort and achieving micro results doesn't sound like a good deal, yet some people follow this pattern for the duration of their careers. Some career professionals are caught up in a cycle of giving activities relatively equal weight. They continue to devote 80 percent of their efforts to that which only provides 20 percent of their results.

Be on the Lookout for High-yield Activities

Sometimes you have to deal with the 80 percent of activities that are of low yield. They might be assigned, or they could be your responsibility; so they could be minor but urgent tasks. That's okay. Nothing about effectively applying the Pareto Principle implies that all of the low-yield tasks will disappear. Quite the contrary, many will be with you day in and day out for the rest of your career.

`The vital notion is to spend a greater degree of your time on high-yield activities, the important stuff, so that in time it won't take a lot of time; the habit is so fully developed within you that it becomes an all pervasive discipline and part of your character.

Dyna Moe

When you look upon even a simple to-do list that you drew up this morning, rank the items. You can put them into numerical order, you can assign them "I"s for important and "U"s for urgent, you can circle items and highlight items: whatever floats your boat.

Recall Alan Lakein's statement, "What is the best and highest use of my time?" With free will each minute is new. You're not an extension of what came before. You can make new choices about where to devote your time and attention. Alfredo Pareto opened the door to higher personal productivity for each of us. It's up to each of us to make the decision to walk in.

The effective, get-things-done type of professional continually seeks the 20 percent of his or her activities that prove to be the most strategic and yield the greatest results.

If you're in sales and twenty different ways are available to make contact with potential clients, perhaps 20 percent or four of the ways prove to be most effective. Hence, you logically gravitate to those four methods and away from the other 16.

With the continual information and communication bombardment that you face, and the array of projects and tasks that come your way, sometimes it's hard to identify the 20 percent of activities likely to be most effective. This is where review and reflection can be helpful. Review file folders, projects, or cases, and ponder what worked and why. What particular strategy or technique proved to be effective? Conversely, what was ineffective?

What activities, rituals, and behaviors do you still engage in because you've always done so? Maybe they're pleasing or comforting. Maybe you've seen others do them, but upon reflection, they yield little in terms of actual results.

Implications of the 80-20 Rule for Leaders

If you're a manager within an organization or an entrepreneur running your own firm, the application of the Pareto Principle can come in handy. Ask yourself, what are 80-20 axioms in my industry or line of business? Where do organizations or rival firms make above average profits, or even outrageous profits?

Find Your Specializations

No matter what you have to offer, in every market ways exist to do things in a superior manner than everyone else. The 80-20 Rule implies that specialization is more often the wiser path than generalization.

What are you so good at that you could be among the absolute best? Stake out a leadership position by taking bold and decisive action. Make it your business to be an expert in your chosen field.

Dyna Moe

By capitalizing on what you do best, you might be able to create not merely a small edge, but a spectacular edge.

Keep it Rolling

Where are you or your organization receiving far more in return than you're inputting? Identify that opportunity area, exceed it, and perhaps you can achieve double or triple the results. When you're on a roll, stay on a roll. Grease the skids, do what you can to up your efforts because you've already identified that this is a high pay-off activity.

If something isn't proceeding so well, examine why, and move decisively. It's better to re-plot your course early, cutting losses if you have to, than doing so too late.

Dyna Moe

The Pareto Principle asserts that being in the right place can be as important, if not more so, than anything else you do. Stay focused on your desired outcome and often an appropriate means will appear.

Feed Your Strengths

You can expend considerable time and effort seeking to cover up your weaknesses, but your weaknesses tend to stay with you for the duration of your career. It would be better to simply acquire help with those areas you are weak.

Depending on where you work and the stage of your career, you likely need the support of others to be successful. In terms of business relationships, be selective with whom you affiliate. Allies are fundamental; the right allies are essential.

Realizing what you want to accomplish, often requires partners or a full-fledged team. The right team on the right mission with the right resources can achieve tremendous results. These are the kinds of groups that have posters on the wall that say "Miracles happen here" (see Chapter 22 and 24).

Cultivate relationships and revel in your shared experiences. Find areas of common ground. When someone does a favor for you, reciprocate in kind.

Coming Undone

Feed your strengths and shore up your weaknesses. Don't make the mistake that so many people do by trying to be well-rounded when the attempt is ill-concieved.

Catapult Your Efforts with Leverage

Leveraging involves making connections between what you've already accomplished and what else you can accomplish as a result of your earlier victory. Perhaps taking a small action can yield a large result.

While the Pareto Principle compels you to seek the 20 percent of activities that yield 80 percent of the results, the concept of leveraging "ups" your efficiency to yet another level.

Implement and Reuse

Suppose you have to make a presentation at work, telling your staff how they could do better at collecting data. The notes or outline that you prepare for that presentation can be used again, as a form of leverage, to create an article. By stripping any company-specific references, you might be able to craft your in-house presentation into a generic piece on effectively collecting data that's good enough for publication.

If you record your presentation to your staff, use a transcription of the presentation and be that much closer to having a finished article. In this manner, you're making your work count more than once—the essence of leveraging.

Generalize Your Findings

In your career, whether or not you have writing aspirations, consider what you've done or what you want to get done and all the other places where such accomplishment applies. Actually, to not do so is a form of waste.

If you've solved some dilemma for your department, and other departments might be facing a similar type of situation, does it make sense for you to make yourself available so that they can benefit from your solution? Would helping your co-workers be a feather in your career cap? Offering such assistance is clearly in alignment with the Pareto Principle. One action that you took that proved highly effective for your own department can now be dispensed to other departments with predictably great effect.

Gain Leverage from Outside Resources

Sometimes, you can leverage who you know and how you know them for a mutual win. Suppose someone in your office is adept at software that represents a stumbling block for you. Have that person advise you, and you in turn advise them in some area where you are adept. With the Pareto Principle in mind, if you are on good terms with 20 people in your office, 20 percent or 4 of them likely represent those with whom you can have a high-leverage relationship.

Recognizing Resources

What new ways could you use your current software? What resources and assets do you have at your command that you could use to optimal effect, but thus far have barely engaged?

➤ How about your phone, printer, copier, e-mail, web connections, or other equipment in your office?

Dyna Moe

Think of high leverage as wealth and no leverage as poverty. When you expend considerable energy with little results, you feel badly and you're no further along. When you expend minimal energy with great result, you feel wonderful and since you have not depleted your resources, you're in a position to accomplish more.

➤   What about your office relationships, information resources available to you, your know-how, or projects you've completed?

➤   Have you barely tapped human resources within your company, such as . . . an information officer? A librarian? A technical assistant? An opinion leader? A mover and shaker?

If you want to get things done and be known as such a person, expand your horizons, and include others. Open up your vistas. Seek ways to combine resources that can add up to spectacular accomplishments.

Catalog Who Is Beneficial to You

If it helps, catalogue the potential resources all around you. Can you connect with others in your same job category? Make a roster of the potential mentors, gurus, and advisors employed by your organization. Make a roster of those outside of your organization.

➤   What top information resources do you have at your disposal?

➤   What does your organization already subscribe to that you could be reading?

➤   What could you be subscribing to and, alternatively, what's worth dropping?

➤   Which online sources are you not tapping?

➤   Which online subscriptions are worth acquiring?

➤   What professional trade, civic, and social organizations do you already belong to, and with your expanded awareness, what resources do they provide that you can now take advantage of, when you hadn't even considered them before?

➤   What personal contacts within those groups represent resources for you?

➤   Which organizations might be worth investigating?

➤   What's worth joining because the knowledge, skills, contacts and exposure that you will receive will help you become more knowledgeable, skilled, or accomplished?

When perceiving the world and resources around you in new ways, the path to getting things done takes different turns. Often, it's a trail you would have missed by proceeding each day as you have been doing. You have to step out and step wide sometimes.

Learn From Others

Consider the barters, trades, swaps, loans, and exchanges that could greatly accelerate your progress towards desired ends. What paths have others already tread, what lessons have they learned, and what wisdom can they impart to you to make your journey shorter and easier? This is leverage at its finest. This is making 20 percent or *less* of your activities yield 80 percent or *more* of your results.

Once you accomplish something, can you teach or train others, or record, package, copyright, trademark, or patent it? Can you standardize, modernize, refine, and use your system or approach again and again?

Stay Vigilant about What is Important

On a continual basis, ascertain what is important, and important and urgent, versus what is simply urgent, versus what doesn't need to be handled at all. In this manner, you can fuse the advice you've gleaned from this book thus far.

Put everything on paper, create the super to-do list, then apply the daily or short-term to-do list, and keeping the Pareto Principle in mind, assess what is important and urgent. At intervals throughout the day, undertaking this exercise will keep you focused.

Remembering the work of Peter and Rosemary Grant, even small changes in your immediate environment, such as being mindful as to where to devote your time and attention, can quickly add up to a huge payoff. Consistently dealing in such thinking can lead to regular, desirable action. Such action on a daily basis can add up to habits, which in time help develop your character and ultimately your destiny.

Dyna Moe

Rather than view the Pareto Principle as an over-sighted business dictum, embrace it as an unfolding, empirical, groundbreaking approach to getting things done. This is your route to mastery.

Your assignment hereafter is to consider the 80-20 rule in regards to everything that you've accomplished, everything that you want to get done, and everything to which you could aspire.

 # Blasting Through Procrastination

In This Chapter:

➤ You aren't the only procrastinator.
➤ Why do we procrastinate?
➤ Techniques for starting on tasks.
➤ Sometimes it's acceptable to put off a task.

This chapter is all about overcoming procrastination, which is the act of putting off something until a later time, either by not starting a task, or by not finishing what you have started. Procrastination can be a major stumbling block to those who would otherwise fancy themselves adept at getting things done.

The Best Laid Plans

Sometimes even the best laid plans run askew: You have this grand project you want to tackle yet week after week, month after month, and even possibly year after year you don't initiate it. Jamie Foxx portrays this to a "T" in his sensitive performance in the otherwise ho-hum movie *Collateral* with Tom Cruise.

Foxx plays a long-employed taxi driver who harbors notions of starting his own limousine service. He's been driving a cab for 12 years. As the plot unfolds, we see that he's not making any tangible progress towards his dream. Rather, he's letting the idea bounce around in his head, using it as fantasy, and barely moving in the direction of his desired end.

He keeps a catalogue of new limousine models with him in the front seat and refers to it while he waits for passengers and, specifically in this drama, during tense moments. He flips through the pages and looks at the models intently as if he's going to acquire one.

All the while, we can see that with his present state of mind such a purchase is not going to happen.

We don't know if he saved enough of his cabby earnings, has been actively seeking outside capital, or has assembled a business plan. Still, it's clear that nothing is going to occur until he overcomes some mental hurdles that he has allowed to linger in his path for years. Any movie fan who witnesses his situation and has fallen into a long-term rut in regards to something he wants to accomplish can feel this cabby's pain.

Everyone Procrastinates . . . Especially at Work!

Procrastination plagues business executives and entrepreneurs, retirees, students, and everyone else in between. Thankfully, no one procrastinates on everything, and each of us has a bevy of work-related tasks where we practically never procrastinate.

Some people procrastinate because they're leery of the high-stake tasks they face. Too easily, these people let themselves "get down." Of course, you're not like that . . .

Institutional Impediments to Getting Things Done

Many office environments today contribute to procrastination. The widespread installation of workplace cubicles multiplies the noise and confusion that permeates the modern workplace and has made Scott Adams, author of *Dilbert*, a rich man.

With so much bombarding us all the time, you have to wonder: will attention spans, concentration, and focus ever be what they used to be? Working all day in an environment, ripe with noisy distractions from co-workers, does little to help the individual whose powers of concentration are already strained.

Coming Undone

Researchers have discovered that procrastinators often are those types of individuals who reflexively "give up" too easily, which is most of us on selected occasions. They might also be perfectionists, continually seeking autonomy and approval, and could have a high fear of failure. Even if you're a committed procrastinator, however, in some areas you shine.

If You're So Inclined to Procrastinate, You Will

While the web, instant messenger, and a smartphone are but a few in a long line of vehicles that procrastinators have employed, in the rice bowl of life they are but meager kernels. In the future even more enticing distractions will be available. If you are unfocused and have a high proclivity to procrastinate, the means at your disposal is immaterial.

Identify the Real Issues

As you saw in Chapter 16, leaving things incomplete contributes to a climate where other things are left incomplete. The more incompletions, big and small, all around you, the harder it is to begin anything. Procrastination becomes the norm.

Dyna Moe

When you identify reasons for procrastination, you have a better chance of sailing past them than if you didn't fathom the issues.

Give yourself the mental edge by seeking completions, one after another, even on small accomplishments, and mow them down.

If you're honest with yourself and acknowledge when you are procrastinating, you're that much closer to taking useful action.

Find Out Why

Sometimes you can't get started because you haven't identified lingering issues that impact your feelings.

➤ Perhaps you're ambivalent about the task.
➤ Perhaps you think it's unnecessary or unworthy of you.
➤ Perhaps you resent doing it, i.e. you weren't able to say no in the first place, and now you have to make good on your earlier promises.

Whatever the reason, when you identify some of the reasons behind procrastination, you have a better chance of leaping over them and getting started than when you don't articulate the issues to yourself and remain in a quandary.

How Can You Solve the Problem?

If the fears you experience in certain situations are holding you back, try one or more of the following tips:

Word Power

To articulate is to express and idea or a concept accurately and coherently.

➤ Permit yourself to experience the fear of whatever task you've been delaying, and you set yourself up to more readily initiate the task at hand. Delve into the fear, don't mask it!

➤   Use uplifting language when you are reticent to begin a task that needs to be completed. Use phrases such as "I will," "I choose," and "I'll be happy to." Say them aloud to yourself.

Another option when you can't get started: Identify a wise, trusted guide or mentor who can give you a jump-start—an encouraging word where it's seldom heard. Such assistance can make all the difference to you.

On other tasks, find a reliable partner who can both help you start and remain on course.

Lead Thyself: Identify a Starting point

When starting a task or project, people might procrastinate if they don't have a clear starting point or a logical sequence of steps to take. Don't become all flustered about how or where you start. Identify a starting point, even if it's not the perfect starting point. For example, if you have a large job, break it down into individual tasks, each regarded as a distinct entity.

If it helps, seek an early, easy win—for whatever you're seeking to accomplish, and pick some aspect of it that you can complete quickly and easily. Take the easy "win," which is an easier approach to starting than tackling some difficult portion head on.

Facing Challenges: Pick an Easy Entry Point

What if everything about some project is difficult for you? It happens. How could you score an easy, early win? Open the file folder, review the contents, and seek something/anything that is familiar to you. Often, that represents an easy entry point. Sometimes merely organizing materials, allocating them to smaller file folders, paper clipping items, or shuffling their order serves a suitable early win. At least you've gained a better idea of the project.

Coming Undone

Some people think that if they can initiate tasks at the "right time," won't that be grand? For most tasks, objectively speaking, there is no "perfect" time, so rise above it.

Suppose you're experiencing a difficult time initiating a project. If so, promise yourself that you will delve into it for only four minutes. By the fourth minute, often you won't want to stop! Strange how that works.

When you tackle a 5-minute job, and gain the completion for having it all done, you have more energy, focus, and direction for, say, another 5-minute job. Likewise, if you do five 5-minute jobs, each job feeling a sense of victory, however minor, you're spurred on by the next and the next. As such, five 5-minute jobs can be easier to tackle than one 25-minute job.

Give Yourself the Edge

In many office environments today the noise and "hub-bub" directly contributes to procrastination. For virtually any task or project you're working on, less distraction adds up to less procrastination!

Suppose you have many tasks to handle, each of which would only require about five to ten minutes to complete. Singularly, none of these tasks would be that difficult to tackle. The thought of grappling with all of them, however, becomes discouraging. As the task roster grows, you feel yourself slipping behind.

Coming Undone

If you find yourself in a work setting where you're hit by distractions and interruptions, even tiny tasks combined with others, can seemingly loom far larger than they actually are.

Remember: Even the smallest step in pursuit of a desired goal is better than nothing. And, in perspective, much of what you face requires only a few minutes to complete.

Who Can Help

Action-oriented role models could be near by. Is someone in your office a take-charge type? Consider the value of observing the behaviors of the action-takers around you. Alternatively, is someone in reach who is seeking to finish the same sort of task? If so, you could have the ideal partner to join you.

Whenever you can identify someone who's facing the same challenge as you are, you have good potential for getting things done faster and easier.

Bust Ruts with Regularity

When you're well-rested and well-nourished you have the best chance of doing your best work. Conversely, when you don't have enough sleep and haven't eaten well, even simple tasks can loom larger than they actually are. Half the time you can't begin on something, it is due to fatigue.

Approaching the Ruts

Here is a variety of rut-busting approaches, one or more of which could prove to be effective for you:

➤   If you face many items competing for your attention, trade one project off against another. Suppose you have to do project A, and you've been putting it off. Along comes project B. It's more difficult, involved, and scary. All of a sudden, A doesn't look so bad. Now, tackle A headlong. You'll still have B to worry about and that could keep you humming along on A.

➤   If you have somebody waiting for your results or, at least, waiting to hear about your progress, you increase your ability to start and stay on the task at hand. One reason that you don't procrastinate at work as often as you might at home is that at work you generally report to a boss who awaits the results of your efforts and who pays you based on your efforts. If you don't complete your work, there are identifiable penalties.

➤   Having too much in your visual field can be an impediment to starting on something. When you have only one project or one task at hand, your odds of maintaining clarity and focus increase. This works even better if you're not in your own office but at a conference table or at some other post where you only have the project materials at hand.

➤   Suppose you know you have to tackle a project on Monday, and you're dreading it. How can you make the project more palatable days beforehand? An effective maneuver is to review the project contents on, say, the Friday before. Over the weekend, you don't have to do anything.

Unbeknownst to you, by reviewing project contents on a Friday, you're already in the germination state. When it's time to start the project on Monday, you find that you can begin with greater ease than you anticipated. The early preview you gave yourself on Friday was the key.

➤   Suppose your car conks out on the side of the road, and your battery receives a jump-start. All of a sudden, the engine is revving and this is certainly not a time to turn the car off. You want to keep it on for a good twenty minutes. Sometimes a mere gesture of turning on your computer or popping a DVD into the player is enough to start on a task that you have avoided.

In essence, flipping on the switch to your PC, having it boot up, and perhaps taking it to the appropriate folder and file, is analogous to jump-starting your car.

➤ Pain is a great motivator, perhaps the greatest of all. What are the consequences of not starting? If you can identify the pain that you will experience as a result of not doing the task or not starting the project, and if the pain is sufficient, that could be an incentive for you to start.

➤ Sometimes the only way to start on a task is to dive into it headlong, cold turkey, not allowing yourself the opportunity to stray. Surprisingly, when you practice the cold turkey approach to procrastination, it's not as upsetting as it sounds. In fact, it can be a great relief.

Capitalize on Your Progress

COO or newly hired, the more items that vie for your time and attention, the larger even smaller projects can loom. Who among us does not feel the crush of what he needs to get done, even when the accomplishments could be nothing but the mundane?

If you still have trouble starting, consider the times you had trouble getting started in the past. What happened once you finally begun, and how good did you feel once you accomplished what you set out to accomplish? If you can evoke those feelings of satisfaction, happiness, and the sheer joy of accomplishment, you might have the winning formula for starting right now.

Does This Have to Be Done at All?

Every now and then you procrastinate because the issue at hand does not need to be handled. I'm not introducing this as an easy way for you to duck out of tasks and responsibilities. Rather, you recognize that occasionally the root of your procrastination is based upon sound reasoning. The task you have been putting off either doesn't need to be done, done by you, done in this way, or doesn't need to be done now. It's worth taking a look.

Factoid

Some people will never be good at playing the piano, some will never be good at programming, and some people will never be good at creative writing. This is simply human nature.

Delegate Challenging Tasks

Consider if you can delegate a portion of the task (see Chapter 21) . . . particularly the part you don't like to do, or are not good at doing.

If you want to "nurture your nature," as author Jim Cathcart says in his book *The Acorn Principle*, capitalize on your strengths and shore up your weaknesses by obtaining help.

When Procrastination Is Merited

In some situations it makes sense not to proceed. Here are a few:

➤ The benefits of proceeding are not abundantly clear to you—sometimes a great notion that seems worth embarking upon is merely that, a notion, and upon reflection, is not something to which you're willing to commit time, energy and effort.

➤ By postponing action, a clear strategic advantage emerges —this could be the case where, say, by beginning three weeks from now, you'll be better prepared, stronger, smarter, or have greater resources.

➤ You haven't made the internal commitment—there are times when it makes sense to begin half-heartedly on an otherwise worthwhile project. The momentum of your start often will carry you to a full gallop. If you recognize that your underlying commitment to the project is woefully inadequate, then you might have reason to pause. Don't in any way use this as an all-purpose excuse for procrastinating. Rather, determine why more groundwork or reflection might be necessary before proceeding.

Many Techniques to Draw Upon

Having completed this chapter, you now have many techniques to draw upon for any given task, if you have difficulty starting. Not all techniques work for everyone all the time. Still, employ one or another until you're rolling.

CHAPTER 20

 # Key Queries to Keep on Course

---

In This Chapter:

➤ The magic of questions
➤ What you've created
➤ Lessons from an unlikely source
➤ On not beating yourself up

The subject of this chapter is how you can devise simple questions that you ask of yourself, to great effect on the high road to getting more done. In short, questions can keep you productive. Sounds too easy, right?

"You want me to ask questions of myself, and that is somehow going to help me get things done?" Precisely! Asking yourself key questions helps you become more honest and gives you a more objective view about the accomplishments you wish to achieve.

What Is the Most Effective Use of My Time?

The question, "what is the most effective use of my time" is something you want to ask of yourself anytime you feel the need. This insightful question helps you to automatically re-direct yourself when you feel as if you're not being as productive as you could be, or somehow have strayed from your intended path.

Suppose you face a variety of unrelated tasks. Or, you face a variety of related tasks on the same project. Asking yourself, "what is the most effective use of my time?" helps direct you to the task that, at present, merits your attention.

Dyna Moe

Not to be too Zen-like, every moment you have the opportunity to make a choice. Even if a task or project is going particularly well, you can make the choice as to how to use your time starting at that moment.

Escape from the Past to Make Free and Clear Choices

In a study published in the *Annual Review of Psychology*, researchers Rachel Karniol, Ph.D. at Tel Aviv University in Israel, and Michael Ross, Ph.D. at the University of Waterloo in Ontario, found that "People less able to relate the person of the past to the person they are now could be at greater psychological risk because they are thinking only in the present and their view of the future could not be developed."

"Individuals often react to the present as if they were living in the past," say the researchers. To make free and clear choices about what we want in the future, it behooves each of us to draw accurately upon our pasts, but also note what's different about today. This means that you do not have to proceed as an extension of what came before.

If you're unable to recognize how you've changed, you're likely to allow your past to over-influence your decisions.

Boldly Take a New Direction

Rather than living life by looking through a rear view mirror, boldly go where you've never gone, and you'll accomplish what could have once seemed beyond your grasp.

You can proceed in a totally new direction if that is what makes sense at this moment. You can make a slight twist or turn. Or, you can continue as you have been doing.

Dyna Moe

When the question "what is the most effective use of my time" arises, it's an indication that you're facing some sort of quandary and probably need to re-direct your efforts.

Will it Be Any Easier Later?

When faced with a situation I would prefer to put off, I ask myself: "Will it be any easier later?" If the task will be easier later, then I have justification for not proceeding now on that particular task.

For example, if I have to organize all the receipts related to a certain project that will be in progress for another week, I can put off this task for another week. Then, with all the receipts collected, I can organize them accordingly. If the task won't be any easier later, then it makes sense to proceed now, especially if it might be more difficult later!

If you have the option of taking work home with you, will you still be as prepared for the task at home in a different, potentially more distracting environment as you would be in the work-related atmosphere of your office? If you will be as capable, okay, take the work home. More often, the task will not be easier later, so seek to handle it right where you are.

Who Created That?

I once took a course based on the work of Robert Fritz, a musician turned accomplishment guru. In his book, *The Path of Least Resistance*, he discussed how to employ self-imposed questions to move from where you are to where you want to be. One of the questions that he advised people ask of themselves is:

"Who created that?"

Any time of day, if you ask yourself "who created that?" the answer comes back that you did. Allow me to explain.

You are experiencing a stringent deadline and are working diligently, but feel intense pressure. Who created that situation? You did for many reasons. You applied for a job with your present employer. You assumed the post, took on the assignment, allocated available resources in some manner, and now find yourself at 10 a.m. with five hours to go before a vital project is due.

Sure, you can blame your parents for not passing on the proper genes to you. You can blame your previous employer for having a less-than-palatable work environment, prompting you to seek your present position with a new employer. You could blame your boss for not introducing the assignment hours or days earlier, and you could generate a dozen other reasons why you are a victim.

Dyna Moe
When you clear away the rubble, and become completely honest with yourself, most of the time, most of the situations you face are your own doing—a truism for nearly everyone.

We play in the sandbox and claim we didn't step into it, we didn't pick up the shovel, and we didn't cause that spec of sand to fly into our eye. If you milk it for all its worth, you can labor under this delusion all your life. You can credit your current situation to your boss.

Over the course of your 20,000 to 28,000 days, most of what transpires in your life is the result of choices you make. Yes, occasionally stuff happens from out of left field. Mostly, you make the choices that impact your life.

When you accept responsibility for the situation, you put the locus of control back

Word Power
Locus of control refers to a pivotal point when you can take action, as in "calling your own shots" or "being your own person."

where it belongs, in your own head. From there, miraculous things can happen. You created the situation, and sure as heck you're going to resolve it. No more second guessing, no more recriminations, no more lost time on the path. Take charge and get it done.

What Is this Problem Teaching Me?

In his book, *Love Medicine and Miracles*, Dr. Bernie Siegel discusses how one's illness can be a path to greater health, understanding one's self, and greater humanity. Siegel suggests to his patients that they ask themselves: what is this illness forcing me to learn? Some patients are stunned. Some understand what he is driving at immediately.

Joined by others in the medical community, it is Siegel's belief that illnesses don't simply arrive in people's lives. They occur for a reason. Most of the time, people "invite" the illness as a result of how they live, which could mean what they eat, how they treat themselves, or even how they think.

Once cancer or heart disease has been diagnosed, Siegel maintains that a patient has much to learn from the illness in terms of how to treat one's self, how to conduct one's life hereafter, how to treat others, and how to embrace a higher level of spirituality.

As a variation on a theme, Robert Fritz suggests a different kind of question: what is the problem forcing me to do or to learn? Suppose you need to finish something, but you keep encountering stumbling blocks. Fritz suggests that to achieve breakthrough solutions, particularly in the face of recurring problems, sincerely embrace each problem you have as a best friend.

Regarding a problem as a best friend enables you to benefit from what Fritz calls the Law of Reversal. This means you're using the negative energy surrounding the problem to propel you forward, to tap into the positive forces available and achieve a solution.

Is the Answer Right Along Side the Problem?

Thomas Kettering, a founder of the Sloan-Kettering Institute, perfected the diesel engine, automobile ignition systems, chrome painting procedures, and a host of other innovations that transformed the auto industry in the 1920s and 1930s.

Kettering's approach to problem solving was unsurpassed. He believed that the major difference between a problem and a solution was that people more readily understood a solution.

Kettering felt that solutions involved a strategic shift in perception, since the solution to the problem must have existed all along within the problem itself. A problem-solver's role was not to master a problem, but to make it generate its solution.

When it comes to problems that you experience, perhaps long standing problems, a solution exists, likely in tandem with the problem itself.

Factoid

In perfecting the diesel engine, Charles Kettering commented that his team had little part in it. Instead, the team "offered" the engine six different types of pistons and, in essence, let the engine "choose" the one "it" liked best.

Cooperate with the Forces at Play

In Fritz's view, since we help initiate most of our problems, the surest path to resolution and to accomplishing what we want is to cooperate with the forces at play. Treat obstacles as your best friends, rather than resist them. You might even say, the bigger the problem, the greater your creative potential.

The problem you're facing can be your best friend because it will help to bring out the best in you. Keep asking yourself: what is the problem forcing me to learn or to do? For some people, it is learning to trust

Dyna Moe

If you find yourself falling off the path in pursuit of a specific goal, use the energy of your plight to leap on to higher ground.

themselves or involving others in the solution. It could also mean approaching the problem in a different way. As answers emerge, keep asking questions.

By regarding problems as a stepping stone for opportunity and not a roadblock, you might view the problem as beneficial and the problem might start to lose power.

A Simple Exercise to Try Anytime

As a simple exercise, think about three things right now that you want to complete that, for whatever reason, have remained undone for quite a while.

Now, identify the major problem involved in completing each of these three tasks. For each situation, ask yourself what is the problem forcing me to learn or do? Have pen and paper ready as the answers start to come forth.

1._____

2._____

3._____

What Would a Paid Consultant Say?

You face a challenging work-related situation and are unsure which way to turn. Now, suppose someone hired you to be a consultant to yourself, and that your job is to advise this person as to which way to turn. As a paid consultant to yourself, what advice would you render? A silly exercise perhaps? Actually, quite the opposite.

Surmising what another party would suggest to you gives you an added measure of objectivity.

By taking on the posture of a consultant, you gain a measure of objectivity that might not otherwise be available to you. After all, a paid consultant, ideally, is impartial. He or she is retained to render an opinion based on a diagnosis of the issue.

When a friend asks you for advice and you offer your opinion, it's a form of

Factoid

President Richard Nixon often referred to himself in the third person. He'd ask himself, "Now, what should Nixon do next?" This generated a measure of objectivity for him that he wouldn't have otherwise had, and he often found that he generated different answers than he would have if faced with the question, "What should I do next?"

consulting. Giving your child or your spouse guidance is a form of consulting, although they don't always appreciate the advice. In a manner of speaking, when you're asked to render an opinion, you're acting as a consultant of sorts. Now, you're simply applying the process to your own work to derive answers that might not otherwise have been forthcoming.

What Else Can I Handle?

Any time you've completed a task or project of significance is a good time to contemplate what else you are able to address.

Likewise, when you recognize that you have six or eight minutes before a meeting, at the end of the day, or at the end of the work week, keep a keen eye out for anything you can take care of right now. The key factors will be the actual time available, your frame of mind, location, and available tools or resources.

Stay on a Roll

You've probably heard the expression "If you want to get something done, give it to a busy person." We're all so busy today, I question the value of that once sage advice.

On the other hand, the best time to get something done is when you are already on a roll. Fresh from the accomplishment of one task, and the resulting confidence and good feeling that imbues within you, you're primed to take on something else.

When a small pocket of time emerges, use it to "short-circuit" the to-do list, or as I often do, simply peruse your master to-do list, looking for everything and anything that might be handled during this opportune moment.

Dyna Moe

You can plot and plan all you want, but sometimes a small task emerges that begs for immediate action. In tending to that matter on the spot, you'll feel more in control, more productive, and even more creative. Getting things done during these small pockets of time also can help to alleviate stress.

Clearing Your "In-bins"

What about handling personal affairs at these emerging moments? The boundaries of our professional and personal lives frequently intersect. It would be unrealistic, and even draconian, to suggest that an unrelenting, 100 percent focus on professional tasks will keep you productive, focused, balanced, and happy.

One of the most pleasing tasks I encountered during these opportune moments is clearing "in-bins," either the physical in-bin on my desk or more likely an e-mail in-bin. Other worthwhile tasks include breaking down the mail, or straightening up some aspect of your office—not obsessively—to enhance your productivity for subsequent projects.

When you take on that extra something else and complete it, go a step further. Again ask yourself, what else can I handle? Continue for as long as you can with this procedure.

Soon enough, the answer that you derive will be "nothing else." Or more likely, you'll stop asking yourself. That's a good indication that you've run the rack. Thereafter, you can ask yourself questions such as what do I want for dinner tonight or what movie do I want to see?

What Would it Take to Feel Good about Departing on Time?

Why bring up the words "feeling good?" Because any given day is significant and how you feel about your accomplishments are equally as significant.

If you finish many things that you set out to do, day after day but don't feel good about your productivity, then what is your life, your career, and each day, all about?

A handful of things surface, which you wish to accomplish by the end of the day, when yourself ask this question.

Cut Yourself a Deal

A wonderful strategy for getting things done is to continually "cut a deal" with yourself. It's a self-reinforcing tool for achieving a desired outcome that you've identified within a certain time frame, as in the end of the day.

Suppose you want to leave the office by 5:00 today. You ponder, "What would it take for me to feel good about ending work on time today?" Today your answer to the question might be to finish three particular items on your desk. If the boss drops a bomb on your desk late in the day, you automatically cut a new deal with yourself, given the prevailing circumstances.

Your new deal could include merely making an initial foray on the project that's been dropped in your lap. You could also accomplish two of your previous three tasks and some fraction of this new project.

By cutting a deal with yourself, you avoid what too many people still confront all the time: leaving, on most workdays, not feeling good about what they've

Coming Undone
Anyone can throw his time or energy into a task to complete it, but at what cost? Your energy? Peace of mind? Quality of life?

accomplished, not having a sense of completion, and bringing work home. You want to earn raises and promotions but not have a lousy life in the process!

And Keep Dealin' by Not Adding More Items

Most people have several things they wanted to accomplish and actually manage to accomplish some of them, crossing them off the list. Rather than feeling good about their accomplishments and leaving on time, they add several more items to the list—a great way to guarantee that they'll still leave their offices feeling beleaguered. Thus, you have the perfect prescription for leaving work every day not feeling good about what you've accomplished: if you always have a lengthy, running list of "stuff" you have to do, you'll never have a sense of getting things done.

Regardless of projects, e-mail, phone calls, or other intrusions into your perfect world, continually cut a deal with yourself so you leave the workplace on time and feeling good about what you accomplished!

Becoming More Effective at Work

Part 6
Becoming More Effective at Work

In this sixth portion of the book, we focus on how you can become more effective at work, which after all is one of the most important arenas of your life regarding getting things done. The four chapters included here are each compelling and illuminating.

CHAPTER 21

Working with Peers, Subordinates, and Bosses

In This Chapter:

➤ Working effectively with others is everything
➤ Fair and square managers finish first
➤ Become a delegation sensation
➤ The care and feeding of bosses

In this chapter, we'll discuss what it takes to function effectively with others.

Having to work with peers, subordinates, and bosses can be as challenging to getting things done as anything else. On any given day, you might have little leeway as to with whom you work.

The New Guy or Gal

Let's start with the scenario that you're the new kid on the block. When you're hired for a new position, specifically one where you supervise others, in many organizations you are 'given' an unofficial 100-days window of opportunity. During this time, you can plead ignorance on key issues, and ask questions that you wouldn't dare to ask if you had been with the company for years.

This 100-day grace period represents the best time to achieve some early wins. In seeking to get things done, concentrate on projects that represent sorely needed improvements that others would like to see resolved. Establish a clear vision of what you want to accomplish and let others in on your plan.

Take advantage of this one-time window of opportunity to set the tone and you could achieve an operating advantage in the months and years to follow.

Supervise Successfully, Lead to Succeed

In many ways, your effectiveness on the job, new or old, is defined by how adept you are at working with others. Above all, the key element to working with peers, subordinates and bosses, has to be interpersonal skills. If you communicate effectively, offer clear and precise directions, elicit feedback, and listen well, you're going to go to the head of the class when it comes to managerial effectiveness.

Now is a good time to recall an observation made in Chapter 2 about effective managers. This is the person who is keenly focused on how his staff proceeds throughout the day and how well they harness ideas and insights, knowledge and wisdom, and energy and enthusiasm to accomplish the tasks at hand.

Dyna Moe

The effective manager seeks to achieve powerful results, while recognizing that sometimes, if not often, progress is uneven, endures twists and turns, and starts and stops.

Throughout business and industry, workers everywhere hunger for leadership. In today's business world, CEOs and top executives come and go, and people are likely to pass the buck as quickly as they receive it.

The manager or supervisor who is willing to step up to the plate and take a vested interest in the division, team, or staff, and the well-being of each participant, while staying focused on the work to be done, can win over hearts and minds.

While scads of books and articles have been written on being an effective manager, supervisor, or staff worker, paying homage to the traits and characteristics in the following sections will serve you well.

The Marine Corps "Rule of Three"

The Marine Corps uses a method of command called the "Rule of Three." A corporal is in charge of managing three privates. A sergeant manages three corporals. A lieutenant manages three sergeants and so on. Each officer in the chain of command needs to stay focused on three other people.

The workaday world operates differently. Still, there is a management lesson or two we could learn from the Marines about staying focused and not over-reaching. Today, what if you focused on the three most significant tasks or projects confronting you?

What if you focused your attention and poured your concentrated effort into making progress on the first of these tasks?

If you're managing others, what if you were able to clearly and precisely direct your troops so that they were ably prepared to tackle the task at hand? In our quest to handle so many things, too often we fritter our attention in too many directions. If we're managing others, we convey this sense of frenzy to them.

By limiting the scope of what we wish to achieve in any given unit of time, such as an eight-hour work day, we give ourselves a strategic operating advantage. If we manage others, we enable them to have a greater degree of focus and clarity that perhaps they sorely desire but have heretofore never articulated.

Being Fair and Consistent with All

Clearly, the people with whom you work are not alike in terms of their skills and background, competence and dedication, or even outlook and enthusiasm. It's easy to play favorites. Who wouldn't be more likely to act favorably towards consistent performers, or those with a winning personality, or those who you seem to get along with easily?

Being unfair or inconsistent with even one other staff person has ramifications that can undermine your effectiveness as a manager. People see and hear and know when someone else in your department is being treated unfairly. If it can happen to one person, then why not again and again? What's more challenging is to be fair and consistent with everyone.

When someone with whom you're not necessarily favorably disposed messes up in some way, can you approach the situation in the same way you would if one of your favorite people messed up in exactly the same way? Can you give equal time, attention, and caring to each staff member? If so, be prepared for the pleasant experience of working with a staff that, overall, could prove to be more productive than you would have supposed.

Dyna Moe
Your quest is to fight for objectivity in dealing with staff so that your emotions don't take over.

Use Language Accepted by All

Have you ever worked for someone who tossed about corporate buzz words that he or she apparently didn't believe in, but was trying to foist upon you? You know, the type of person who would win a Razzy for bad acting? Who wants to work around people like that? It makes you feel like they are insincere and fake."

If you're supervising younger staff, you don't need to know all their lingo. Indeed, you'll come across as a poser if you attempt to talk their talk while not being in their world. You don't need to enroll in "Communication 101," simply be yourself, keep it real, and speak to a staff person as you would a good friend.

You wouldn't use jargon with a friend, would you? You wouldn't submit your friends to organizational psychobabble would you? Then don't do it among your charges. Be real with the people with whom you work or supervise. Use terminology or phrases to which they can relate.

Your Words, Your Actions

For reasons that probably only cultural anthropologists can describe, people tend to become more upset about promises that were made to them and broken than almost anything else that transpires between individuals.

If you say it, mean it. If you promise it, work like a trucker on a deadline to ensure you deliver. If you can't make good on your progress, explain why and explain what you will do to rectify the situation, either this time or next time. Then, make sure that you deliver on the next promise, because the people with whom you work, and especially who you manage or supervise, can more easily recall the promises you've made than you can. So, write them down.

Delivering on your promises is an effective way to ensure that your staff delivers the type of performance you seek. After all, if they're rewarded accordingly, time after time, then they know that you'll deliver.

Factoid

In the Tylenol scare years ago, several people died because someone had poisoned a few bottles. As soon as it became apparent that the deaths were due to poisoned Tylenol, McNeil Consumer Healthcare, the distributor of Tylenol, for for the manufacturer, Johnson & Johnson took action with a full-disclosure public relations campaign.

McNeil Consumer Healthcare's campaign candidly revealed the entire situation related to the Tylenol scare with little or no spin on the facts and not a trace of defensiveness. This unorthodox approach maintained the public trust during the company's darkest hour.

Soon, McNeil became the leading manufacturer of over-the-counter cold medicines in the U.S. Its public relations campaign is still being studied in business schools as a perfect example of being straight with people.

At all costs avoid offering a continuing promise. That means that you delay that which you said you would. Worse, you might up the ante, suggesting that ultimately the reward will be even bigger than you first introduced, and that can backfire on you as well.

Keep things simple, keep things above board, and keep your word. When in doubt, tell the truth, accept responsibility, and be a stand-up kind of manager.

Instill a Group-Like Atmosphere

We'll cover the issue of assembling a winning team in Chapter 24. Here, focusing on working with an intact team, what can you do to ensure that each member of the team feels that he or she plays a vital part? Whenever practical, involve the team in decision making. Include everyone in the discussion. Depending on the issue, encourage a variety of ideas in brainstorming sessions.

When you include people in this manner, they have a more vested interest in ensuring that the task or project is completed on time and within the budget. If decisions are always made by you, you and only you, that can work in the short term, but after a while it can be kind of grating. People feel stifled; they want to express themselves and to know that their ideas matter.

Dyna Moe

When you include the group in the decision-making process, you also generate new ideas that you could never have come across by yourself.

Successful corporations pay employee bonuses for ideas put into the proverbial "suggestion box" because these organizations recognize the value and power of fresh perspectives, innovative ideas, and cost-saving solutions. Not everyone has a great idea all the time, but it only takes a few ideas that squarely hit the mark to realize that soliciting feedback from knowledgeable others makes great sense.

When it's obvious that the path described or solution proposed by one of your staff offers great potential, act on it. Effective leaders produce results and your role is not one of manipulation; it is one of increasing participation and cooperation, while offering guidance, recognition, and praise when merited.

Provide Challenges, Offer Guidance

Working with others would be a piece of cake if the only tasks you ever requested of them were simple to tackle, easy to complete, and well within their capabilities. In today's workplace, this is a fairy tale. Increasingly, you have to make an unreasonable request and the individual(s) assigned such a task could, at first, squawk. Anticipating such resistance will serve you well.

Your role is to offer staff guidance on how to begin, generate momentum, avoid pitfalls, and proceed to completion. The more challenging the task, the more you need to stay in touch. In the early stages of the project, you could be putting in ten "units" of energy for every one "unit" of output you receive. That's okay. You and your staff are in a concentration mode.

Later, as the project is rolling, you could be putting in ten units and receiving a commensurate return. Ideally, when the project is humming along, one unit of energy then offers ten units of output. Now you've achieved momentum! When the people you supervise experience momentum, your odds of succeeding on the next challenging project increase markedly.

Secrets of Effective Delegators

One of the key approaches to getting things done is to delegate effectively. This presumes that you have others to whom you can delegate. In my work with more than 850 organizations over the last two decades, managers increasingly have fewer resources, a lower budget, and less staff people. To get something done, often they have to do it themselves!

Assuming you have others to whom you can delegate, the first or second time you personally tackle a particular task yields valuable information. You learn more about the nature of the task, perhaps how long it takes, whether you enjoy doing it or not, and so on.

Coming Undone

In the course of your workday there should be only a handful of tasks that you alone need to do because of your experience, insight or specialized knowledge. Everything else that can be delegated should be delegated, otherwise prepare to spend long, intense days attempting to handle everything yourself.

By the third time, a task of the same ilk as those you've handled before often becomes best handled by someone reporting to you. Such tasks could involve entering names into a database, completing an interim report, or assembling meeting notes.

What Can be Delegated, Ought to Be

On the path to getting things done, identify all those tasks that you can possibly delegate to others and then prepare those others so that they have a high probability of succeeding.

Many managers and supervisors fail to delegate effectively because either they don't fully trust the people with whom they're working, or they've always been get-it-all-done-by-myself types. Some managers feel they have to take care of everything themselves and never break the habit of "doing it all."

If someone like that is in your seat right now, recognize once and for all that as a category of "one" you can only accomplish so much.

Media mogul and influential editor H. L. Mencken once said, "For it is mutual trust, more than it is mutual interest that holds human associations together." If you want to rise in your career, assume increasing responsibility, and look forward to raises, master the art of delegating and trust that others can do the job. You might as well start now.

Dyna Moe

People on your staff right now likely can help you with tasks you've been dying to hand off to someone but didn't see how or when you could put them into play.

Delegation Starting from Zero

Sometimes your delegating task poses no mystery. It's part of your job description. Or, based on the type of organization where you work and the job roles assumed by you and your staff, areas for delegation are obvious. Otherwise, here are general guidelines for being an effective delegator:

➤ Prior to delegating anything to anyone, take the time to actually prepare your staff for delegation. This would involve assessing an employee's skills, interests, and needs.

➤ You could even ask people what new tasks and responsibilities they would like to assume. You might be surprised at the wide variety of responses you receive.

➤ While you want to delegate to staff people who show enthusiasm, initiative, and interest, or have previously demonstrated the ability to handle and balance several tasks at once, sometimes you have to delegate to someone who has not exhibited any of the above. In that case, delegate on a piece-meal basis. Ensure that the staff person is able to effectively handle the small task or tasks he's been assigned and does not feel swamped or overloaded.

➤ When a staff person demonstrates competence, you can increase the complexity and frequency of assignments.

Walk Them Through It

The first time you delegate anything to anyone, walk them through exactly what you want them to achieve. Paint a vivid portrait of what things will look like once the task or project is completed.

You could have some instructions to provide or training to offer, but otherwise don't be concerned with how the staff person will proceed. He or she could have a notion or two out of your realm that prove to be suitable and appropriate for the task.

Match up the tasks you wish to delegate with those staff people who have the requisite skills and background. However, don't be afraid to assign someone a task that represents a stretch. This is the way people learn and grow, and a method for developing an increasingly competent staff.

Empower that person by offering guidance at critical junctures. Be available as much as practical, although be careful not to encourage an environment of constant interruptions in which you cannot get anything done. If it helps, plot times for when you two will meet to compare notes. Monitor project progress and offer guidance.

As staff members demonstrate their capabilities on the projects you've delegated, give them more slack in terms of how they'll approach and complete the assignments. Forsake over-controlling.

Ideally, you've delegated enough authority for your staff to successfully complete the tasks by allowing them to make their own decisions and take initiative. You know you've delegated effectively when they're able to operate even in your absence.

Word Power
If something is requisite then it is needed to achieve a desired outcome.

Your Toughest Customer: Your Boss

Unless you run your own organization, you report to someone else, a boss. Your boss is your toughest customer, the person who you have to impress day in and day out. For however long it lasts, your career is linked to this individual regardless of his or her level of competence, personality type, or daily disposition.

Fortunately, your boss is human, same as you. So, it's possible to diagnose your boss to learn how he or she operates and expects others to operate, what makes his day and what ruins it.

Make Your Boss Look Good

To observe and understand your boss, you draw upon the same skills that you've tapped your whole life, and have used with your parents, friends, lovers, teachers, professors, coworkers, and everyone in between.

Per Chapter 3, practice Mark McCormack's notion of "aggressive observation." Specifically, you "read" others by paying attention to their needs. Anyone can do it and become better at working with others. Without even knowing your boss, I'll bet he seeks praise for the work he does. Yet how often do you praise your boss? If your boss has been supportive of you, tell him or her you appreciate it. Be honest in your praise . . . sycophants can be easily spotted.

Dyna Moe

To make your boss look good is no secret — handle your work efficiently and effectively.

Offer Solutions to Your Boss

Regardless of your boss's operating style, he'll be appreciative when you are able to both succinctly identify a problem and have some viable solutions to that problem in mind.

By having solutions ready to propose, you avoid a classic dilemma faced by too many otherwise competent staff people. They are bright, alert, and eager to point out ways the company might be losing customers, market share, or revenue. However, with no solutions in mind, they are simply sirens sounding warnings. Warnings have value, but they mark an individual as rather one-dimensional.

By having solutions in mind, you do both your boss and yourself a favor. Your boss has other issues to handle and is grateful to have ideas about addressing some new problem that emerges. Concurrently, your solution-oriented style conveys the message that you have solid promotion potential. You demonstrate that you are thinking ahead and considering what's best for all.

What if Your Boss Is a Career Roadblock?

If your boss is a terrible taskmaster, a tyrant of the office, insensitive to individual needs, or merely callous, you can still turn gain an advantage.

Working for a boss you don't like could strengthen your ability to deal with people, including good and bad future bosses, and could help you hone your diplomatic skills. If you can coexist with such individuals, your chances of dealing successfully with all others improve.

When your supervisor is an incompetent boss, lacks creativity, and has trouble making decisions, turn the situation to your advantage by taking on more responsibilities.

Perhaps you're working for an insensitive boss who bawls you out for minor mistakes or takes credit for your achievements while neglecting to praise your efforts. It might seem like nothing positive can come from this experience, but don't despair. You're learning one of the most valuable of business lessons: "don't take it personally."

Nothing stops a career achiever in his tracks faster than the tendency to take every callous remark or each instance of a lack of recognition as a personal affront. Don't dwell on these things, move on.

Dyna Moe

Keep doing a good job and uphold the name of your organization. Be professional and take your experiences in stride. Learn and benefit from them, but don't waste energy resurrecting the past.

You're not the only one who notices if your manager's behavior is volatile. Your ability to stay cool and perform well, contrasted with your boss's temper tantrums, could win you kudos from colleagues and from top management. Sometimes you can learn as much from a negative example as from a positive one. Instead of wasting mental energy on the things your boss is doing wrong, contemplate how they could be done right in the future.

CHAPTER 22

Meetings, Meetings, and More Meetings

> ## In This Chapter:
>
> ➤ Pre-interviewing participants
> ➤ Circulating an agenda at the outset
> ➤ Encouraging promptness
> ➤ Conditioning your meeting environment

If you regard meetings as an unproductive way to pass the time and a major intrusion to your day, this chapter is for you!

Some people have such great dislike for meetings that they feel stressed and anxious the moment they learn they have to attend one, let alone conduct one. Despite the fact that many managers dislike calling meetings, and staff often dread attending them, studies show that more people today are spending more time in meetings on a variety of topics and objectives than ever before.

Meetings: Now More Than Ever

The number of meetings being held is on the rise and this is borne out in recent years by workers who report attending an increasing number of meetings, not fewer meetings as one might have expected in this age of audio and video conferencing technology.

It seems that John Naisbitt had it right in *MegaTrends* when he said that as the business world develops more sophisticated technology, the need for face-to-face interaction will increase. He called this phenomenon "high-tech, high-touch."

Factoid

The typical U.S. employee spends about one-third of his or her time in meetings. On any given day in the U.S., about 11 million business meetings are held.

In a 20- to 21-day work month, a typical career professional is likely to attend about 60 meetings of various lengths. Some will be impromptu, small meetings, others will be longer, more formal, and more difficult to endure.

Meetings: The Potential Versus the Reality

Meetings are designed to inform, update, plan, negotiate, sell, and/or review. The typical meeting is arranged by one person to convey information to many people. Ideally, the attendees will contemplate what they heard, generate wonderful ideas, and take bold, decisive action to the delight of the meeting chair. Well, I did say *ideally*.

The realities are that people shuffle in and listen dully to some "stuff" that they have to do or learn, or take back to others. They also doodle, guzzle coffee, clean their fingernails, sneak text messages, and fail to stay awake. Most of what they hear is quickly forgotten.

Senior executives who arrange meetings are more likely to deem them effective than those who were summoned to the meeting. Meeting chairs seem to be more optimistic in their assessment of both the value and results of the meetings they conduct, compared to others attending the meeting. Often, however, whatever the meeting participants are supposed to do is rarely done on time or in the fashion that the meeting manager had sought.

Despite your feelings towards meetings and experience in them, they can serve as an effective and efficient way to aid you and your staff in getting things done.

Let the trumpets sound: a better way exists to conduct meetings to and encourage staff to get things done.

Factoid

Nearly all meeting participants say that they daydream sometimes during meetings and 73 percent of meeting participants admit to doing other work during meetings. Nearly 2 in 5 admit to dozing off at some time during a meeting, hopefully without anyone else noticing.

Get Involved with Participants

The key to conducting a successful meeting is preparation, which you probably didn't want to hear. One study determined that "the amount of time spent on preparation for a meeting characterized as highly productive" was nearly double that of "the preparation time for a meeting described as not very or not at all productive." So, let's talk about preparation . . .

In successful meetings, the person conducting the meeting spends about one unit of time for every two units of meeting time, and one unit of follow-up time. In other words, for a two-hour meeting, about one hour of preparation time is expended, matched by about one hour of follow-up time.

Rope'm in Before It Starts

An effective and organized way to conduct a meeting, and a vital element of preparation, is to elicit in advance the participation of those who will be part of the meeting. It only takes two to four minutes per attendee for you to . . .

➤   speak with people who will be attending the meeting,
➤   prep them as to what's going to occur,
➤   hear their views about what they're going to receive from the meeting, and
➤   make them, in general, partners as opposed to subjects.

If your group meets regularly, pre-ask participants:

➤   What's worked well for you in previous meetings?
➤   How can we proceed so as to involve everyone?
➤   What would you like to derive from this meeting?

Does this sound like more work than it's worth? Consider that meetings aren't held to simply gather a bunch of people in one place; they're held to accomplish something worthwhile.

Pre-Interviewing Boosts Results

Beyond conducting the meeting itself, some managers dread the thought of having to pre-interview the participants. Yet, the process doesn't have to be strenuous if it's conducted in an organized fashion.

If discussing meeting objectives with participants will greatly accelerate progress, why wouldn't you want to do this? The meeting is likely to take less time, and result in greater participation and advancement towards getting more done.

Dyna Moe

Participants routinely report enthusiasm about pre-interviewing. It makes them feel valued, that their input matters. They can anticipate the meeting with a new perspective, since they know that "this one" is going to be different.

Pre-interviewing attendees offers clues on how to proceed:

1. You design a custom agenda that focuses on topics identified as vital to the entire group.
2. You arrange the topics in an order conducive to achieving the group's overall objectives.
3. You pre-circulate the agenda so that participants offer ideas on how and when they can best contribute.

When you implement pre-interviewing, your meeting is more likely to stay on course, end on time, and encourage participants to be more enthusiastic for the next meeting.

Winning Pre-Meeting Points!

Your participants tend to regard you as an organized, competent manager when you pre-interview and provide them with an agenda. As you'll see with the next meeting, when participants have a vested interest in the content of a meeting and when they receive an agenda in advance that specifies the precise starting time, they have another indicator of the importance of being there.

If you're requested to attend a meeting, ask to have the meeting agenda sent to you in advance. If the other party does not have one, ask for a brief outline that highlights the key topics to be covered. Otherwise, you're going in blind.

Staying on Schedule: Not a Minute Too Long

An increasing percentage of meetings now occur within the confines of an organization itself, i.e. fewer meetings are held at conference centers, hotels, and outside facilities, and more meetings within the offices, boardrooms, and the auditoriums of the organizations employing the meeting's participants.

When meetings are held off-site, away from the organization's facilities, and require business travel, most professionals report that they're concerned about their work responsibilities that pile up back at the office during their absence. Yet, long meetings can prove to be satisfying to everyone.

In a study conducted by InfoCom, the longer a meeting's length, surprisingly, the more likely it is deemed to be effective, based on the responses of all those who attend meetings.

For long meetings, the preparation involved might help to increase everyone's focus.

Begin as Scheduled

Regardless of your meeting's length, it is necessary for you, as the meeting manager, to start meetings on time so that stragglers will realize that they are late and that the others, indeed, arrived as scheduled. Organized managers start meetings on time!

Business meeting specialist Robert Levasseur suggests that at the start of any meeting, "participants reach a common understanding of what they're going to do and how they're going to do it." Hence, everyone needs to be present at the start. Levasseur says that this normally takes ten percent of the meeting time, so if you meet for 30 minutes, you need 3 minutes to deal with basic issues such as . . .

➤ the main purpose of the meeting,
➤ the participants' desired outcomes,
➤ the actual agenda itself, and
➤ the key meeting roles, which for smaller groups is understood at the outset.

Issue "Tardy Slips"

Several techniques, which work to varying degrees of effectiveness, encourage promptness. Here are a few:

➤ Require tardy people to apologize to the group. It then becomes their responsibility afterwards to catch up with the group for the parts they missed.
➤ Do not backtrack for late arrivers, it forces everyone to wait while the guilty party receives a personalized briefing.
➤ Lock the meeting room doors (only for the bold!). Anyone who tries to enter late has to knock on the door. Depending on how charitable you're feeling, the knocks could or could not be answered on the first round. Tardy attendees then sheepishly take their seats.
➤ Hand out plum assignments in the first few minutes so that tardy people are left with the least desirable tasks. This is a great incentive for arriving early.

Even after you illustrate how necessary it is to be on-time at your meetings, some individuals might arrive late.

Devise Your Own Method to Encourage Promptness

On my first job, if you were late for a meeting you had to throw a dollar into the kitty for every minute you were late. Nobody ever walked in more than five minutes late. (I have no idea where the money went!)

Learn what works for your participants and determine what steps you'll take to encourage promptness. No coercion is as effective, however, as pre-interviewing

Coming Undone

In some organizations, and this is not my preference, the tardy are the subject of early discussion: they are the target of jokes, gossip, and innuendo. So be late, and be vilified!

participants, circulating an agenda, and repeatedly demonstrating that meetings start as scheduled.

Use Agendas as Game Plans

Most participants honor time frames if they know in advance that a particular item will be allotted five or ten minutes. A tight agenda helps them to stay on track. If someone admits in advance that only three minutes are needed for a particular issue, then that individual is less likely to run on and on and on . . .

Follow the agenda strictly and elicit others' input as needed. Encourage the attendees to participate and as each agenda item is discussed, ask participants to keep in mind: what is the specific issue being discussed, what does the group want to accomplish in discussing the item, and what action needs to be taken to handle the issue?

Dyna Moe

Schedule meetings around breakfast, rather than lunch or dinner. Early in the day, most people will get down to business if they can depart on time. Also, some of the topics that emerge in the meeting can be carried out during the course of the day.

Define, Resolve, and Keep it Moving

When your group identifies the needed action for a particular issue, key questions include who will act, what resources are needed, when will the issue be resolved, and when will the group discuss the results. Upon successful conclusion of these questions, the group moves on to the next issue, then the next.

Not every question needs to be addressed for every issue. Often an agenda item represents an announcement or a report to the group that doesn't require any feedback or discussion. Other times the issue at hand represents an executive briefing, because the matter has already been resolved.

On occasion, discussion ensues and an item ends up taking twice as much time or more than originally allotted. Thankfully, participants often make up for the overflow in one area by being briefer in other areas.

For agenda items that have a corresponding objective, seek progress towards the objective: what else needs to be done, by when, to meet the overall objective? As with any goal or objective they need to be written, quantified, and assigned specific time frames.

Don't Fall Off the Track

You can use a variety of techniques to keep the meeting organized and on track:

➤ Ask participants to keep their remarks within the allotted time frames. Some groups keep a timer in plain sight to encourage everyone to keep their comments brief. Others meet in a room with a wall clock in plain view.

➤ Announce who will speak next and how many minutes are allocated for that topic.

➤ Ask participants to circulate summaries of their comments, charts, or exhibits in advance that illustrate the points they wish to make.

These techniques will vary in effectiveness based on the purpose of your group, how often it meets, and your group's history.

Undershoot So You Can Overshoot

A wise meeting manager might allocate five minutes for a topic that he or she will personally be covering, knowing that it will actually require about three minutes. Hence, several minutes can be saved.

For a meeting that lasts longer than 30 minutes, schedule a break in the middle. Otherwise you'll lose attention of participants who are thinking about sex, getting a tissue, making a phone call, or answering nature's call.

Condition Your Meeting's Environment

The quickest way to lose the participants, other than being a crashing bore, is to conduct your meeting in a room where the environment can be distracting. When the temperature is too high, there is poor ventilation, and the meeting room is dark, you encourage people to fall asleep. It's anthropological —as soon as it's dark, the brain receives a message that it's okay to doze off. A warm, stuffy room only aids the process.(See Chapters 5 and 6 on environment).

Ensure that your meeting room is well lit with excellent ventilation. If you have a choice between having a room be slightly warm or slightly cool, opt for cool. A cool room will keep participants fresh and alert. The discomfort could prompt attendees to complain, but at least no one will go to sleep.

Regardless of where you meet, here are other room-related organizing techniques:

➤ Meet where participants won't be disturbed by ringing phones, people knocking on the door, and other intrusions. You want to achieve a meeting of the minds and accomplish great things; distractions do not help.

➤ Meet in a room with wall-to-wall carpeting and walls adorned with pictures, posters, or curtains to absorb sounds and offer a richer texture to the voices being heard. Contrast this environment with a meeting held on a tile floor, with cold metal chairs, and blank, thin walls. No matter what's being discussed, participants can't wait for the meeting to end when the meeting room feels like a holding cell.

➤ Meet where the seats are comfortable and support the lumbar region of the back. However, overly comfortable seats could have a detrimental effect and encourage people to nod off.

Have Sufficient Equipment Available

Meeting participants appreciate well planned meetings that serve as a forum for them to contribute their thoughts and ideas. Such meetings can make a meaningful contribution to employee job satisfaction.

If participants need to take notes or work from laptops or tablets, make sure there are effective flat surfaces on which they can work. Pens, pads, cold water, and possibly tea or coffee should also be available.

Set up and double check out recorders, projectors, slides, chalkboards, whiteboards, and any other equipment long before the meeting begins. Also check for replacement batteries, light bulbs, extension cords, and all supporting equipment in advance.

Avoid Conduct Becoming of a Leader

Maintain a supportive atmosphere for all participants; otherwise, comments come off as edicts (i.e. "I say, you do," "I command, you obey, insect"). Edicts don't encourage people to attend meetings even when vital and interesting topics are covered.

Serve as a facilitator. You elicit the best of responses from participants, encouraging them to cooperate with one another, and encouraging them to function as a team (see Chapter 24 on handling conflict within teams).

Word Power

A facilitator is a person who assists an assembled group of people to identify their common goals and help them to achieve such goals without assuming a particular viewpoint.

Follow-up with Your Attendees

Effective meeting managers speak with participants afterwards to learn if participants thought the meeting was useful, what could be added, what could be dropped, and how the meeting could be improved. The manager collects these suggestions, ruminates on them, and incorporates those that offer a notable contribution.

Some managers, in the erroneous attempt to "save time," don't bother to gather any feedback from participants following a meeting. They figure that their own observations were plenty, so why bother taking the time to consult with others?

Software to Keep You on Track

Meeting management software has grown in popularity. Such software is designed to help manage all meeting functions such as initial planning—even helping to determine if there needs to be a meeting at all—meeting objectives, and meeting outcomes.

Meeting management software provides a web-browser interface that allows the meeting planner to disseminate the agenda and meeting materials prior to the meeting, as well as to assign tasks for before and after the meeting. Such software also helps the meeting planner make decisions, establish action steps, archive meeting notes and ideas, address follow-up issues, and identify topics and agenda items for future meetings.

Examples of meeting management software include www.smartworks.us and www.mba ware.com/meetmansof.html. If you conduct lots of meetings, it pays to check these out.

 Influencing With or Without Authority

In This Chapter:

➤ They like me, they really like me

➤ Emotion precedes logic

➤ Doing everyone a favor

➤ Self-confidence works wonders

In this chapter, we discuss exerting influence without necessarily having authority (based on your job position). Happily, such methods work more than well when you do have job position authority.

Being Liked Is Half the Battle

Ten years and seven score ago, Abraham Lincoln said to "win a person to your cause, convince him that you are his true friend." Did he mean you're supposed to feign friendship? Can you elicit cooperation and participation only when others regard you as a true and lasting friend? Unless you're liked or respected, you won't be able to win others to your cause?

"D," none of the above.

Inducing others to be on your side or to participate with you when you can't otherwise compel them to do so, in part, requires that they have some degree of affinity with you, what you're seeking to accomplish, or the situation itself.

> ## Coming Undone
> When working with others to get things done, much of the time you're not necessarily in a position of authority. The people with whom you're working might not report to you, be responsible to you, or care about what you're seeking to accomplish.

Robert Cialdini, Arizona State University Regents' Professor Emeritus of Psychology and Marketing, who has studied persuasion for 30 years says, "Though we don't always realize it, we're more likely to be influenced by people we like or identify with."

I Like You, Do You Like Me?

In his book, *Get Anyone to Do Anything and Never Feel Powerless Again*, David Lieberman states that "how someone feels about you is greatly determined by how you make them feel about themselves. You can spend all day trying to get them to like you and to think well of you, but it is how you make them feel when they are around you that is the key."

> ## Coming Undone
> Hard-driving, get-it-done-at-all-cost types can miss the forest for the trees in associating with others, more so if they regard people as a means to an end rather than unique individuals in association with each other to pursue common objectives.

Hmmm, have you given any thought to how peers, co-workers, or staff, feel when they are around you? Or are you too concerned with how you feel when you're around them?

Lieberman describes *reciprocal affection* which means that when we learn that someone thinks well of us, we're unconsciously driven to think that person is more likeable. It is simply human nature to do so. When those individuals whom you want to influence are aware that you actually like and/or respect them, you increase the probability that they will like and/or respect you as well. Then, all kinds of things are possible.

Second and Lasting Impressions

Amazingly, you can induce people to like or respect you even when you've long known them and the relationship hasn't gone well. Lieberman poses the question "Who says you can't get a second chance at a first impression?" If you did something completely inappropriate, by leveling with the other party—"I feel so embarrassed"— you open the door to future participation and cooperation.

Studies show that leaders of countries, from a U.S. President to the leader of a small and distant sovereignty, achieve higher approval ratings when they own up to their blunders, however grave they could be, as opposed to attempting to whitewash them.

Dyna Moe

Extending yourself after acting inappropriately demonstrates that you're aware of your previous, unacceptable behavior. This conveys to others that you're not likely to repeat the behavior. It also shows that you have the potential to be one of the "gang," someone who takes responsibility for your actions.

At work, when you're willing to admit to a previous faux pas, you win psychological strokes that reduce people's barriers to participation and cooperation, not that you do this as a ploy. Still, it's fruitful to understand how and why people are persuaded.

Emotion First, Logic Second

Bert Decker, who wrote *You've Got to Be Believed to Be Heard*, says that "people buy on emotion and justify with fact." If you're old enough to remember President Jimmy Carter, you could recall that his primary approach to influencing others was to appeal to their intellect, using logical explanations and rational thought. The problem with this approach is that people first need to be won over emotionally.

David Lieberman remarks that 90 percent of the decisions we make are based on emotion. "We use logic to justify our actions," says Lieberman. "But if you appeal to someone on a strictly logical basis, you'll have little chance of persuading them."

Carter's successor, Ronald Reagan, knew how to appeal to people's emotions. For

Factoid

Speaking coach Bert Decker says, "Likeability is the shortest path to believability and trust." The fastest and easiest way to start this train in motion—to be liked—is to smile.

openers, he smiled a lot and the smiles seemed sincere. To influence others, he told stories, employed facial expressions, and injected personal warmth and magnetism.

When people were primed and ready, Reagan then would deliver the rational portion of the argument. He'd hold up a chart or refer to some data. By waiting until he had first made the emotional connection, he was then able to make the logical connection.

Bert Decker succinctly observes, "If you don't believe in someone on an emotional level, little if any of what they have to say will get through."

Reagan was deemed a more effective presenter, and as such, a more effective president than Carter among media pundits from all sides of the political spectrum. Today, Carter's speeches are all but forgotten and his presentation style is emulated by no one, whereas Regan is referred to as the "Great Communicator."

Persuasion as a Science

The aforementioned Robert Cialdini is a pioneer in the study of persuasion and has made breakthrough discoveries. He poses the question, "Have you ever purchased a product or service that proved to be of little value, or have you ever voted for an issue which, upon reflection, you're not in favor of? Of course! We all have, but why?

"Even then smartest people fall prey to sophisticated persuaders," says Cialdini. He has identified ways one can tap powerful instincts within others to both influence and persuade them.

Reciprocity is a Strong Factor Between People

When another person does a favor for you, even a small one, do you feel obligated to offer some favor in return? Cialdini conducted a study where restaurant waiters delivered the bill for the meal along with two free mints for each diner. The results, all other things being equal, were that tips increased by 14 percent.

At work, if you offer to help someone, say in another department, and then in two weeks, a month, or two months later you ask them to help you, their inclination rises markedly.

People are often helpful simply for the sake of being helpful and undoubtedly you have both given and received help under such circumstances. However, if you need the help of others outside of your direct authority, relying on reciprocity works well.

Factoid
Reciprocity is a tool of persuasion that the movers and shakers among us have used since the dawn of civilization and will continue to be a powerful tool in the future.

More than 80 years ago, Dale Carnegie proclaimed that when a person does a favor for someone else, the person doing the favor tends to have positive feelings towards the person he helps. Doing favors for each other increases the likelihood that both parties will have a more favorable regard for the other.

What about those individuals within your organization, or outside of it for that matter, for whom you've already done favors? What about those people who have done favors for you within recent memory? Right now, the people in these two groups represent the universe of individuals who you can most readily influence, even if they are not under your job-related authority.

To increase your circle, do more favors for others and request more favors from others. In each case, proceed with sincerity and a genuine desire to help. Thereafter, don't be surprised if your ability to get things done in participation and cooperation with others rises significantly.

How to Encourage "Buy-in"

Residents of a neighborhood were asked to sign a petition supporting a charity for the disabled. Two weeks later they were asked for contributions for that charity. Double the funds were collected from that neighborhood than in previous campaigns.

"Most residents dug more deeply into their pockets," says Cialdini, "because they wanted to be consistent with how they responded to the petition."

Consistency is also known as buy-in. Induce people to commit in small ways to a product or service, a charity or cause, or even an idea, and later it will be easier to gain greater commitment.

In the workplace, and specifically in your career, if you have an idea that you wish to put into action, or a project that you want to complete, rather than seeking in one motion to influence people to jump in whole-heartedly, instead, seek their approval on some minor component of what you're attempting to accomplish.

Thereafter, you'll have less resistance to their participation at a higher level.

You might divide up your appeal into steps, although inducing one or two small incidences of buy-in could be sufficient. Inducing buy-in, or applying the consistency principle ties into another tool of influence, social validation—the "bandwagon" effect.

Social Validation Impacts Us All

You've been exposed to social validation techniques since you were a toddler. Every time you watch a television commercial, you see images of happy, satisfied people whose lives have improved dramatically as a result of using the product being advertised.

When you watch an infomercial and the voice-over says, "Our switchboard is jammed, please call back in a few minutes," this is a not-so-subtle way of conveying that the item for sale is in such demand that other viewers can't wait to make a purchase.

Yeah, right . . . Nevertheless, people are notably influenced by what other people are already doing.

Cialdini refers to a study conducted by City University of New York which revealed that when a single person on the street stared up at the sky, only one in 25 passers-by looked up. When several people were staring at the sky, 20 of 25 passers-by looked up to see what the group was looking at.

Word Power
Social validation occurs when people make choices by observing the decisions others have made before them.

In the workplace, particularly when you are not in authority, if you have already won over others on your project, inducing others can be easier. The advocates you have won over—as a result of exchanging favors, or otherwise inducing them to buy in—increases your odds of getting others to jump on the "bandwagon" to where ever you are leading it. Your converts can serve as missionaries, selling others on your ideas. This is how all religions started.

Authority is a Powerful Influencer

When you visit the doctor's office for the first time and see a wall full of degrees, licenses, and diplomas, even if you know nothing else about that physician, you have been influenced.

Similarly, when someone comes into your office to repair the copier or some large, complex piece of equipment, the fact that he or she is wearing a uniform with the manufacturer logo or insignia increases your readiness to trust that person, even if you have never worked with him or her before.

Whether or not you have a position of authority, in influencing others in the workplace you can increase your level of perceived authority by displaying appropriate symbols and trappings. What would these include? If you have any degrees, licenses, or diplomas, put them on the wall. If you've won awards, been cited for any reason, have received plaques, been featured in articles, display those as well.

Pedigrees after your name, such as Ph.D. or MBA, or a professional certification such as CPA (certified public accountant) or CMC (certified management consultant) work well. Such degrees, awards, and

Dyna Moe
Have you ever had a photo taken with a politician or celebrity? If so, a picture with a nice frame, positioned so that others can see when they enter your office, conveys that you are someone of prominence.

designations take years to earn, but some people who have them, for whatever reason, downplay them.

What academic and professional distinctions and kudos have you earned that you are not employing to optimal advantage?

Just the Basics: Write and Speak

Beyond degrees, awards, and designations, other ways to establish your authority are to get published in newspapers, magazines, journals, and even your own organization's in-house publications.

Writing articles for publication is a proactive strategy for establishing your career. If you've ever considered writing an article but hesitated, be assured that it's not as difficult as it could seem. Most publications routinely edit your material. They're more interested in receiving interesting themes and concepts submitted by people with the right qualifications.

Your Byline, Your Credentials

Regardless of your field, you have information that will be of interest to your peers or clients. Don't make the common mistake of thinking, "Who would want to read something written by me?" That's a defeatist and unrealistic attitude. With thousands of magazines, newspapers, journals, and newsletters in print, and web-related publishing opportunities, several million bylined articles appear in the U.S. alone each year. A significant number of those are by first-time authors.

All other things being equal, if you've had a couple of articles published, you're better positioned to influence others than someone who hasn't. In a nutshell, getting published . . .

➤ positions you as an expert in the article subject area.

➤ makes for attractive reprints—you can create a favorable impression by supplying co-workers, peers, staff members, and bosses with reprints of an article you've had published. Of course, be discreet to avoid seeming egotistical.

➤ enhances visibility for you and your organization: always mention your organization in your bio when you write an article. For example, "Joe Smith is a manager of XYZ Corporation." Your article therefore will market both you and your organization.

Coming Undone
Some organizations are sensitive about publicity and would prefer not to be mentioned in connection with an employee's activities. Check out your organization's policies before proceeding.

Thereafter, appropriately displaying or circulating reprints will further add to your air of authority. The benefits of getting published can continue for a surprisingly long time.

Lend Me Your Ears: Power Speech

Speaking to groups, even groups outside of your organization, ultimately will enhance your status as an authority within your organization. Bruce Barton, an American congressman in the mid-twentieth century, once said, "In my library are about a thousand volumes of biography—a rough calculation indicates that more of these deal with men who have talked themselves upward than all the scientists, writers, saints, and doers combined. Talkers have always ruled. And they will continue to rule. The smart thing is to join them."

What you say could be less important than the fact that you are able to say it with confidence. Others will pick up on your knowledge and devotion to the issue.

At the most basic level, as you improve your speaking abilities and your level of self-confidence—the two generally go hand-in-hand—you register a notable impact among those you encounter on the job. Even if you don't pursue opportunities to speak to groups internally or externally to your organization, increasing your level of self-confidence has a succinct and highly favorable effect on others, particularly others you wish to influence.

Self-Confidence: Vital to Influencing Without Authority

Self-confidence, and lack thereof, is the difference between a chocolate cheesecake and Jell-O. When you do not have job-related authority, self-confidence is a prerequisite to influencing because you become a more appealing employee and co-worker, and hence your likeability factor rises.

To increase your level of self-confidence learn from and emulate those who already have it. Psychologist Dr. Judy Kuriasky says, "Imitation is, after all, a key to learning. If you're attracted to self-confidence in others, it's a good bet that you have the capacity for greater self-confidence in yourself. That which we like or envy in others usually reflects our own values."

Imitation is a major part of learning in our early years of life but can still work well in adulthood. Simply identify the people around you who seem to have the attention of others, and watch how they behave. Is it how they work, what they say, or how they carry themselves that attracts attention?

Select one small behavior at a time and emulate it!

"I Will," not "I Could"

Self-confidence comes from feeling that you deserve to have and be what you want. A confident person writes a project proposal that says, "My project will accomplish xyz for our organization." A less confident employee says, "My project could accomplish xyz"... phrasing that might communicate the employee's own doubt.

Confidence means taking a positive approach that rubs off on other people, causing them to view you as more appealing, whether you work on software applications, in accounting, or with a forklift in the warehouse. Others around you will sense your confidence and buy in to what you're selling.

Whatever you do on the job or in your personal life, you are more likely to do it well if you expect to succeed than if you expect mediocrity or failure. While others are consumed by self-doubt, belief in yourself and your ability to generate solutions to nagging problems can be one of your strongest attributes.

Self-doubts compromise your appeal. Worse, it's difficult for you to effectively market yourself. It's like trying to sell a product you don't believe in. Your doubt hobbles your efforts, ultimately sabotaging your progress.

So much of what we do, both at and away from work, is in cooperation with other people. When others sense that you are confident, they want to be around you, support you, and even be like you. Conversely, people tend to avoid someone who is continually worried, hesitant, or skeptical.

In the workplace, many co-workers could know next to nothing about one another. Conversant people are more likely to be viewed and treated as confident people. Getting to know the people around you will make it easier later to approach others with a project idea or to ask for a favor. A self-confident person attracts fellow employees and creates positive partnerships within the company, thereby strengthening the overall fabric of the workplace instead of weakening it.

> **Dyna Moe**
>
> It's enticing for people to be around someone with a positive, enthusiastic, can-do attitude. They will go to bat for you and generally assist you in being as effective as you can be.

Accentuate the Positive

When you dwell on your mistakes, they can drag down your positive attitude. Instead, see them as lessons, stepping stones to a higher vantage point from which you can obtain more knowledge and wisdom. Be glad you've learned a lesson, and seek to avoid making that mistake again.

Becoming confident is not about perfection; confidence is about recognizing your ability to achieve your goals and weathering the occasional storms you encounter. Consider everything you typically accomplish in a day—even the small tasks. When you add it all up, you might be surprised at the length of the list of and complexity of the tasks.

Perhaps you have capabilities and skills you hadn't previously acknowledged or valued sufficiently. Don't think all is lost if the big victories elude you for now.

Dyna Moe

Conveying your best qualities in the workplace can help you to influence others that you normally would have no authority over.

The smallest achievements can provide solid building blocks for increased confidence and appeal. From there, effectively influencing others is well within your capabilities.

CHAPTER 24

Assembling a Winning Team

In This Chapter:

➤ Work with the best or suffer like the rest

➤ When teams gel

➤ Negotiation comes in handy

➤ Conflict is inevitable

This chapter discusses how each team is a unique entity in the universe, the members of which thrive on understanding, autonomy, responsibility, and supervision.

Assembling a winning team means being able to lead your team through the rigors of challenging projects. It's more than scheduling meetings, speaking to your team members, and broadcasting e-mail messages. It calls for an interpersonal connection with each member of the team.

Veteran team leaders understand that their overall ability to get things done is largely dependent on the quality level of the individuals added to the team. You want to start with good people—there's no substitute for this! A team is more than the sum of the individuals who comprise it. Still, the more competent your staff members, the more competent your team.

Nurturing-type Organizations Enhance Your Ability to Succeed

The organization where you're employed can help propel or thwart your efforts. Good organizations help you be your best. Such organizations have a track record for supporting teams, reward team leaders for taking appropriate risks, and have a realistic notion of what types of resources you'll require in pursuit of your task or project. Unsupportive organizations tend to do the opposite.

You have the best chance to succeed when each of your team members reports to you and no one else. Unfortunately, your team members could be reporting to you as well as other team leaders. You might have one staff person on board for 60 percent of his time, another for 20 percent and another for 100%.

If your staff is pulled in many directions with responsibilities for other tasks and projects, and cannot offer the requisite concentration and energy for your project, you'll have to make the best of the situation. Your job as team leader will be more difficult, with slower progress and likely less enjoyment.

Teams of Different Stripes

In simplest terms, a team is an assembly of individuals who gather together to accomplish a particular objective. Presumably, these individuals working in unison will accomplish more than any single individual could accomplish, and if the team is effective, will create a synergistic effect.

Word Power
Synergy is when one plus one equals more than two.

Two people working as a team should be able to accomplish much more than the sum of what each individual would accomplish on his own. A group of three should accomplish more than what three individuals working on their own would accomplish.

Different types of teams are more suited for different types of tasks:

➤ *High performance teams*, which can be anywhere from four, five, or six people up to as many as 12, are committed to both achieving the team's overall objectives, as well as to one another's individual growth, success, and personal experience.

➤ A *team* has been described as a small group of people with complimentary skills. While holding themselves mutually accountable, they are focused on a common goal or objective, and strive effectively to achieve their objective.

➤ A *workgroup* consists of individuals who exchange information, perspectives, or procedures that help one another perform more competently in his or her area of responsibility. Members of the workgroup generally don't share a common purpose and do not participate with one another in joint projects, at least those that would otherwise require a team approach. Nevertheless, members of a workgroup can be highly supportive of one another and offer support on a continuing basis.

Of these three types of assemblies, the high performance team has the greatest potential for synergy and superior performance in pursuit of specific accomplishments.

For the discussion hereafter, the term "team" will be used to mean two or more people who have assembled to accomplish a specific task or project.

Dyna Moe

Depending on where you work, what you're seeking to accomplish, and how large or small your team could be, nearly endless variations exist as to what form your team will take and what they're capable of accomplishing.

More Members, Greater Complexity

The larger the size of your team, the more complexity. This could seem obvious, but perhaps you have not contemplated the level of complexity as a team moves from, say, three to five members. On a two person team, there's only one connection, between you and the other person. With a three-person team, the number of connections is three, as indicated in the diagram below.

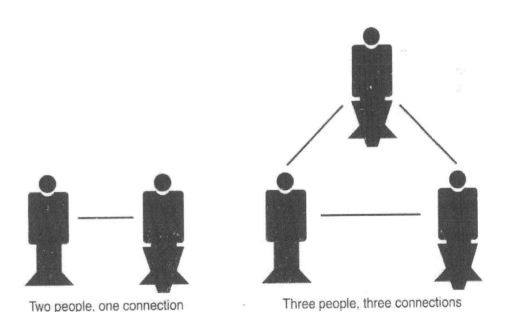

Two people, one connection   Three people, three connections

As the number of team members increase so does complexity

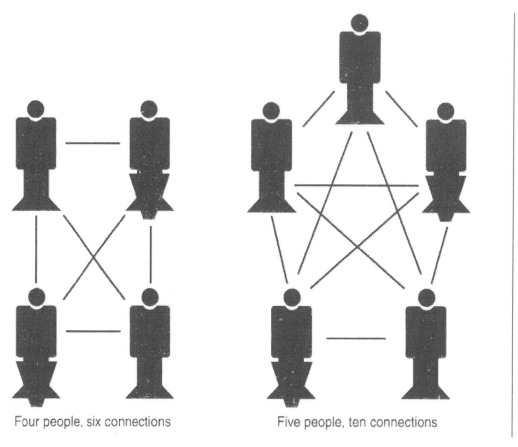

Four people, six connections   Five people, ten connections

As the number of team members increase so does complexity

With a four-person team, the number of possible connections grows to six, and with five it grows to ten. With a six person team, the number of interpersonal connections grows to a whopping 15.

The fewer number of team members you require to accomplish what you seek to get done, the fewer connections, the less complexity, and potentially the greater harmony. Not that great things can't be accomplished with teams of six or more people. Still, you have to pay homage to the increase in geometric complexity as more people are added to a team.

Assembling the Highest Quality Team Members

Starting with you and no other team members, you seek to recruit the highest quality team members you can, assign them roles and responsibilities commensurate with their skills and capabilities, and ensure that they work smoothly with one another.

You are fortunate if you're given the opportunity to pick your own team members. You have a decent chance of choosing staff members who have the skills and capabilities, as well as strengths and weaknesses that compliment other team members.

Dyna Moe
By deploying your staff members for the highest good—in a manner that is both worthy of them and supportive of you—you increase the probability of accomplishing the desired objective.

Are There Safe Selections?

If you can choose people who you already know, or with whom you've already worked, you're ahead of the game. Perhaps as a result of exchanging favors with individuals throughout your organization (see Chapter 23 on influencing with or without authority), you have a reasonable idea of who to select.

If people who wind up on your team are complete strangers to you, fear not. You can still achieve admirable results. Many a team assembled out of the blue, never having worked with one another, find their groove and accomplish great things.

The downside of being able to choose your own team members is that your built-in biases and prejudices will prevail. You might end up choosing people who think like you, act like you, or even talk like you.

As many team managers learn, whether you choose staff members or have them assigned to you, you don't know how things will proceed until you're tested by fire. Once you begin working on a project, with long hours together, have many opportunities for cooperation or lack thereof, you then see whether or not the team has the potential to gel, meet the project challenges, and prevail.

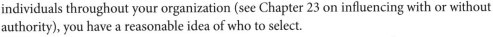

Build a Foundation

Whether handpicked, assigned, or some combination of the two, team members need to know one another. First-time team leaders can be overly eager to tackle the tasks at hand. The longer the project, the more critical it is to devote time and effort in the early stages to forming bonds between team members, defining and clarifying roles, and learning about one another as individuals. From there, communication patterns emerge. You can more easily formulate a schedule that all team members understand and follow.

Getting-to-know-you sessions allow and encourage team members to speak up, share their views, and feel at ease about being on the team. Particularly for long campaigns, it makes sense to establish an orientation plan.

Orientation Sensation: Enable Team Members to Bond

The time and energy you invest in helping team members to establish bonds with one another and to feel as if they're part of a cohesive unit is seldom wasted. The payoff comes in the level of cooperation among team members.

If some or all of your team members already know each other, then obviously the time you have to invest in orientation can be shorter than if a group of complete strangers is getting together for the first time. In either case though, it behooves you to review the fundamentals, such as who reports to whom, how resources are allocated, how to order supplies, and so on.

As the new team is assembled, you can call upon each member of the group during orientation to introduce themselves. If team members already know one another, have each team member speak about what he would like to accomplish or air any concerns he might have.

Ground Rules for All

When it's your time to speak, after saying a little about yourself, focus on the team ground rules, such as how time will be allocated and how much money will be spent. Also talk about the internal hierarchy within the team in case some team members might report to others, rather than to you.

Team members could have more questions that need to be addressed, such

Dyna Moe

The more issues you air at the outset, the greater your chance of heading off potential problems such as individual power-plays, hidden agendas, and bottled up frustrations.

as the following:

➤ Can we get in touch with you after hours?
➤ Will other team members be added later?
➤ What if we need to add outside resources?
➤ How do we authorize payments for needed supplies or equipment?
➤ Where will we store project resources?
➤ To what degree can we share team information with outsiders?

If it helps, establish common terminology, so that team members know the difference between, say, putting a rush on something versus handling it as soon as possible. Craft your own exhibits such as the example shown that follows and share them group wide so that everyone is singing from the same hymnal!

A Hierarchy of Requests

1. As Soon As Possible: Drop everything else, and finish as quickly as you can.
2. Highest Priority: Put this at the top of your to-do list.
3. Please Rush: Please complete this and report back quickly.
4. Priority: Put this task high up on your to-do list.
5. Crucial: Handle this when you can, but soon.
6. For Your Information: Look at it once, if you want to.

By surfacing basic operational issues at the outset, burdens that you alone might have had to assume can be alleviated.

You Can't Think of Everything.

You're not omniscient. You can't be on top of it all. It is to your benefit to have team members conversing, sharing ideas, and surfacing issues early in the game. In general, issues identified at early-round meetings help to head off problems that likely would have emerged later.

Everyone wants to feel as if he or she is a valuable addition to the team. And no one wants to be completely managed. People prefer to collaborate. They are more than willing to acknowledge you as the team leader, but they don't want you to be autocratic.

Their highest level of contribution often directly relates to the degree to which they believe managerial information is shared freely with them.

Competent and responsible professional staff members increasingly seek to gain access to the reports and management documents that you, as team leader, are privy to. If you've been a play-it-closely-to-the-chest type of manager until now, you might want to let go of the reins a little.

Chart Progress Individually and Collectively

To increase the propensity that you're all working in unison toward a final objective, each team member needs to have access to the project management tools that you employ, such as Gantt or milestone charts, PERT charts, flowcharts, calendar tracking, and any project management or scheduling software (see Chapter 13).

When team members have the opportunity to review Gantt or PERT charts and can observe how their current progress impacts the progress of fellow team members, the probability increases that each team member will perform as required. After all, no one wants to look at a chart and discover that he or she is holding up the works!

Dyna Moe

Project management charts offer a pictorial look at how individual team member contributions support the overall project. Often, meetings, discussions, memos, and messages can't convey the same immediate impact.

When all players have a vivid understanding of their roles and how they are interrelated, then group cohesiveness, uniformity, and peer pressure can generate significant input. As much as anything, sticking to the project schedule is fueled by each team member realizing the importance of his individual role, what it means to the team as a whole to stay on track and how responsibilities interconnect.

As team leader, once you're assured that each of your team members possesses this level of realization, the potential for you to complete the project on time and within budget rises markedly. Peer pressure alone can often do the trick!

Something Borrowed: Teams Members

More often than not, you will be asked to assemble a team that consists mostly of individuals who participate only on a part-time basis. It's not the best of all worlds, but depending on the talents and skills of team members, you might have more than enough to see you through to successful completion.

If you have to borrow staff from other departments and divisions within your organization, dust off your negotiation skills. To recruit your staff, you could find yourself bargaining with the people in production, marketing, accounting, or finance. Even if successful, you might then have to negotiate with team members themselves as to how much energy and effort they can realistically expend on your project.

Make One Sale After Another

In some instances, you might have to sell your project to others if it is going to start at all!

If there is predictable resistance from other managers to letting go of their good staff, why do they do it at all? They could be loyal and dedicated employees of the organization who recognize it's for everyone's good. Some managers realize that they might have to make the same types of requests of you. Some are forced to partially let go of staff people. Some see it as inevitable.

Factoid

The people you would like to have on your team often are the most skilled and talented around -- the same people that other project managers are least likely to want to share.

As a team leader, don't be surprised if you find yourself in a continuing tug-of-war with other team leaders for talented staff people. This is the terrain of contemporary management and it's not likely to change in the short run.

Paint the Picture for Your Staff

As mentioned, even when you get clearance from other managers to recruit talented staff for your team, you have to sell your team on the mission. Here, you draw upon every ounce of influence you can muster, everything you've learned about persuasion, whatever you know about packaging, positioning, merchandising, and successfully luring others.

You use your passion as a driving force. See Chapter 3. You paint a picture of what it will be like to realize the achievement. You convey a sense of excitement while remaining honest and above board.

You don't want to over-sell or make promises that you can't keep. It is one thing to successfully recruit people to be on your team, it's quite another when they realize that you lied about how the project would unfold and what their experiences would be.

Telling the Truth Works Wonders

Once you've successfully recruited talented staff, maintain your passion. Until they embrace the project as their own, team members will feed off of your energy. You'll know if you've assembled a winning staff when their energies feed off of one another, much like a baseball team proceeding toward the pennant in late September.

Just as you were truthful in recruiting skilled and talented employees to be part of your team, be truthful as you proceed along the path to getting something done.

When you leave out critical facts, or paint a rosy picture on how the team is progressing, you could hinder performance because you're preventing your staff members from seeing reality. How can each of your team members succeed at their assigned roles if they don't know the true situation? As your project ensues, telling the truth becomes more vital than merely relating good news.

Learn to Roll With the Punches

It's frustrating for team leaders when they assemble the right people, establish the right action plan, and find that progress isn't anywhere near what they envisioned. You've got to stay loose, and be willing to turn on a dime.

Flexible team leaders finish first. Inflexible team leaders are mired in what went wrong. Adopt the mind set that setbacks and mistakes are inevitable, and they also represent opportunities for learning, redirection, and growth.

Coming Undone

If you convey to team members that mistakes won't be tolerated, they play it safe, proceed with caution, and do no more than is asked of them. When fear prevails, your role is more challenging.

Mistakes Happen, It's What Happens Next that Counts

Create an environment that says, "We strive to do our best, but sometimes mistakes will happen." When team members know that you won't blow your top and can handle some of the inevitable bumps in the road, they're more willing to: 1) take appropriate risks, 2) accept responsibility for their mistakes, 3) learn from them, and 4) move on.

The more challenging the project, the tighter the time frame, the more restrictive the budget, the more likely that mistakes will occur. Seek to have everyone acknowledge them for what they are, and ascertain if any opportunities result from the mistake.

Dyna Moe

When team members receive support for assuming responsibilities for the mistakes they've made, they find it easier to critically self-assess their own performance. That tends to make them even better employees than they were before.

The knowledge and even wisdom that team members gain as a result of their mistakes, shared with the group can sometimes benefit the entire project.

How Am I Doing So Far?

People at all levels prefer to be held accountable for the work they do. They also want to receive regular feedback as to how they're doing. When you give them appropriate feedback, they know what they're doing right, they know what they're doing wrong, and they can learn and improve. If you go too long without giving people feedback, they wonder if you're noticing at all, or if you even care.

Some team leaders make the mistake of not giving feedback to highly competent staff, figuring they already know they're doing a good job, so why bother with excess verbiage? Like partners in a loving relationship, people want to know on a continuing basis that their partners still want them above all else. So too, your team members want to hear from you, even if you only offer performance feedback as infrequent as once a day.

When Conflict Arises

If you have the knowledge and skills of Peter Drucker, Ph.D., the premiere management guru of the twentieth century, conflict between you and team members, or between team members themselves, still, is unavoidable. Many team leaders regard conflict as something to be avoided at all costs—not a sound approach to team leadership.

When conflict is left untouched, it can fester, grow at an alarming rate, and upend a team's progress.

The Basic Types of Conflict

It's best to identify conflict as it emerges. Generally, you encounter two basic types of conflict. With the first type, a single team member has problems relating to someone else on the team, or the entire team itself. Such conflict can result in jealousy, hostility, distrust, disharmony, or withdrawal.

The other type of conflict you'll encounter has to do with the appropriateness of a procedure or a particular task or assignment, or how the group itself is managing its resources. Since this type of conflict is not based on personalities of team members, conflict could have resulted regardless of who is on the team.

Anecdotes for Each Conflict

Fortunately, with both types of conflicts, antidotes abound. By allowing underlying issues to emerge, a team can sweep away some barriers early in a project, while they're still relatively easy to deal with, and hence help to establish an environment that leads to project success.

With conflict between individual team members, by surfacing the issues and having both parties air their grievances, the entire team can benefit. Sometimes you're able to identify and dislodge other issues that would have come up much later.

In a climate of exploration and of mutual understanding, you can deal with the conflict. This opportunity won't emerge in a climate of passivity or ignorance.

In addressing the second type of conflict, recognize that it can be constructive, energizing, and motivating. In some instances, this type of conflict fuels progress rather than thwarts it.

Dyna Moe

Sometimes it's best to take time out from the overall project, perhaps have a half-day retreat, and let team members join together in an atmosphere of cooperation and trust.

You can help members to recognize that they share some deep-rooted values and common aspirations.

The synergy that you derive from holding such sessions can pay for itself in terms of team member's increased energy and renewed commitment to the project.

 # Partnering Strategies to Get Things Done

This chapter discusses how it helps if your and your partner(s) proceed with the same intensity as you strive to get things done.

"United we stand, divided we fall."
"Birds of a feather flock together."
"No man is an island."
"Either we all hang together, or we all hang separately."

Partnering with those around you might determine whether or not you accomplish something big. There is something encouraging, stimulating, and inspiring about partnering with others who are seeking to achieve the same goals that you are. It also helps if you're striving for the same goal at the same time, such as two workers studying for a career-related exam.

Potent Professional Peers are All Around

Of all the possible others with whom you could combine forces, your professional peers are your easiest to identify and join in partnership. Your peers consist of co-workers, other people in your line of work, and others with whom you have a rather natural and easy communication channel.

Peer group partnerships tend to be more fluid, though potentially as powerful as any of the other types of groups. Undoubtedly you already belong to one or more peer groups consisting of two or more people.

A peer group by any other name . . . below is a sampling of the names attributed to peer groups although, what you call your affiliation is not nearly as important as how you work together and what you're able to achieve.

Partners All

• Affiliates	• Friends	• Partners
• Comrades	• Team members	• Colleagues
• Principals	• Co-venturers	• Joint venturers
• Cohorts	• Collaborators	• Class mates
• Help mates	• Mates	• Group members
• Founders	• Crew members	• Staff members
• Contributors	• Associates	• Helpers

Terms of Affiliation

• Band	• Team	• Crew
• Union	• Unit	• Assembly
• Conglomerate	• Party	• Council
• Task force	• Skunk works	• Commission
• Committee	• Board	• Advisory board
• Cabinet	• Congress	• Parliament

Managers and staff people in other departments and divisions who have no formal role in what you're working on could serve as valuable resources. Depending on their education, background, and experiences in general, you could find selected individuals who can serve as ad hoc trail guides, at least pointing you in the right direction.

Dyna Moe

Every time you encounter another co-worker you potentially open yourself up to a world of opportunities, knowledge, contacts and influence that you can not realize based on a brief encounter.

Consider this: a quick well-delivered phone call to one of these valuable contacts, a one-line e-mail, or a brief encounter in the hallway could result in you getting the right input at just the right time to propel your project or task forward.

The Care and Feeding of Partners

In professional services, accountants, dentists, doctors, attorneys, engineers, and real estate agents usually launch firms as business partnerships. Changes in tax, liability, and estate planning have combined to make the corporate form of organization more viable for many professional service firms.

Coming Undone

Fifty-fifty partnerships sound fine but can lead to far more squabbles than when there is a clear leader. When parties have equal rank and no one is in command, the chance of stalemates rises on given issues.

When two friends form a partnership, trouble can loom because their friendship itself can hinder them. If they've gotten along well for years, each could assume that the same relationship is possible in a business setting, however it's wise to be wary. Partnerships at work are a different animal.

Despite the pitfalls, something special can occur between partners who draw out the best in each other.

As long as partners respect the capability or contributions of the other, partnerships can go on and on, independent of what type of relations the individuals have otherwise.

Partnering With Customers or Clients

Partnering with customers or clients can prove to be rewarding as well. From the standpoint of achieving effective solutions, how often do you consider the knowledge, operating experience, and resources of your organization's best customers or clients?

When it comes to getting more done, customers can offer fresh perspectives and keen insights that could mean the difference in the case of, say, developing a new product or service. Also, customers or clients could have policies and procedures in place which could be worth emulating.

Appeals for Participation

People respond to high appeals for participation. When Colin Powell assumed leadership at the U.S. Department of State in January 2001, his closed-door 90-minute session with top agency officials reportedly was the stuff of legends.

Although Powell didn't allow a recording of his speech, lifelong state department employees allegedly re-dedicated themselves to the agency's work. Now that is recruitment. Likewise, you hear of coaches who give half-time pep talks that rally their teams on to victory despite the pounding they took in the first half.

You might not possess legendary alliance-building skills, but elements of your personality and communication style can be harnessed to win people over, and get them to partner with you. You can start on this road, the next time you attend a meeting or business function within your organization or outside of it. You can even start with total strangers!

Enlisting Others at Everyday Activities

Those who have achieved success at work or in life often seem to know something special about connecting with other people. They say the right things, and associate with the right people. They have a knack for keeping up with what is going on, and they find ways to use that knowledge to form alliances.

High octane persuaders can adapt their styles depending on degrees of formality, levels of seriousness, and people involved. They have subconscious ideas of their desired outcomes in the back of their minds. These ideas might range from negotiating a business deal to successfully completing an involved project.

Dyna Moe

Those with a knack for forming alliances know the importance of using a person's name. It has been said that our names are the "sweetest and most important sounds in the English language" to many of us.

The accurate use of names is crucial in greetings, and alliance builders are especially adept at remembering and using them. Some naturally have good memories; others take memory enhancement courses to learn and practice the many tricks for remembering. They know how important this skill can be. Addressing someone you have recently met with confidence, without mixing up his or her name, opens the door of opportunity.

One manager at an electronics company instructs his assistant to make calls before a meeting and create a list of the names of people who'll be in attendance. He studies the list prior to the event so that he'll be at his networking best when he arrives.

The Value of Exhibiting Host Behavior

At a business reception small pockets of people congregate between the bar at one end of the room and the table at the other end. The chance to make new business contacts here is ripe.

You'll spot at least one person, smiling and gracious, moving around the room fluidly, shaking hands and introducing himself with direct eye contact and a warm smile. This person spends some time with each individual he or she greets, listening carefully while the other talks. This person's ability to form alliances and partnerships is miles above the others in the room.

Dyna Moe

Many people feel too awkward to even say who they are. Say your name and position with enthusiasm. Then give enough information to lead the other person into an engaging conversation. All this takes only a matter of seconds. Practice will take away the awkwardness you could feel at first.

Whatever his job title, he understands a critical factor in human relations, described by Dr. Adele Scheele in *Skills for Success*—the importance of exhibiting host behavior. In other words such people don't wait to make connections. They know when to take the initiative to make others feel comfortable in a meeting environment.

To make new quality contacts, you have to take advantage of the opportunities that come your way. When you have the chance to meet someone in person, first, introduce yourself. Some alliance builders have a focused agenda and seek occasions for making business contacts or improving business relations.

Alliance builders seldom have the problem of having nobody to talk to; if left alone momentarily, they have a knack for acting in a commanding manner. Rather than sinking into the woodwork, they stand straight and, sipping a drink, survey the room with a look of alert interest and even slight amusement. They're never left out because they don't act left out!

Being Open to Empowering People

Some people, me included, rely heavily on empowering people to gain the kind of insights, input, and feedback that enable us to propel ourselves forward. These include peers, affiliates, and a wide variety of others, drawing from the best of those you might encounter at work and in life, as well as coaches.

Essential to having empowering people in your career is to be open to having them! This sounds simple, but many career professionals don't embrace the notion. Who at your workplace always:

➤   looks forward to hearing from you?
➤   listens to you closely?
➤   heeds your advice? and
➤   is appreciative for having received it?

Word Power
An empowering person helps energize, authorize, or encourage another individual to act.

Is this the kind of person you want to be around? Of course. That's the kind of person I am to my empowering people. They know that I want to hear from them and that I value what they tell me. I often act on what they recommend so rapidly that they're amazed how quickly their advice took effect.

You for Me, and Me for You

People who empower you are also empowered by you in some way. Otherwise the relationship would not continue. The way that you empower them can vary. Perhaps simply valuing what they say in a way that few others do fulfills a need in them that prompts them to want to keep the relationship going. Here are other reasons that you could be empowering to those who empower you:

➤   Perhaps few others value them the way you do.
➤   The energy, discipline, and enthusiasm you exhibit in pursuit of your projects could be inspiring to them.
➤   What you want to get done in and of itself could be of notable interest to them.
➤   The questions that you ask of them could require answers that they previously could not have articulated and they value this interaction.
➤   They value being exposed to elements of your world and your insights.

Empowerment Is Where You Find It

You can find empowering people in your career nearly everywhere you turn. Your peers, the list of groups earlier in this chapter, the next function you attend—all represent fertile arenas. Here are some more ideas:

➤ Professional association meetings, i.e., if you're a financial planner, perhaps you meet somebody at the state chapter meeting of the Institute of Certified Financial Planners

➤ At civic, social, or charitable association meetings.

➤ At an adult-ed course you take.

➤ Through friends.

➤ At conferences, particularly if they're a presenter.

➤ On airplanes, especially if you're seated in first class.

➤ When you serve on the same task force, special committee, commission, or other elected or appointed group.

Dyna Moe

The process of identifying and nurturing relationships with empowering people is dynamic, you're always bringing new people into the fold, while encountering yet others you suspect will become empowering people in your life.

You can only connect with so many people on a regular basis. The relationship with each of your empowering people requires some type of sustenance. So, what efforts will you undertake to maintain the relationship?

Advisory Boards: Empowerment Formalized

I have an advisory board of directors and I suggest that you devise one as well. Your initial response might be, "Okay, Jeff, you're an author and a speaker. I can see why people might want to be a member of your advisory board. I simply work at XYZ organization assembling computer chips. Who wants to be on my board?" Many people would like to be on your board!

If you poll most people whom you know, you'll find that they've never been asked to be on a board in their entire lives. They've heard about people on boards, but they're never asked.

Look for people in your immediate surroundings who can be members of your advisory board. These could include people in local associations, one or two people from work, perhaps some one from your church or community group, perhaps a mentor.

I'll briefly describe my advisory board so that you'll have ideas as to who you might choose to be on yours. I have two people from radio: a radio host and a radio station manager. I also have a few people from associations, both national and local. I have a lawyer, a magazine editor, a newspaper editor, a professor, a high school teacher, and three entrepreneurs.

I invite the whole group to dinner twice each year. It doesn't cost as much as you might think; you can feed everyone for under $280.00. I let everyone know in advance what career and business challenges I'd like to tackle at the session.

First we have dinner, usually some kind of a buffet. Afterwards, I pass out the agenda, which is a repeat of the questions I circulated to them in advance before that evening. One by one we discuss my goals and they freely give me their ideas. I record everything and later carefully transcribe each of those gems.

You might think, "People will come to my advisory board dinner once or twice, but would they come over and over again?" My board has met numerous times and I almost have to laugh because I get requests from people I've never met who have said, "So and so is on your board and suggested that you might invite me to be on it as well."

Keep Eliciting Participation

What if assembling an advisory board is a bit much for you right now? For whatever you're trying to accomplish, when you want or need to recruit others, you can appeal to people's reasons for participating. The following list, origin unknown, frequently appears in chamber of commerce newsletters under the title "inducing people to volunteer."

1. To fill time
2. Repay a perceived indebtedness
3. To benefit someone they love
4. To set an example for children
5. To work as a family
6. Someone they love is also involved
7. To meet people
8. To please someone else
9. To have fun
10. To gain skills
11. To gain experience
12. To be visible
13. To gain credit
14. To express their religion or belief
15. To find happiness
16. Because of tradition

17. To employ otherwise unused gifts or skills
18. As part of a group
19. To maintain health
20. To explore new learning, ideas
21. To heal
22. To avert loneliness
23. Because of interest
24. As a hobby
25. Out of concern
26. To receive a tax benefit
27. To counter-point paid work
28. As an extension of a job
29. Because they were assigned
30. To survive tragedy (cope)
31. To test leadership skills
32. To gain recognition
33. To acquire self-confidence
34. To be a change agent
35. To right a wrong
36. To work in a safe place
37. To save money
38. To have a purpose
39. To be a good neighbor
40. To get out of the house
41. To keep active
42. To experience new lifestyles

The breadth of items on this list, speak for themselves. Note the linkage between many of the reasons sited and the principles of persuasion discussed in Chapter 23.

Partnerships Worth Exploring

Have you ever thought about teaming up with a coach to receive the big-picture type of guidance that you might not otherwise be attaining on the job? Considering the kinds of things you want to achieve on the job and throughout your career, could a coach be helpful for you?

Psychologist Harry Olson, based outside of Baltimore, Maryland, says that virtually all professional and Olympic athletes have personal coaches to help them perform to their maximum potential and deal with competition.

The better such athletes become, and the more elite their status, the more they need and rely on coaches. Why? Because the higher they rise in their fields, the more critical their moves become, and the more vital personal feedback is in avoiding mistakes. A personal coach offers the competitive edge!

Olson says that a career coach can help "diagnose and sort out your situation and opportunities, offer new strategies for dealing with office politics and competition, and help you with vital stress management skills."

Factoid

Many high-achieving individuals from speed skaters, to concert pianists, to top executives in business rely upon the aid and instruction of coaches, mentors, or other advisors to both improve performance and to capitalize on new opportunities.

"A good career coach helps you discover and capitalize on new opportunities, provides new tools to improve communication, and helps chart your goals and career path." A career coach can serve as your personal counselor, confidant, and consultant.

Dyna Moe

Deb Giffen, based in Philadelphia, has coached many high achievers in many different professions. "The fundamentals of coaching others stay the same from person to person, almost independent of what the student is trying to achieve," say Giffen. "That's why I can help one person in one field, and another person in another, even if I personally don't have a background in those fields."

I Did it "My Way!"

"We don't question the wisdom of using tools to fix our cars or build wood projects, yet often we balk at using all the resources available to build our careers," says Olson.

Many achievers value "doing it on my own." They see using outside help as a weakness, as if they are dependent on the helper; as if using a personal consultant or counselor somehow takes something away from them. Far from it. The career counselor works behind the scenes, helping you so that you can do your job better.

Self-analysis is limited and faulty because of self-protective "blind spots." A coach increases your objectivity. Because of his or her background and training, a coach can address a broader range of issues than you'd be inclined to do. The coach's primary role is to be a trainer, a listener, an observer, a motivator, and a sounding board.

Your Ambition as the Driving Force

What *you* want to get done is the foundation of your relationship with the coach. A good coach commits to helping you succeed.

Ultimately you alone decide if a coach or career counselor is for you. Olson says, if you encounter any of the following, the answer is probably "yes":

➤ Organizational changes where you work, especially if they have a direct impact on you.

➤ Expansion into new markets or diversification into new products or services.

➤ Increased competition for your company from other firms trying to take over your market share.

➤ Increased management or supervisory responsibility.

➤ Increased leadership opportunities.

➤ A new boss or leadership shake-up above you.

➤ Changes in your role or assignments within your company.

➤ Corporate intrigue, jockeying for position, turf protection—especially if you're on the rise.

➤ Blockades of your progress by internal feuds or informal political processes.

➤ Excess stress on the job.

➤ Increased production or sales quotas.

➤ A new project you lead or participate in developing.

Dyna Moe

A good coach will help you map out your goals and strategies, and will monitor your progress. You will receive objective, honest feedback on an adult-to-adult basis without judgments. The coach will neither command you to do something nor let you flounder. He or she will help you sort out options. The ultimate decisions and actions are always your own.

If you have a strong desire to advance in your organization or field regardless of whether you experience any of the above, you could probably benefit by partnering with a coach.

Mentors as Partners

Having a mentor, like having a coach, can be wonderful and can accelerate your path to getting things done. Many books and articles have been written on mentoring, but I can save you a ton of reading. Mentors generally emerge from those people in your career who are already among your empowering people.

Like a coach, a mentor can help to broaden your horizons. He or she might be pleased to introduce you to associates garnered over the years, key and interesting people—the kind it could have taken you years to meet on your own.

You might prefer to stick with only engaging empowering people because problems often arise in the mentor-protégé relationship. One survey revealed that only about a third of mentor-protégé relationships last more than three years.

When the mentor was the immediate supervisor to the protege, many times the protégé ended up getting fired!

The following issues are worth knowing about, at the least, so that you can avoid them:

➤   A career or business failure by one person could embarrass the other.

➤   Each person risks getting involved in the other's career battles (in which neither belong) because of the bond that develops.

➤   Confidential information exchanged can leave one or both sides vulnerable if a rift occurs later.

Coming Undone

A mentor is usually not your boss. Having a mentor outside your organization or your division is best in the long run. However, always be wary of a potential problem this could cause with your own boss, especially if he or she feels threatened by someone else giving you advice.

Some protégés develop accelerated expectations. A mentor can often make things look too easy; he or she simply calls someone on the phone and presto!, wheels are in motion. Realize that it probably took your mentor a decade or more of experience and alliance-building to be able to do that. Also, as with any partner, hold up your end of the relationship to keep it vibrant!

CHAPTER 26

Reflect and Decide

In This Chapter:

➤ The battle for your own mind
➤ The attachments we don't even know about
➤ Creativity is inexhaustible
➤ The science to following your gut

This last chapter provides you with the appropriate closure and inspiration you need to both finish the book and embark on that golden path to getting things done more easily.

Here is a key realization: In a world that constantly bombards us with distractions and temptations taking the time to pause and reflect, listen to your small, quiet voice, tap your internal intelligence sources and visualize your desired results, separates the high achievers from the rest.

When you win the battle for your mind, you can win at nearly everything. Undoubtedly, you have a fine mind, and it has brought you to where you are today. All that you've accomplished and haven't accomplished, largely has been a result of your ability to tap your most vital get-it-done resource: your mind.

Leaders Win the Internal Battle

When you contemplate the challenges that you face and the things that you want to accomplish, consider that many other people experience the same kind of quandaries that you do. It's easy to lose sight of this perspective. The best and brightest action-types among us at work win the internal battles first and then go on to accomplish great things, at which time the results of their efforts become noticeable.

Do you remember the scientific concept of inertia from your seventh-grade Earth Science class?

The longer a body is at a rest, or more specifically attached or immobile, such as a person, the harder it is to get moving. If you're trying to break new ground, being rooted in the past is a potentially major obstacle for everyone involved.

Human beings, as creatures of habit, custom, and convenience, often become attached to conditions around them, the equipment they use, procedures, and how things are supposed to be. This is true even when their surroundings are not pleasant.

John Kenneth Galbraith, Ph.D., a noted economist from Harvard, wrote *The Nature of Mass Poverty* in 1979. While researching his book, he visited four continents to learn why some civilizations remain poor and some groups had stayed poor, even for centuries.

Galbraith found that poor societies accommodate their poverty. As hard as it is to live in poor conditions, unfortunately people find it more difficult to accept the hardship—the challenge—involved in making a better living. Hence, they accommodate their poverty, and it lingers from year to year, decade to decade, and even century to century. Organization, departments, divisions, teams, and even small groups, if not careful, are all subject to accommodation.

Anyone Can Succumb to Attachment

On a personal level, getting stuck in a rut is no less difficult. Attachment reigns supreme to achievers of all ages. When my daughter Valerie was four years old, her mother and I bought her an old, upright piano. It was a little banged up and missing a few keys, but for a four-year-old, it was fine.

To our amazement, she played well. At age six, she began piano lessons. The teacher encouraged us that our little girl had a special talent.

Two years later, the piano teacher told us it was time to buy a grand piano for Valerie. It would be quite expensive, but she was now winning awards, so it seemed like the right thing to do.

We went to a large piano emporium and Valerie tried all of them! Finally we came to a piano that proved to be "the one." She loved it and we bought it. We told Valerie that the piano movers were going to take the other piano in trade, but it didn't register with her. Days before the new one arrived, we cleaned up the old one, and then talked to Valerie about how that piano would be leaving and the new one would be arriving.

Factoid

Psychology tells us the older you get, the harder it is to let go of attachments. The way we do things and how we think starts to become embedded into the brain in the form of neural pathways. These pathways serve as paths of least resistance that prompt us to take mental shortcuts in response to stimuli.

The old had been her piano from the age of four and she was now eight. In other words, she had been with this piano for half of her life. She broke into a sob—not just a kid crying, but a deep mourning sob, as if she had experienced the death of a parent or a close friend.

"It's the only piano I have ever known, I have been playing with it since I was four! Why do we have to get rid of it?" Trying to be a good father, I explain to her that realistically we couldn't keep both pianos. The house is a good size, but two pianos are a bit much.

We took photos of the piano and we videotaped her playing—we made sure we had it covered. I explained to her that once the old piano departed, she would start to play on the new one and she wouldn't even think of the old one. But, this is not an argument for an eight-year-old. For days she lamented, "Why do we have to get rid of the old one?"

Finally the day arrived. The piano movers came to deliver the new piano and take away the old one. Something in me, I don't know where it came from, finally got through to her. I was able to communicate with her in a way she could understand and accept. Or, it could be she got there on her own, I don't know.

After another tearful outbreak I said, "Val, when the piano goes back to the store, then some other parents will see it and maybe they'll buy it for their little girl. She'll learn how to play, and have that piano several years before she gets a bigger one."

Now, Val's expression started to change a little. She was still sobbing, but I knew that she was ready to forsake her attachment when she said to me, "Or maybe it will be a little boy."

To me Valerie's ability to adapt represented an extraordinary chain of events. Here was an eight-year-old willing to give up her attachment to something she had for half of her life. In my own life, I have had far more difficult times with attachment. I have had attachments to objects, to people, and even to opinions, as do we all.

I once couldn't stand Elvis Presley. I thought he was a country bumpkin. One time, 25 years following his death, a TV special about him showed him discussing his acting ability and he said, "If I were as talented as James Dean . . ." I stopped in my tracks, I just froze, as Elvis Presley had used the past conditional, "if I were", which is correct English. Not one person out of ten knows that this is correct grammar.

Most people would say, "If I was as talented as James Dean," but "if I were" is correct because he knew he would never be as talented an actor as James Dean.

Suddenly I gave up my attachment to having Elvis be some kind of bumpkin. A small issue you say?

Further on in the special, Elvis was shown going through 28 takes for one song. Everybody in the studio was saying, "Yeah, we got it, there is at least one take on the reel that is fabulous."

Elvis says something like, "Wait, we don't have the right version yet." He went on for 35 takes in all, and later the group selected one of the takes in the 30s!

Are you so attached to the way you do things that when you're exposed to another way you fight tooth and nail? Do you resist seeing things another way and gravitate back to what you've been doing, even if it doesn't help you to get things done?

Acknowledging and Overcoming Neural Pathways

As one passes 35, 40, 45, and 50 years of age, slowly we each become familiar with certain thought and activity patterns that form neural pathways in the brain. All the while, we don't realize what is occurring. These patterns become second nature to us although they are not necessarily permanent . . . unless we allow them to be.

It's not that people can't change in the advancing ages, it's that their neural pathways become more firmly entrenched. Fortunately, you can change, at any age, but it requires effort.

Simply knowing that neural pathways exist and that they can be re-routed helped to free me from some of my own preconceived notions regarding work, life, and what I want to get done.

Years ago I set out on a course which I think has paid off and could work for you as well. I take different paths home, hence helping to form new neural pathways. I listen to classical music occasionally, although it is not my favorite type of music. I read magazines that are outside of my immediate interest area.

I attend movies, plays, and concerts that are not necessarily my first choices. As long as I am exposed to different plots, characters, scenery, sounds, and other ways of seeing the world,

I consider the experience to be beneficial. I visit websites that display viewpoints contrary to mine. I read articles by authors whose bias is obvious. I ask young people for their opinion and I ask people older than myself for their opinion.

Coming Undone

If you're not careful, the neural pathways you develop—will define and eventually rule the rest of your career.

Flexing Your Creative Muscle

I know people who will take courses on topics completely out of their field, who try new dishes at restaurants, and who strive to keep themselves open to new ideas. You can do all kinds of new and different activities in your personal life that will serve to stimulate your creativity at work, break free of attachment, and overcome immobility when you want to get things done.

Here are a few ideas . . .

At work:

- Take a planned 15-minute break twice daily
- Eat away from your desk
- Brainstorm with people not in your department
- Furnish your workspace with plants, pictures, or art that inspires you
- Learn some aspect of the organization that is completely foreign to you

Away from work:

- Change your magazine subscriptions
- Read a literary novel or epic
- Dress differently for different occasions
- Relax on your porch
- Install a hammock in your backyard

In general, to develop your awareness:

- Take an impromptu weekend trip to someplace you haven't visited
- Enroll in a course
- Join a book discussion group
- Volunteer at a charity
- Take up a new sport

The payoff that these types of activities generate is the ability to have an open mind, to make decisions on reasonably accurate observations, and to draw upon one's collective experience.

One Decision Leads to Another

Rebecca Merrill, in her book *Living in Yes*, regards effective decision-making as the quintessential skill in life and in one's

Dyna Moe

In a *Fast Company* article "Decisions, Decisions," writer Anna Muoio said, "Stripped down to essentials, business is about one thing: making decisions. We're always deciding something, from the small and daily such as which emails to answer, what meetings to have, to the macro and strategic such as what product to launch and when . . ."

career. Merrill says that we make decisions all the time, and "we never get to stop doing it." It's vital, she says, to understand that "every new decision leads to more decisions. It's merely a question of how well or how poorly they set you up."

In this day and age, as discussed throughout this book, it's increasingly difficult to make effective decisions because of the surplus of information that is available. In many respects, it works against our ability to choose and creates an intelligence deficit. Choose, we must. Merrill says, "With every decision you'll experience some loss, even, and especially, if you choose to do nothing."

Since the quality of your life is directly related to the quality of your decisions, it's well worth your while to learn how to make good ones. Merrill says, "You can only make a decision you are capable of making when the decision is called for." The paradox of it all is that there are no "right" or perfect decisions. Said another way, "All decisions are a function of who you are at the time you make them." The more clear your thinking process, the greater the quality of your decisions.

Factoid

Rebecca Merrill states that although we spend a small percentage of our lives actually making decisions, they determine the course of our careers and the rest of our lives.

Thinking Is a Process That You Do All the Time!

In his book, *Thinking for a Change: 11 Ways Highly Successful People Approach Life and Work*, John Maxwell points out that since our decisions are based on the way we think, it's crucial to understand the nuances of the thinking process itself.

Maxwell cautions that the biggest challenges most people face, for example, when it comes to making effective personal decisions are their feelings. "They want to change, but they don't know how to get past their emotions," he says. Maxwell offers a syllogism that helps people to readily understand that they are in control:

Word Power

Merriam-Webster Online says that a syllogism is a formal argument in logic that is formed by two statements and a conclusion which must be true if the two statements are true.

Major Premise: I can control my thoughts.
Minor Premise: My feelings come from my thoughts.
Conclusion: I can control my feelings by controlling my thoughts.

Maxwell says that if you're willing to "change your thinking, you can change your feelings. If you can change your feelings, you can change your actions."

The action that you take based on good thinking can change your career and your life.

An Analytical, Intellectual Approach that Works Well

Using one's intellect for intelligent analysis certainly has its benefits when it comes to decision making. The scientific method first introduced in 1592 by Sir Francis Bacon, an English philosopher, was improved upon a generation later by Rene Descartes, a French philosopher and mathematician, who provides the most fundamental approach to analytical thinking.

Recalling your seventh-grade science class, the scientific method consists of six steps including observation, asking questions, formulating a hypothesis, experimentation, gathering and recording data and results, and forming a conclusion.

This stuff is pretty cut and dried, so I won't elaborate on it, however the list that follows succinctly captures the essence of the six steps:

1. Observation—Observation involves the use of your five senses. As you observe, you begin to formulate certain questions.
2. Ask Questions—Ask questions concerning how and why certain things occur. Keep a record of your questions and take notes as you seek to answer them. Eventually, state the specific problem that you want to solve and conduct research to learn what the experts have to say about it.
3. Form a Hypothesis—Make an educated guess about the answers to your questions. One option is to keep a journal of your thoughts.
4. Experiment—Visualize experiments that could be used to test your hypothesis. After careful thought, design and perform experiments that will best serve to test this hypothesis. Repeat each test several times.
5. Gather and Record Results/Data—As you gather your data, make precise measurements. Record them carefully and accurately so that you can analyze them later and draw appropriate conclusions. This step requires unbiased observation.
6. Conclusion—Use your data to support, disprove, or leave inconclusive the original hypothesis. Report any complications that arose, or possible improvements to be made, in your experimental procedure. Make your findings available to others.

Remember, if your conclusion disproves your hypothesis, it is not necessarily a failure!

Shackled by the Paralysis of Analysis

Analytic and scientific approaches to decision making certainly are worth knowing and using in many instances. Many people overly rely on such analysis, which takes the form of seeking reams of data before making a decision. In an overly informed society —regardless of whether you're making a purchase, hiring someone, or opening a drive-thru restaurant— you'll find enough information to persuade you to go both left and right. You'll find so much information that a clear-cut decision is nearly impossible.

A study was completed on the use of information in making decisions. Two groups of individuals had to make purchase decisions. One group was given data, analysis, and articles —everything they thought they needed. The other group made the decision based on instinct. After a few weeks, the two groups were able to see the results: each group felt nearly the same about its decision. More data does not necessarily produce the best answer.

If you are forty years old, forty years of data is brought to bear when you make a decision. Instinct, then, is not based on a moment's whim—it's everything you've ever learned during your existence. Each of us has the ability to make intuitive choices, but for many, the word intuition or instinct is taboo. Yet the top C.E.O.s of large companies often make decisions based on what feels right.

Find Your Own Path

When we're consumed by too many details or too much information, it makes sense to switch mental gears and employ all of our faculties, especially the power of intuition.

Intellect is significant, but so are instinct, intuition, and gut feelings. In fact, recent discoveries have demonstrated that there's more to instinct, intuition and gut feelings than you might imagine.

Robert Cooper, Ph.D. observes, "Gut instincts are real and warrant listening to." For most things that you want to get done, even highly involved projects, you already have a strong idea as to how to best proceed.

Dyna Moe

Time and time again, astounding achievements have been realized by people who were able to look beyond what was known or accepted as true, use their intuitive faculties as well as current observations to arrive at current decisions.

Follow that Notion

Evidence is mounting that it's okay to rely on your instincts more often! If you're figuring out how to accomplish something, it's often okay to simply start and let your intuition guide you.

All the cellular intelligence throughout your body goes into a decision based on instinct or intuition. Your decision isn't whimsical, random, or foolish.

Decisions based on instinct and intuition automatically encompass *all of your life experiences* and *acquired knowledge*.

FURTHER READING

Benton, Deborah. *Lions Don't Need to Roar.* New York: Warner, 1993.

Bliss, Edwin. *Getting Things Done: The ABCs of Time Management.* New York: Scribner, 1991.

Bliss, Edwin. *Guide to Getting Things Done.* New York: Bantam Books, 1977.

Bossidy, Larry et al. *Execution: The Discipline of Getting Things Done.* New York: Crown Business, 2002.

Cathcart, Jim. *The Acorn Principle.* New York: St Martins, 1998.

Chang, Richard. *The Passion Plan at Work.* San Francisco: Jossey Bass, 2001.

Cialdini, Ph.D., Robert. *The Psychology of Persuasion Influence: The Psychology of Persuasion.* Chicago: Longman, 2000.

Covey, Stephen. *The Seven Habits of Highly Effective People.* New York: Fireside, 1990.

Daniels, Aubrey. *Bringing Out the Best in People.* New York: McGraw-Hill, 1994.

Davidson, Jeff. *Breathing Space: Living & Working at a Comfortable Pace in a Sped-Up Society.* New York: MasterMedia, 2000.

Davidson, Jeff. *The 60-Second Organizer: Sixty Solid Techniques for Beating Chaos at Home and at Work.* Avon, MA: Adams Media, 2004.

Davidson, Jeff. *The 60-Second Procrastinator.* Avon, MA: Adams Media, 2004.

Decker, Bert. *You've Got to Be Believed to Be Heard.* New York: St. Martin's, 1993.

Fritz, Robert. *The Path of Least Resistance.* New York: Ballantine, 1984.

Galbraith, John Kenneth. *The Nature of Mass Poverty.* Cambridge, MA: Harvard University Press, 1979.

Glickman, Rosalene. *Optimal Thinking: How to Be Your Best Self.* New York: Wiley, 2002.

Gordon, Robert. *Macroeconomics (9th edition).* New York: Addison-Wesley, 2002.

Grant, Peter. *Ecology and Evolution of Darwin's Finches.* Princeton, NJ: Princeton University Press, 1986.

Huxley, Aldous. *Brave New World.* Garden City, NY: Doubleday, 1932.

Labovitz, George, and Victor Rosansky. *The Power of Alignment: How Great Companies Stay Centered and Accomplish Extraordinary Things.* New York: Wiley, 1997.

Lagatree, Kirsten. *Checklists for Life: 104 Lists to Help You Get Organized, Save Time, and Unclutter Your Life.* New York: Random House, 1999.

Laird, D. A. *Technique of Getting Things Done.* New York: McGraw-Hill, 2000.

Lakein, Allen. *How to Take Control of Your Time and Your Life.* New York: Wyden, 1973.

Lieberman, David. *Get Anyone To Do Anything and Never Feel Powerless Again.* New York: St. Martin's Griffin, 2001.

Maxwell, John. *Thinking for a Change: 11 Ways Highly Successful People Approach Life and Work.* New York: Time Warner, 2003.

McCormack, Mark. *Staying Street Smart in the Internet Age.* New York: Viking, 2000.

McEwen, Bruce. *The End of Stress as We Know It.* Washington D.C.: Joseph Henry Press, 2002.

Merrill, Rebecca. *Living in Yes: Helping Smart People Make Good Decisions.* Philadelphia: Xlibris, 2004.

Pascale, Richard, Mark Millemann, and Linda Gioja. *Surfacing the Edge of Chaos.* New York: Three Rivers Press, 2001.

Paulson, Terry, Dr. *They Shoot Managers Don't They.* Berkley: Ten Speed Press, 1991.

Pound, Ezra. Confucius, *The Great Digest and Unwobbling Pivot.* New York: New Directions, 1951.

Posner, Gerald. *Case Closed.* New York: Random House, 1993.

Rosen, Larry and Michelle Weil. *Technostress.* New York: Wiley, 1997.

Siegel, Bernie. *Love Medicine and Miracles.* New York: Quill, 1990.

Sugarman, Joe. *Success Forces.* Chicago: Contemporary Books, 1987.

Toffler, Alvin. *Powershift.* New York: Bantam, 1991.

Yanagi, Soetsu. *The Unknown Craftsman.* New York: Kodansha International, 1972.

Useful Directories

National Trade and Professional Associations. Washington DC: Columbia Books, 2015

Oxbridge Directory of Newsletters. New York: Oxbridge Communications, 2015.

State and Regional Associations. Washington DC: Columbia Books, 2015.

Made in the USA
Middletown, DE
21 June 2015